DIPLOMACY AND IDEOLOGY

The Origins of Soviet Foreign Relations 1917-1930

For information address

SAGE Publications Ltd
28 Banner Street
London EC1Y 8QE

SAGE Publications Inc
275 South Beverly Drive
Beverly Hills, California 90212

British Library Cataloguing in Publication Data

Uldricks, Teddy J
  Diplomacy and ideology. – (Sage studies in 20th century history; vol. 9).
  1. Russia – Foreign relations – 1917-1945
  I. Title
  327.47   DK266   78-63142

ISBN 0-8039-9848-1
ISBN 0-8039-9849-X   Pbk

DK
266.3
U42

First Printing

DIPLOMACY AND IDEOLOGY

The Origins of Soviet Foreign Relations 1917-1930

Teddy J Uldricks

University of California, Riverside, USA

SAGE Studies in 20th Century History *Volume 9*

SAGE Publications • London and Beverly Hills

For
Fritz T. Epstein
and
Barbara Jelavich

CONTENTS

ABBREVIATIONS AND ACRONYMS

Tsentrosoiuz	All-Russian Central Union of Cooperative Societies
Cheka (or VCheka)	All-Russian Extraordinary Commission (i.e., Political Police) [Vserossiiskaia Chrezvychainaia Komissiia]
Comintern	Communist (or Third) International [Kommunisticheskii Internatsional]
CPSU	Communist Party of the Soviet Union
DVP	*Dokumenty vneshnei politiki SSSR*
GPU (or OGPU)	State Political Administration (i.e. Political Police) [Gosudarstvennoe Politicheskoe Upravlenie]
Narkomindel (or NKID)	People's Commissariat of Foreign Affairs [Narodnyi Komissariat Inostrannykh Del]
NKVD	People's Commissariat of Internal Affairs [Narodnyi Komissariat Vnutrennykh Del]
Politburo	Political Bureau [of the Central Committee of the CPSU]
Polpred	Plenipotentiary Representative (equivalent to Ambassador) [Polnomochnyi Predstavitel']
PSS	*Polnoe sobranie sochinenii*
RSFSR	Russian Soviet Federated Socialist Republic
Sovnarkom	Council of People's Commissars [Sovet Narodnykh Komissarov]
SRs	Socialist Revolutionaries
USDS	United States Department of State

PREFACE

The works of Marx and Engels, as well as the prerevolutionary writings of Lenin, made no provision for 'socialist diplomacy'. The militant revolutionary would seem to be the antithesis of the striped-pants diplomat. When the Bolsheviks seized power in October of 1917, they confidently expected that the world revolution would quickly sweep away the capitalist states and, with them, the need for the devious arts of bourgeois diplomacy. The anticipated European revolution never materialized, however, and the Soviets were soon forced to come to terms with the outside world by traditional diplomatic means. Revolutionaries had to become diplomats.

It is the purpose of this study to chronicle and analyze the origins and early development of the Soviet diplomatic corps. The work will trace the structural and organizational evolution of the People's Commissariat of Foreign Affairs under the first two Commissars, Lev Trotskii and Georgii Chicherin, and attempt to assess the significance of these developments for Soviet foreign policy. The Soviet diplomats themselves (their social and political background, education, career patterns, etc.) constitute another important focus of the study. Biographical data have been compiled on well over six hundred Soviet diplomats and Foreign Commissariat officials in order to create a profile of the men who carried out Soviet foreign policy from 1917 through 1930. The nature of this collective biography and the sources upon which it is based are discussed in the Bibliographical Essay. Other topics dealt with include the relationships among the Narkomindel, the executive and legislative organs of the Soviet state apparatus, and the Communist Party, as well as the process of foreign policy formulation and execution. Finally, the style and methods of Soviet diplomacy and the role of ideology in Soviet foreign policy are assessed.

Dates listed in this study are given according to the Western calendar beginning with 26 January 1918. Prior dates are given according to the Russian 'old style' calendar. In matters of transliteration, the Library of Congress system, though without diacritical marks, has been employed throughout. Although Soviet diplomatic representatives in the period from 1917 to 1930 never bore the official ranks of Ambassador or Minister, they are often referred to as ambassadors in the text since they fulfilled all the functions of that position.

It is a pleasure to acknowledge my debt to my mentors and friends, Professors Fritz T. Epstein and Barbara Jelavich. The topic of this book, together with much of the initial research design, was suggested to me by Dr Epstein. Professor Jelavich directed my work during the dissertation stage. Whatever value this study may have is due in no small part to the demanding, yet always patient and charitable, supervision of these two distinguished scholars. I am also indebted to Professors Stephen Cohen, Richard Debo, Anthony De Luca, Ernst Ekman, Charles Jelavich, Bernard Morris, James Parsons, Alexander Rabinowitch, Alfred Senn, John Thompson, Ronald Tobey and Irwin Wall for their helpful suggestions and penetrating criticisms.

John Sontag, Eugene Magerovsky and Vernon Aspaturian were kind enough to permit me to peruse their unpublished manuscripts dealing with Soviet foreign policy. I also gratefully acknowledge permission from the editors of the *Slavic Review* and the *Jahrbücher für Geschichte Osteuropas* to include material (though in revised form) which appeared previously in their journals. My thanks are due to the staffs of the Indiana, Columbia, Yale, Princeton and Harvard University libraries and of the libraries of the Berkeley and Riverside campuses of the University of California, the New York Public Library, the National Archives, the Auswärtiges Amt, the Hoover Institution, the Institute for the Study of the USSR (Munich) and the Institut für Auswärtige Politik in Hamburg.

I greatly appreciate the assistance I have received from the Russian and East European Institute at Indiana University, the Woodrow Wilson Foundation, the Humanities Fund, Inc., the Academic Senate of the University of California, the Russian and East European Center of the University of Illinois and Mr and Mrs Paul A. Salmonson. My thanks also go to Mrs Mary Smith and Mrs Connie Young who typed the final version of the manuscript and to my children, Aaron and Evangeline, who patiently endured my long absences while working on this book. Finally, to my wife Gail, who provided both encouragement and direct assistance, I owe much more than any formal statement can possibly convey.

Riverside, California
February 1978

INTRODUCTION

Soon after the Bolsheviks seized power in October of 1917 they created the People's Commissariat of Foreign Affairs, or Narkomindel.[1] The birth and early evolution of this new Soviet foreign office were strongly conditioned by two factors. First, the new regime inherited the Foreign Ministry of its Imperial and Provisional Government predecessors. This heritage entailed not only a central bureaucracy and its network of foreign outposts, but also a tradition of established administrative practices and diplomatic styles which influenced the molding of the new Commissariat. Although the Bolsheviks thought of themselves as thorough-going revolutionaries, they would never be able to abandon entirely the legacy of the past. Secondly, the corpus of doctrine elaborated by Lenin and his faction in the long years before their rise to power also provided guidelines for the evolution of Soviet diplomacy. Before the October revolution, the Bolsheviks did not have a detailed blueprint for restructuring the Russian government, but they had developed a sophisticated analysis of politics within the imperialist state system. This Marxist-Leninist interpretation of international affairs served as the fundamental reference point for fledgling Soviet diplomats.

THE IMPERIAL MINISTRY OF FOREIGN AFFAIRS

The tsarist foreign office was charged with conducting political relations with all foreign governments, protecting Russian interests, and facilitating legitimate business between Russian citizens and foreigners. The organization was headed by the Minister of Foreign Affairs who was appointed by the tsar and who sat on the Imperial Council of Ministers. The central institutions of the Ministry included its Council (where the Minister, his Deputy and other ranking officials deliberated policy issues), a Chancellery which handled diplomatic correspondence with Western states, an Asiatic Department which conducted relations with Eastern countries, a Department for Internal Communications, a Department

for Personnel and General Management, and the archives. The
Ministry, of course, controlled the network of Russian embassies,
legations and consulates around the world. The great expansion of
the Russian Empire in the eighteenth and nineteenth centuries also
necessitated the opening of Foreign Ministry branch offices in the
outlying provinces and port cities of the Empire. In 1913 the Ministry
employed 689 officials. Places in the diplomatic corps were generally
reserved for men of gentry birth.[2]

The Ministry of Foreign Affairs had neither the constitutional nor
the customary right to formulate Russian foreign policy. That was
entirely the prerogative of the tsar. In practice, the policy-making
powers of the Foreign Minister depended on his abilities and, most
importantly, on his personal relationship with the tsar. The foreign
office also had to share its authority with certain other departments
of government — especially the Ministries of War, the Admiralty
and Finance. In addition, the irresponsibility of some tsarist
diplomats further weakened the Foreign Minister's authority. The
laxity of discipline in the foreign service, combined with the difficulties of long distance communication, occasionally produced a
situation where a maverick diplomat could affect the course of Imperial policy despite the will of St Petersburg.

The February revolution of 1917 wrought few structural or personnel changes in the old tsarist Ministry of Foreign Affairs. Pavel
Miliukov, of the liberal Kadet party, replaced the last tsarist appointee, Nikolai Pokrovskii, as Foreign Minister. Except for a minor
reorganization and the retirement or transfer of a handful of veteran
officials, things remained almost unchanged at the Ministry's central
offices in Petrograd.[3] The same was true at Russian embassies
abroad. The new Minister published an appeal on 5 March 1917 asking the staff of the Imperial diplomatic service to stay at their posts.
Most of them responded favorably to his request. Only a handful of
intransigent monarchists resigned their positions or were fired by
Miliukov. The great majority of tsarist diplomats proved willing to
serve the Provisional Government. The Ministry was severely
criticized, in fact, by left-wing political groups for its failure to effect
a more thorough house cleaning.

It is little wonder that many of the former tsarist officials remained to serve under Miliukov, for the new Minister intended to pro-
secute the war vigorously and to reaffirm tsarist war aims. Since
tsarism had been discredited by its bungling of the war effort and by

the rumors of treasonable Germanophile tendencies at the court, many diplomats actually regarded the Provisional Government as an improvement over its Imperial precursor.

Miliukov so strongly and outspokenly opposed the anti-war sentiments of the Petrograd soldiers and workers that his pronouncements on foreign policy brought on a crisis, with huge protest demonstrations filling the streets on 21-22 April. On this account, a new cabinet was formed on 5 May with another Kadet, M.I. Tereshchenko, replacing Miliukov as Foreign Minister. However, Tereshchenko effected no major changes in foreign policy or within the Ministry.[4] He continued the policies of his predecessor, which included a refusal to publish the secret treaties revealing the tsarist and Entente war aims. Thus, when the Bolsheviks took over the Ministry of Foreign Affairs in October they inherited an institution which had changed little in terms of structure, personnel or foreign policy orientation since the fall of the monarchy.

PRE-REVOLUTIONARY BOLSHEVIK VIEWS
OF DIPLOMACY AND WORLD POLITICS

The views on diplomacy and world politics expressed by leading Bolsheviks before the October revolution constitute a second important influence on the founding and early development of the Soviet foreign service. It is not surprising that the Russian communists had very little to say on the arts of diplomacy per se. After all, they believed that the hoped-for revolution would be a European affair, sweeping away all bourgeois and feudal governments within a very short time and thus ending the need for relations (hostile by definition) with capitalist states by the devious and tainted methods of bourgeois diplomacy.

Bolshevik leaders did, however, have much more to say about world politics. As early as 1905 Lenin argued that a proletarian revolution might well come to power first in Russia and that it would serve as the detonator for a general European upheaval.[5] But, he was not at all clear about how much time might separate the two events, and he warned that the revolution might, '. . . first win its victories in one or several countries with the rest remaining for some time bourgeois or pre-bourgeois'.[6] Lenin also felt that any Russian revolution would certainly encounter the combined opposition of the 'property-owning classes of Russia' and of their international allies. He believed that the building of socialism in Russia would be '. . . almost hopeless for the Russian proletariat alone. . . if the European socialist proletariat should not come to the assistance of the Russian proletariat'.[7] As will be seen later, Lenin's pre-1917 ideas on the international situation were mirrored in the obvious working assumptions of early Soviet diplomacy, especially in the expectation of hostility from reactionary Europe, the belief that many temporary sacrifices must be made to buy time for the new regime, and the feeling of urgent necessity in Bolshevik attempts to encourage the revolutionary process in western Europe.

Agreeing with Lenin, Trotskii maintained that the Russian working class would be incapable of sustaining its revolution without the support of the European proletariat.[8] The threat to the power of the international bourgeoisie posed by any successful revolution in any major state would lead to a world-wide coalition of all the forces of reaction — the bourgeoisie, gentry, monarchy, militarists, etc. — aligned against the growing militancy and solidarity of the workers' movement.[9]

The only pre-revolutionary Bolshevik works which directly and solely concerned themselves with questions of world politics were Nikolai Bukharin's *Imperialism and World Economy* and Lenin's *Imperialism, the Highest Stage of Capitalism,* written in 1915 and 1916, respectively. Lenin argued that the continued concentration of capital and production had led to a new economic formation, monopoly capitalism. In this stage the need for constantly expanding markets created incessant pressures for the export of capital and the acquisition of colonial empires. Since the globe had already been divided by the imperialist powers, the dominant theme of contemporary international politics was the continued struggle for a redivision of the world. Under these conditions the world situation could best be characterized as extremely unstable, while treaties and alliances could be little more than temporary truces between wars.[10] Bukharin claimed, in dialectical fashion, that the very destructiveness of these wars would herald the advent of socialism in Europe.[11] The obvious corollary to this analysis, which would soon find an important place in Soviet foreign policy, was that heightened imperialist conflict was bound to lead to the emergence of serious discontent among the colonial peoples. Such movements would weaken the capitalist powers still further.

In 1915 Lenin had written that in the field of international politics, if the Bolsheviks could seize power, '. . .we would propose peace to *all* the belligerents on the basis of the liberation of the colonies and of *all* the dependent, oppressed and disfranchised peoples'.[12] Lenin felt that none of the major powers would accept such peace proposals and that this would make revolutionary warfare incumbent on Russia,[13] though he had obviously changed his mind by the time of the Brest-Litovsk negotiations. However, he did not see the possibility of combined intervention by all the powers against revolutionary Russia because he felt that their imperialist rivalries ought to divide them.[14]

Thus, before 1917 the leading Bolsheviks had not ventured to discuss what socialist diplomacy might be like and had only sketched the barest outline of their vision of the international situation after the anticipated revolution in Russia. They expected their own impending struggle to ignite the fires of revolution all over Europe. The forces of the old order might gird themselves for one last stand, but over-extended and internally divided by the crisis of imperialism, they would be no match for the aroused proletariat and their allies in the oppressed peasantry and exploited peoples of the colonial world. The triumph of world revolution seemed inevitable. Therefore, the Russian communists did not feel it necessary to formulate a more elaborate analysis of bourgeois world politics or any body of diplomatic procedures to use in that arena. Future Bolshevik representatives might engage in traditional diplomacy only to expose the falseness and class content of the high-sounding phrases of the bourgeois diplomats. Diplomacy would become the servant of revolution.

The Bolsheviks were not seeking to master the bourgeois state system, but to replace it with a new system. The future Third International would be both the tool to coordinate the world-wide assault on the old regime and the agency which would facilitate international socialist collaboration after the total victory of the revolution. There was no room in such dreams for striped pants, secret negotiations or Satow's *Guide to Diplomatic Practice*.

NOTES

1. The name Narkomindel is a contraction of the Russian title *Narodnyi Komissariat Inostrannykh Del* (People's Commissariat of Foreign Affairs), abbreviated NKID.

2. For the evolution of the Imperial Ministry of Foreign Affairs see its official centennial history, *Ocherk istorii ministerstva inostrannykh del* (St Petersburg, 1902); V.A. Polenov, 'Obozrenie prezhniago i nyneshniago sostoianiia ministerstva inostrannykh del', *Sbornik imperatorskago russkogo istoricheskago obshchestva* (St Petersburg, 1867-1917), vol. XXI, pp. 163-96; Sergei S. Tatishchev, *Iz proshlogo russkoi diplomatii: Istoricheskie issledovaniia i polemicheskie stat'i* (St Petersburg, 1890); and Robert M. Slusser, 'The Role of the Foreign Ministry', in: Ivo J. Lederer, ed., *Russian Foreign Policy* (New Haven, 1962), pp. 197-211. For the structure of the Ministry in the twentieth century see A.A. Dobrovol'skii, ed., *Polnyi svod zakonov rossiiskoi imperii* (St Petersburg, 1911), 1st edn., vol. I, part II, book V, division IX, articles 786-838.

3. See Thomas Riha, *A Russian European: Paul Miliukov in Russian Politics* (Notre Dame, 1969), pp. 294-97; and Rex A. Wade, 'War, Peace and Foreign Policy During the Russian Provisional Government of 1917', Ph.D. dissertation, University of Nebraska, 1963, pp. 35-39.

4. For a full discussion of the policies of both Miliukov and Tereshchenko see Rex A. Wade, *The Russian Search for Peace, February-October 1917* (Stanford, 1969); and A.V. Ignat'ev, *Vneshniaia politika vremennogo pravitel'stva* (Moscow, 1974).

5. V.I. Lenin, *Polnoe sobranie sochinenii* (Moscow, 1960), vol. XI, p. 45 and passim [hereafter *PSS*].

6. Ibid., vol. XXX, p. 133.

7. Ibid., vol. XII, p. 157.

8. Leon Trotsky, 'Prospects of a Labor Dictatorship', in: *Our Revolution: Essays on Working Class and International Revolution, 1904-1917* (New York, 1918), pp. 136-37.

9. Ibid., pp. 139-40.

10. Lenin, *PSS*, vol. XXVII, passim and esp. pp. 417-18.

11. Nikolai Bukharin, *Imperialism and World Economy* (New York, 1973), esp. pp. 144-70. Also see Stephen F. Cohen, *Bukharin and the Bolshevik Revolution: A Political Biography, 1888-1938* (New York, 1973), pp. 25ff.

12. Lenin, *PSS*, vol. XXVII, p. 50.

13. '. . .the victorious proletariat of [one] country. . .would stand up against. . .the capitalist world. . .raising revolts in those countries against the capitalists, and in the event of necessity, coming out even with armed force against the exploiting classes and their states', ibid., pp. 50-51.

14. Ibid., vol. XXXIV, pp. 233-34. Also see Arno J. Mayer's discussion of Lenin's ideas up to 1917 in his *Wilson vs. Lenin: The Political Origins of the New Diplomacy, 1917-1918* (Cleveland and New York, 1959).

1

THE BIRTH
OF A PEOPLE'S COMMISSARIAT

The armed uprising of party cadres, workers and soldiers which took place on 24-25 October 1917 shattered the Provisional Government and swept the Bolsheviks into power. The most immediate task facing Lenin and his party was the consolidation of their fragile hold on that power. The Bolsheviks had been working toward a revolution ever since the founding of the Russian Social Democratic Workers Party at the turn of the century, but they had made few plans for the organization of their hoped-for workers' state or the implementation of their policies.

During the first days after the revolution, executive authority was exercised by the Military-Revolutionary Committee of the Petrograd Soviet, whose Chairman was Trotskii. But this was only a provisional administration, meant to function until permanent governmental organs were set up. Trotskii's oft-quoted conversation with Lenin provides an interesting perspective on the formation of new socialist institutions:

> It is necessary to form a government. We have several members of the Central Committee. A meeting of the Committee quickly opens in the corner.
> What will we call it? — Lenin muses aloud. — Anything but ministries: a foul, worn-out name.
> — Perhaps commissars, — I suggest, — but there are so many commissars right now. Perhaps supreme commissars?. . . No, 'supreme' sounds bad. How about 'people's'?
> — People's commissars? That might do, Lenin agrees. And the government as a whole?
> — A council [*sovet*], of course, a council. . . . The Council of People's Commissars, ah?
> — The Council of People's Commissars? — Lenin picks it up, — that's perfect: it reeks terribly of revolution![1]

On 8 November 1917 the Second All-Russian Congress of Soviets established the Council of People's Commissars (*Sovet Narodnykh Komissarov* or *Sovnarkom*) as the executive body of revolutionary Russia.[2] The new government included a commission for foreign affairs which was subsequently rechristened the People's Commissariat for Foreign Affairs.[3] Much of the structure of the Soviet government seems to have been modeled on that of its imperial predecessor and, therefore, even though diplomacy had previously played no part in Bolshevik thought, a foreign office appeared on the new regime's organizational chart. There is little evidence concerning the motivations of the Bolsheviks in establishing a foreign service. Such an organization might publish the secret treaties relating to the First World War and also call for a general peace conference, but there is nothing in the available sources to suggest that the Soviet leaders regarded this new Commissariat as a very important institution.[4] In contrast, a good deal of significance was attached to the International Department of the All-Russian Central Executive Committee (VTsIK) of the Congress of Soviets, which was created at about the same time to manage relations with foreign revolutionary movements.[5] Unlike the Narkomindel which, to party militants, seemed tainted by its association with bourgeois diplomacy, the International Department was respectably revolutionary. Only the subsequent failure of the anticipated world revolution and the resulting dependence of the Soviet state on traditional diplomacy would raise the status of the NKID. A year later Lenin would claim that, '. . .from the very beginning of the October Revolution foreign policy and international relations have been the main questions facing us'.[6] True enough, but that development had come as a surprise to the Bolsheviks, even to their leader.

Trotskii's role in the new regime was the subject of a discussion in Lenin's office on 7 November. In his memoirs, Trotskii claims that his work in preparing the October revolution had left him exhausted and that he therefore wished to assume a less demanding post, perhaps in editorial work in the party press. This may well have been false modesty or a clever political pose — an attempt to avoid seeming overly ambitious. Whatever the truth, Lenin wanted him to take an active role in the consolidation of Bolshevik power and the construction of the new Soviet state. Lenin first suggested that Trotskii assume the chairmanship of the Council of People's Commissars, but Trotskii refused the offer and Lenin did not press the matter since, apparently, the other Bolsheviks present were not in favor of the idea. Lenin then proposed that Trotskii take the commissariat of the interior so that he could direct the fight against counterrevolution. Trotskii declined again, this time because he had no sympathy for nationalist aspirations and was therefore unsuited to handle the delicate nationalities question, and because his Jewish background would handicap him in dealing with a population whose anti-semitism was deeply ingrained.

Since Lenin insisted on keeping Trotskii in the service of the party and state at the highest level, and since he and Sverdlov had already earmarked the major editorial position for Bukharin, Sverdlov came up with a solution: 'Lev Davidovich should be counterposed to Europe; let him take charge of foreign affairs.' 'What foreign affairs will we have now?', Lenin retorted. Ultimately everyone including Trotskii himself agreed that he should head the new NKID. He would thus have a seat on the Council of Commissars and, since his diplomatic duties were not expected to be overly taxing, he would be able to rest or to help in other departments when needed.[7] Now the Soviet state had both a Commissariat of Foreign Affairs and a Commissar of undoubted abilities.

Soon afterwards, in answer to a fellow Bolshevik who had asked what sort of diplomatic work a communist state could have, Trotskii remarked, '[I'll] issue a few revolutionary proclamations to the people and then close up shop.'[8] Subsequently, the new Commissar felt it necessary to qualify this bold rejection of diplomacy. 'I deliberately exaggerated my point of view, of course, wishing to emphasize that the center of gravity was then not in diplomacy.'[9] For Trotskii the appointment actually meant freedom from daily departmental work and a chance to cooperate with the other leading Bolsheviks in the overall work of establishing a new regime. When some of his friends offered their services for the NKID, Trotskii suggested that they would find more gratifying and useful work in other departments.[10]

FROM MINISTRY TO COMMISSARIAT

During the first days after the revolution the emergent Narkomindel carried out its functions at the Smolnyi Institute near the Sovnarkom offices. Trotskii received journalists and the few foreign diplomats who sought out the new Commissar in his tiny apartment on the top floor of the Institute.[11] What little work the NKID had at this stage — mainly the issuing of passports and import-export permits and the supervision of customs houses — was handled quite informally under the authority of the Military-Revolutionary Committee.[12] The Narkomindel was forced to operate through the Committee because it did not yet have control of the facilities and staff of the old Ministry of Foreign Affairs. M.S. Uritskii had been ordered by the Military-Revolutionary Committee to seize the Ministry building on the first day of the revolution.[13] Uritskii met no active resistance at the Ministry, but its officials refused to show him the secret treaties which he demanded or to assist him in any other way.[14]

In fact, the officials of the Provisional Government Ministry of Foreign Affairs continued to occupy the Ministry building and to perform a few functions such as the transmission of funds to captured Russian prisoners of war. The Bolsheviks requested that these experienced Ministry employees remain in service under the new regime. Their first major task was to be the translation of Lenin's Decree on Peace into many foreign languages.[15] Deputy Minister A.M. Petriaev, speaking for his colleagues, expressed the staff's total unwillingness to cooperate with the revolutionary regime, although he did offer to continue the prisoner of war work.[16] Most of these officials, whether *chinovniki* of the former tsarist ministry or more recent post-February recruits, supported the liberal Kadet Party, and they favored Miliukov's policy of vigorously prosecuting the war against Germany. They strongly opposed the Bolshevik seizure of power. Lenin's 'defeatism'[17] and his insistence on the rapid conclusion of peace was nothing short of treason in their view.[18] Under the Provisional Government, the civil servants had formed their own union. The Union of Unions of State Employees now called a general strike, refusing to recognize the authority of the Council of People's Commissars.[19] The striking officials were confident that the Bolsheviks could not retain power for long. By boycotting the new regime they hoped to speed the downfall of Lenin's party and to protect the apparatus of government from Bolshevik meddling in the meantime. The Foreign Ministry staff enthusiastically supported the strike.[20] Only a few minor employees (guards, couriers, servants, etc.) refused to take part in the boycott.

Trotskii tried to break the strike by issuing an order on 10 November 1917 that all those not reporting for work by the thirteenth of the month would be relieved of their positions and that their pensions and other civil service perquisites would be forfeited.[21] Even this threat did not shake their resolve. The majority of the *chinovniki* continued the strike. Repeated threats and appeals by Trotskii, Zalkind and other Soviet officials were met with defiance. So, a decree on 13 November announced the dismissal of the bulk of the former officials of the Ministry, 'for their refusal to obey the Council of People's Commissars'.[22] A further order for the arrest of the strike leaders was issued the following day.[23] A few arrests and a show of force by a unit of Red Guards finally convinced the recalcitrant officials to turn over the keys to the Ministry offices, code rooms, archives and safes to Zalkind.[24] High level officials like Prince Ukhtomskii, Deputy Minister Neratov, Deputy Petriaev and Chancellery chief Tatishchev were all relieved of their posts. The event marked the all-but-complete break in the continuity of personnel between the Imperial and Provisional Government Ministries, on one hand, and the new People's Commissariat on the other. When Trotskii arrived at the Ministry headquarters on 27 November, he found only a few minor officials remaining to serve under him.[25]

Lenin later made a virtue of necessity in extolling the character of the Narkomindel:

> . . . this apparatus is an exceptional component of our state apparatus. We have not allowed a single influential person from the old tsarist apparatus into it. All sections with any authority are composed of Communists. That is why it has already won for itself (this may be said boldly) the name of a reliable communist apparatus purged to an incomparably greater extent of the old tsarist, bourgeois and petty-bourgeois elements than that which we have had to make [do] with in other People's Commissariats.[26]

There is some disagreement about the number of former Ministry officers who remained in Soviet service. Zalkind claimed that there were only two such cases, A.I. Dolivo-Dobrovolskii, a former Consul in Czernowitz, and F.N. Petrov, former First Dragoman at the Consulate in Teheran. He noted that a sign was posted at the entrance to the Ministry which read, 'former officials are requested not to trouble themselves with offers of their services'.[27] It seems, however, that there were a few more. Besides Dolivo-Dobrovolskii, at least four other members of the economic and personnel section stayed in office.[28] Other holdovers included D.T. Florinskii, from the Russian Consulate in New York, Murav'ev, of the First Department, Andrei Sabanin, a former legal officer who co-edited the first official Soviet treaty series, and N.P. Kolchanovskii, as well as A.N. Voznesenskii, an Asian specialist. The Bolsheviks were perplexed by this problem. They despised and distrusted the servitors of the old regime but they desperately needed the experience and technical expertise that the veteran foreign service officers could provide.

Trotskii had delegated the responsibility for reopening the Foreign Ministry and creating new machinery for the NKID to his assistant Ivan Zalkind.[29] With the help of N.G. Markin, a Bolshevik sailor, and E.D. Polivanov, a Petrograd *Privatdozent,* Zalkind proceeded to set up the new Commissariat on an ad hoc basis, salvaging as much of the structure of the old Ministry as possible and creating new organs wherever the needs of the Soviet state required them. The small amount of daily correspondence and general paperwork was handled, as before, by the Chancellery, now renamed the Secretariat. A new Western Department, with Zalkind in charge, was instituted to supervise relations with Europe and the Americas. The Soviet negotiating team at Brest-Litovsk operated under the auspices, if not the direction, of this organ. The Asiatic Department, under Polivanov, carried out its traditional functions, while the economic and legal departments managed trade relations and investigated legal questions. Control of foreign visitors and of immigration was placed in the hands of the Visa Department.

The Bureau of Prisoners of War Affairs was created to carry out the double assignment of maintaining contact with Russian prisoners in enemy hands and conducting propaganda among the German and Austrian captives. The latter task was executed with some success, since several important central European revolutionaries emerged from the Russian camps.[30] The most novel of the Bolsheviks' creations were two information agencies, a Press Bureau under Karl Radek and a Bureau of International Revolutionary Propaganda, staffed by Boris Reinshtein and two Americans, John Reed and Albert Rhys Williams. Radek's operation was soon transferred to the Soviet Central Executive Committee, while Reinshtein's group became the NKID Press Department.[31] The complete list of sections and departments of the Narkomindel included:

1 Secretariat of the NKID
2 Department of Relations with the West
3 Department of Relations with the East (including sections for

Far Eastern Affairs and for the Tatar language press)
4   Press Department (which published articles and books on Soviet foreign policy, the contemporary world situation, and international socialism)
5   Prisoner of War Department
6   Legal Department (for the liquidation of Russian foreign properties, matters of inheritances and similar problems)
7   Department of Personnel (for the payment of employees and of expenses, bookkeeping, and drawing up the Commissariat's budget)
8   Department of Visas
9   Economic Department [*ekonomicheskii otdel*] (for import-export problems)
10 Department of Ciphers
11 Department for Currency Exchange and Loan Agreements
12 Department of Bibliography (for maintaining the Commissariat library and selling literature)
13 Department of Economics [*khoziaistvennyi otdel*] (for routine housekeeping chores)
14 Typographical Department (with a lithographic section)
15 Department for the Transmission of the Moscow Archives
16 'Lecturing' Department (for public lectures)
17 Control Department.[32]

Most of these departments must have been very small and several of them probably shared the same personnel. By the end of December, 126 people were employed by the NKID and, surprisingly, the Narkomindel was the first Commissariat to be fully established.[33]

The emerging People's Commissariat of Foreign Affairs received its staff from three principal sources: the few former Ministry officials who agreed to serve the Soviet regime, the Petersburg party committee which assigned a cadre of Bolsheviks to augment the Narkomindel's ranks, and the pro-Bolshevik workers of the nearby Siemens-Schuckert factory, who formed a unit of guards to protect the NKID offices and who fulfilled many minor functions in the Commissariat.[34] The party contingent formed the core of the new commissariat. These were veteran Bolsheviks, men with extensive political experience whose long years in exile abroad had acquainted them with conditions throughout Europe and North America. The list included such dedicated and talented Bolsheviks as Leonid Krasin, Lev Karakhan, Maksim Litvinov, D.Z. Manuil'skii, Vatslav Vorovskii, Iakov Ganetskii, P.L. Voikov, V.R. Menzhinskii, Aleksandr Troianovskii, N.N. Narimanov and Adolf Petrovskii.

For a long time control of Russia's foreign missions remained beyond the reach of the new regime in Petrograd. The Bolsheviks at first hoped that at least some of the existing diplomatic staffs of the embassies and consulates would follow the directives of the new government just as they had submitted to the Provisional Government after the February revolution. With few exceptions, these expectations were disappointed. The diplomats in the field proved to be as reluctant to accept Soviet power as their colleagues in the central Ministry and, of course, they were not directly subject to coercive measures by Bolshevik authorities.

On 5 December 1917 Trotskii sent a wireless message to all embassy, mission and consular personnel requesting that they immediately pledge their readiness to implement the orders of the Soviet regime. Those who refused were instructed to turn over all their duties to lesser, loyal officials.[35] The mission staffs were strongly anti-Bolshevik almost to a man. They refused to submit to the authority of the Sovnarkom and they continued to use state funds for anti-Soviet propaganda and activities. Only a few diplomats, including Baron Ungern-Sternberg, Chargé d'Affaires in Portugal, and Iurii Solov'ev, the acting Chargé in Spain, responded positively to Trotskii's appeal.[36] Therefore, on 9 December 1917 the NKID dismissed twenty-eight ambassadors, envoys and consular officers and ordered the flow of state funds to them to cease.[37] However, the Provisional Government's diplomats, and most of the governments to which they were accredited, continued to ignore these orders.

In response to the October revolution the Provisional Government's ambassadors around the globe organized themselves into a group, variously called the Council of Ambassadors or the Russian Political Conference, to fight against Bolshevism.[38] They did not limit their endeavors to passive resistance to Trotskii's orders, but waged an active campaign to prevent the recognition of the Soviet state by any other governments. Moreover, these diplomats attempted to support and coordinate the work of anti-Bolshevik groups in Russia.[39] The Russian embassies thus became focal points for the diverse forces struggling to undermine Lenin's regime.[40]

Failing to secure their allegiance, the NKID next attempted to displace the non-cooperating tsarist and Provisional Government officials with new appointees. This task was complicated by the fact that no other state had as yet formally recognized the Bolshevik regime. The Council of Commissars simply ignored this problem by naming new ambassadors without first consulting the governments to which they were sent. Because of war-time disruption and blockades, it was almost impossible to dispatch diplomatic agents from Petrograd to the Western capitals. Therefore, the Soviet authorities tried to appoint, wherever possible, men who were already residing in the country of their assignment. There were a large number of Bolsheviks living throughout Europe and in the United States at that time. They had been previously expelled by, or had escaped from, the tsarist police and had not yet been able to return to Russia after the February revolution. Such people, along with a few pro-Bolshevik foreigners, were the obvious choices to serve as the Soviet regime's first new diplomats.

At the end of December 1917 Trotskii appointed Maksim Litvinov, a Bolshevik political exile who had lived in London since 1909, as the new Soviet representative to Great Britain. The British were forced to deal with Litvinov in order to prevent the closure of their own embassy in Petrograd. However, they refused either to oust the Provisional Government Chargé, Nabokov, or to recognize Litvinov officially as the Russian ambassador. Furthermore, the British government would not receive Litvinov at the Foreign Office, but negotiated with him indirectly through private meetings with a minor diplomatic official, Reginald Leeper. Litvinov was dissatisfied with these arrangements, although he accepted them as temporary expedients.[41] Besides Litvinov, the Sovnarkom also nominated a number of consular agents for Britain and the Empire. John Maclean, a radical, anti-war leader of the Independent Labour Party in Scotland, was appointed Consul in Glasgow, and P. Simonov, a former ore miner and trade union official, was made Consul-General in Australia, replacing the tsarist incumbent, Prince Abazov. In addition, a certain comrade Skevensyrev was named Consul-General for India. Both Maclean and Simonov actually took up their duties, mainly assisting émigrés to return to Russia, but the India Office refused to admit Skevensyrev. Maclean was never recognized by the British and constant harassment by the police limited his effectiveness.[42]

V.V. Vorovskii, who was in Stockholm at the time, was appointed

Soviet representative to Sweden, Denmark and Norway. His instructions made it clear that the scope of Vorovskii's authority extended well beyond Soviet-Scandinavian relations: '[Your] task is not to be an envoy to the Swedish king or government, but to be a diplomatic agent of Soviet power, located in Stockholm but empowered to establish ties and conduct talks not so much with Sweden as through Sweden with other countries. . . .'[43] As the representative of a revolutionary regime, Vorovskii did not think it improper to establish his mission in the offices of the International Socialist Bureau, then headed by Angelica Balabanov. In fact, Balabanov occasionally substituted for the Soviet envoy in negotiations with Swedish business interests.[44]

In January of 1918 the NKID informed the American Embassy that 'citizen' John Reed would replace the current Russian Consul in New York. However, the American Ambassador, David R. Francis, objected to the appointment and Lenin cancelled it a few days later.[45] V.A. Karpinskii, a Bolshevik émigré in Geneva, was appointed Soviet envoy to Switzerland. His diplomatic career was almost as brief as John Reed's. He was not able to wrest control of the Russian mission from its Provisional Government incumbents and he failed to establish relations with the Swiss authorities. Meeting no success in Bern, Karpinskii soon departed for Russia.[46] Then, at the end of January 1918, the Sovnarkom announced that it was sending Lev Kamenev to France and Ivan Zalkind to Switzerland in order 'to acquaint the governments and peoples of the Allied countries with the course of the [Brest-Litovsk] peace negotiations'. The French refused to admit Kamenev but, after a long series of difficulties, Zalkind finally arrived in Switzerland. Like his predecessor, Zalkind never attempted to present his credentials to the Swiss government. Instead, he spent his time meeting with Russian émigrés and various Western European radicals. His apparent purpose was to present the Bolshevik view of events in Russia and to gather information on the revolutionary situation in Europe.[47]

The attempt to purge the foreign missions of their tsarist incumbents and replace them with Bolshevik nominees ended in complete failure. The old diplomats remained at the Russian embassies, using them for anti-Soviet activities, and the governments to which they had been accredited continued to treat with them as the legal representatives of the Russian state. The United States regarded Boris Bakhmet'ev, a Provisional Government appointee, as the

Russian Ambassador until 1922, even though the Soviet government had endeavored to replace him with L.K. Martens in January 1919.[48] Most of the would-be Bolshevik diplomats were arrested and deported by the states to which they were assigned. In the few instances in which they were permitted to remain at their posts, the Western statesmen looked upon these Soviet representatives as merely informal and temporary envoys with no official standing. Simonov was the only one of them actually to function in his official capacity, but he too was soon arrested and deported.[49] Thus, during its formative period, the Narkomindel was an isolated central organ, lacking the usual diplomatic outposts.

Deprived of its foreign missions, the NKID was especially anxious to maintain the only remaining channels of diplomatic communication with the outside world — the foreign missions in Russia. The Bolsheviks appear to have been unusually correct and polite in their dealings with diplomats accredited to Petrograd and they also took steps to ensure the safety of the embassies from mob attack and vandalism.[50] The Entente powers did not want to see their ties to revolutionary Russia completely severed, either, since they still had hopes of further Russian participation in the war. At a conference in Paris in November 1917 it was decided that each Allied country should immediately make its own approaches to the Bolsheviks. Bruce Lockhart, previously an Acting Consul-General in Moscow, was dispatched to Petrograd as British High Commissioner and seems to have functioned well. The RSFSR was already represented in London by Litvinov. Neither of these men had an official diplomatic status, but both were involved in important negotiations.[51] Captain Jacques Sadoul of the French Military Mission in Petrograd rendered much the same sort of service for his government, though much less effectively, because he was unable to secure the cooperation of the French Ambassador, Joseph Noulens.[52]

These early, informal relations with the Entente powers were ended abruptly in March 1918 by the signing of the Brest-Litovsk peace. The immediate termination of hostilities was a necessity for Lenin and his followers. They had been swept into power by the workers and soldiers of Petrograd in large part because theirs was the only party which promised an immediate, unconditional end to the war.[53] The pledges had to be honored or the new Soviet regime would have gone the way of its two predecessors in 1917. Failing to convince either the Allies or the Germans of the desirability of a general peace conference, the Bolsheviks were forced to open negotiations for a

separate peace with Germany, despite their weak bargaining position. With all hope gone of bringing Russia back into the war, stri-
dent anti-communist hostility set the tone of the Western powers' attitude toward Bolshevik Russia. A later Commissariat publication
characterized the situation accurately:

> . . .the end of 1917 and [early] 1918 was the period of the gradual dying off of
> the old connections with the foreign states, inherited from the past. No other
> tasks of the Narkomindel organizers, other than those arising from the necessi-
> ty of ensuring its functioning, were commensurate in volume to these connec-
> tions remaining from the past.[54]

The Narkomindel's tasks were mainly confined to miscellaneous
minor duties and propaganda work during November and December
1917. The propaganda barrage had begun on the second day of the
revolution with the broadcasting of the 'Declaration of the Principles
of Revolutionary Foreign Policy'. All the Commissariat's pronouncements returned to two points: the necessity for an immediate,
general and democratic peace, and the importance of ending secret
diplomacy.[55] The NKID scored a major coup on 9 November 1917
with the publication of the Entente's secret treaties,[56] together with
this statement: 'The peoples of Europe and all the world need to
know the documented truth about those plans which were forged in
secret by the financiers and industrialists in conjunction with their
parliamentary and diplomatic agents.'[57] The Commissariat performed a number of minor functions, as well. A decree of 3 January 1918
made it responsible for the prosecution of those guilty of smuggling
contraband across the borders.[58] The NKID also handled the issuing
of passports. To obtain a passport it was necessary to make application and secure the approval of an NKID official (usually Adolf
Ioffe) at Smolnyi, then to procure the document itself at the old
prefecture, and finally to have the passport signed and visaed by the
NKID back at Smolnyi.[59]

The NKID had little substantive work to do in its first months.
Even after Zalkind had gained possession of the Foreign Ministry
building and had begun to organize the new Commissariat, Smolnyi
Institute continued to serve as the hub of Soviet diplomatic activity.
Lenin and Trotskii received foreign dignitaries there, and the party
leadership met there frequently to discuss the international
situation.[60] The most important diplomatic activity at the time, the
Brest-Litovsk talks which began on 22 December 1917, were closely

supervised by the party. Actually, all the major issues of policy concerning these negotiations were thrashed out in the Central Committee, not at the Commissariat of Foreign Affairs.[61] In practice, the Narkomindel was, from its first days, a creature of both party and state, owing responsibility to each. Especially in this early period immediately following the revolution, the line between party and government was non-existent for all practical purposes, although no formal or constitutional link connected them. Lenin, Trotskii and the other prominent Bolsheviks, by simultaneously occupying the chief positions on both the Central Committee and the Sovnarkom, provided this informal linkage.

THE DAWN OF THE CHICHERIN ERA

The People's Commissariat of Foreign Affairs had begun to function during the first two months of Bolshevik rule, but its structure was still skeletal, its duties and goals ill-defined, and its organizational life still an ad hoc affair, dictated by the exigencies of the moment. Such a state was inevitable given the chaotic political and social conditions of early 1918. Soviet power was not yet established in vast areas of Russia, the war with Germany dragged on until March, and the Bolshevik leaders could not foresee what kind of foreign relations the fluid international situation might necessitate. Also, the urgent problems of consolidating the revolution and reorganizing the economy had to receive the bulk of the new regime's energies.

Except for the few holdovers from the former Ministry, the Narkomindel staff at this stage found itself deficient in experience and administrative abilities. Trotskii, though a gifted leader, had too many other responsibilities to solve these problems. Thus, the NKID struggled along from day to day performing only minor functions because of this lack of experienced and energetic leadership, and because of the confused conditions which existed in the emergent Soviet administration as a whole. The situation was further complicated by the lack of any coherent concept of the role which diplomacy and diplomats might play in the evolution of the first 'workers' state'. By March of 1918, however, the Bolsheviks had begun to realize that the anticipated revolution in the West which

would deliver Soviet Russia from domestic anarchy and capitalist encirclement was not a matter of days or weeks away, but perhaps
months or even years.[62] Therefore some mechanism for temporary
and minimal relations with the outside world had become essential
for the new socialist state. This new awareness of the importance of
diplomacy caused the Bolshevik leadership to pay more attention
to the languishing NKID and to allocate greater resources to it. In the
course of 1918 the Narkomindel would take on a firm and rational
structure, elaborate its procedures, and begin to assume its functions
as the official diplomatic representative of the Soviet government.
However, these developments required first of all a new Commissar
who was knowledgeable of the diplomatic arts and who could devote
his full energies to building an effective foreign office.

In Trotskii's absence, the Narkomindel was superintended by his
lieutenant, Ivan Zalkind. Unfortunately, Zalkind had neither the administrative ability nor the tact necessary to serve as head of a national diplomatic establishment. A German diplomat complained
that, 'his manners, even for a Bolshevik, are horrible'.[63] In another
instance, a threat of violence against the United States embassy,
emanating from Russian anarchists who were upset about the jailing
of some of their American comrades, reached the Narkomindel early
in January of 1918. Zalkind in Trotskii's absence forwarded this
threat to the American embassy together with a statement of his inability to offer any protection! Outraged, Ambassador Francis immediately dispatched his unofficial agents Raymond Robins and
Alexander Gumburg to register his displeasure with the Soviet
government. Zalkind was dismissed on the same day (29 January
1918) on which Gumburg and Robins protested to Lenin. However,
this one incident was probably not the sole nor even the principal
cause of Zalkind's replacement, as Francis claimed.[64] It was obvious
to all that the People's Commissariat of Foreign Affairs needed a
new director who could not only fully devote himself to its work, but
also had the sensitivity necessary to deal amicably with the hostile
capitalist diplomats, and the background in foreign affairs required
to help formulate policy in these explosive times.

Fortunately an excellent candidate for the position was available
— Georgii Vasil'evich Chicherin. His background and experience
made him the ideal Bolshevik diplomat; he had both an excellent
education and experience in the Russian foreign service. Chicherin
was born into a gentry clan which traced its noble lineage back to the

fifteenth century. More important, diplomacy was a family profession. His father had been a counselor at the Imperial embassy in Paris, while his maternal uncle, Count Stakelberg, had been Russian ambassador at the Habsburg court during the Congress of Vienna. Even as a boy, Chicherin had exhibited a deep interest in history and international affairs. As a student at the University of St Petersburg, he had distinguished himself in the Faculty of Philosophy and History, and had subsequently become fluent in French, German, Italian, Polish and Serbian, in addition to his native Russian. After graduation he worked in the Archives Division of the Imperial Foreign Ministry, where he wrote a history of the Crimean war under the direction of the noted Russian historian, N.P. Pavlov-Silvanskii. Chicherin also possessed excellent credentials as a revolutionary. He became a fellow traveler with the Socialist-Revolutionary Party around the turn of the century and soon had to flee Russia to avoid arrest. In western Europe he first joined a Bolshevik group in Berlin, then broke with them after the defeat of the revolution of 1905 and switched his allegiance to the Mensheviks. Between 1906 and 1914 he achieved a prominent position in the European socialist movement, where he frequently clashed with various Bolshevik leaders. Chicherin gravitated back toward Bolshevism during the First World War, however, when he found himself unable to support the 'defensist' stand on the war issue espoused by most Mensheviks.[65]

As early as the middle of January 1918 Lenin and Trotskii had discussed the idea of appointing Chicherin as the latter's assistant.[66] Then 'sometime between the 18th and 21st of January, 1918', Lenin telegraphed Trotskii at Brest-Litovsk, asking him to submit a formal request that Chicherin be assigned to the NKID. The Council of People's Commissars granted that request on the 21st of January, appointing Chicherin to the post of Deputy Commissar of the Narkomindel.[67] With Trotskii busy at the peace conference, Chicherin became the de facto chief of the Narkomindel. Chicherin did not remain a Deputy Commissar for long. Only two months later, with civil war impending, Trotskii was given the crucial post of Commissar for Military and Naval Affairs (8 March 1918). Then on 13 March the Sovnarkom officially replaced him with Chicherin as Commissar of the NKID.[68] Trotskii later reminisced, '. . .with a sigh of relief I handed the diplomatic helm over to him.'[69] Lev Mikhailovich Karakhan then relinquished his role as secretary of the Soviet delegation at Brest-Litovsk and returned to serve under

Chicherin as Deputy Commissar.[70]

Chicherin was certainly the logical choice for the NKID command. He was the only Bolshevik with experience in, and knowledge of, the inner workings of a diplomatic chancellery. The few other party members, such as Karl Radek, who were as familiar with the international situation as the new Commissar, either disdained diplomatic work or were needed at even more important positions. It is possible that politics within the party also may have been involved in this appointment. Unlike the independent-minded Trotskii, Chicherin was a reliable and faithful executor of Lenin's foreign policy. As the American Consul-General in Moscow stated, after the collapse of Trotskii's 'no war, no peace' policy, Lenin '. . .turned to Chicherin who was his personal man Friday. He knew he could count on Chicherin — Chicherin was completely devoted to Lenin. . . . Knowing that he could be sure that Chicherin would do as he was told and do it promptly and exactly, Lenin picked him out and made him Commissar of Foreign Affairs. . . .'[71] Chicherin himself admitted that he never took important initiatives on his own authority, but always acted in consultation with Lenin.[72]

Chicherin's appointment as chief of the Narkomindel was not widely popular in party circles, however. His former association with Menshevism and his cautious, almost conservative, nature displeased the Old Bolsheviks and the party's left wing. Karl Radek referred to him as an 'old woman',[73] and Maksim Litvinov seems to have been unhappy at being passed over for the promotion.[74] Ioffe, who had been appointed ambassador in Berlin after the signing of the Brest-Litovsk treaty, was similarly upset and provoked the following outburst from Lenin:

> Chicherin is a magnificent worker, most conscientious, intelligent, and skillful. Such people must be valued. That his weakness is a lack of commanding ability is not a misfortune. Few people are without fault upon close examination!
>
> It is possible to work with Chicherin, he is easy to work with, but it is also possible to make work impossible, even with Chicherin.
>
> You have picked a quarrel with him, but the Commissar of Foreign Affairs justly complains of you, for you do not take him into consideration, and without administration and decisions of the Foreign Commissar, of course, ambassadors are unable to take correctly rational steps.
>
> I hope you will take all steps in order to remove these faults.[75]

Nor did Chicherin's peculiar habits and life style win him any friends. Because of his nervousness and insomnia, his typical working 'day' began around five in the afternoon and might last until five o'clock the next morning! Not only the NKID staff, but the entire diplomatic colony in Moscow was forced to adopt these hours if they wanted to do business with the Foreign Commissar. Chicherin thought nothing of summoning his subordinates from their beds in the middle of the night or of having them fetched from the theater or parties in order to get whatever information he needed from them.[76] According to one foreign correspondent who was close to him:

> Chicherin lived the life of a recluse. His apartment adjoined his office and he rarely left the building except to go to the Kremlin for cabinet or Politbureau meetings. One Sunday afternoon, after he had talked to me for over an hour, he asked me whether I would take a ride with him. We drove out the Tverskaya towards the airport. There he ordered his car to stop, stepped out on the left side, walked around the hood, re-entered the auto on the right side and ordered the chauffeur to return home. He had taken his day's, perhaps week's exercise and air.[77]

Commissar Chicherin's preoccupation with detail and his reluctance to share responsibilities irritated a few of his colleagues. Litvinov once commented that, 'his only weakness, perhaps, was that he found it difficult to delegate authority and wanted to execute all his ideas himself. Often he conceived of a diplomatic note, drafted it himself, then translated it and went to the length of carrying it to the nearest post office. This actually happened during our stay in Berlin in 1922.'[78] Chicherin's nocturnal habits and mania for following up even the most trivial matters also gave some Narkomindel staff members the impression that their Commissar was inaccessible.[79] However, his diplomatic experience, his knowledge of international politics and his dedication to ensuring the safety of the Soviet experiment through diplomacy easily outweighed his faults and eccentricities.

REORGANIZING THE NARKOMINDEL

In 1918, under Chicherin's leadership, the burden of relations with foreign governments and citizens was increasingly shifted away from the Council of People's Commissars, and especially from the personal diplomacy of Lenin and Trotskii, to the People's Commissariat of Foreign Affairs.[80] At the same time the NKID finally received a coherent and rational organization which, though often tinkered with, would remain basically the same bureaucratic structure throughout Chicherin's long tenure as Commissar.

First the bulk of the Narkomindel work force was transferred from the Smolnyi Institute to the building of the former Imperial Ministry of Foreign Affairs. Then on 25 March 1918, the NKID relocated its operations in Moscow, along with the rest of the Soviet government. The Commissariat was housed in the top floors of the old Hotel Metropole, now converted into a government office building and called the Second House of Soviets. During the height of the crisis in July 1918, caused mainly by an uprising of the Left Socialist Revolutionaries, the place was closely guarded by Red Army troops. Machine guns were mounted in the corridors and many Soviet diplomats and staff members wore sidearms (though not Chicherin). The Narkomindel remained in these quarters until 1922 when it moved to a more comfortable and spacious old office building at the corner of Lubianka Avenue and Kuznetskii Most. In addition to its central offices, the NKID maintained facilities for foreign guests and travelers at the Hotel Savoy which operated under its auspices. Moreover, Deputy Commissar Karakhan and his family were assigned the first floor of an opulent mansion on the Moskva River, across from the Kremlin. The upper floors were reserved for visiting Asian dignitaries, for whom the Karakhans served as official hosts.

Like his predecessor, Chicherin also tried to re-enlist some of the former Ministry of Foreign Affairs diplomats and officials, but even his courtesy and tact could not persuade them to serve the revolutionary regime.[81] However, some new cadres of functionaries were recruited, who, at least in Trotskii's opinion, tended to be less revolutionary in their politics than the earliest NKID staff.[82] A few volunteers of liberal or moderate socialist persuasion began to come forward. Such men hoped that the passage of time, combined with their own levening presence, would begin to mellow the Bolsheviks. Doubtless, some new employees may have joined the Narkomindel merely because it could provide lodging and priority ration cards in those difficult times. By January of 1918 the various central departments of the NKID already employed over two hundred workers.[83] Chicherin also began to regularize office procedures, though with only limited success. Staff members continued to complain of inefficiency and confusion throughout the Commissariat.[84]

The establishment of some semblance of bureaucratic routine and the admission of non-Bolshevik elements notwithstanding, the Narkomindel was still an organ of a revolutionary regime. Therefore, as a gesture of communist egalitarianism, the various diplomatic ranks — ambassador, minister, etc. — were abolished. On 4 June 1918 the Sovnarkom proclaimed that:

> The R.S.F.S.R. in its international relations proceeds from the recognition of the complete equality of large and small nations.
> Accordingly. . .the Council of People's Commissars decrees:
> 1) the ranks of envoys, ministers and of other diplomatic representatives to be abolished and all representatives of the Russian government, accredited to foreign governments are to be called plenipotentiary representatives of the R.S.F.S.R.
> 2) in accord with the basic idea of international law, — as to intercourse of governments equal in rights, — to consider identical the authority of the representation of all the diplomatic agents of foreign governments, accredited to the R.S.F.S.R. irrespective of their ranks.[85]

The Soviet Republic thus announced that it intended to deal with all foreign states, both oppressed colonial nations and the great powers, on the basis of equality. This step was taken to demonstrate that Soviet diplomacy, not only in its pronouncements but in its very structure, would be fundamentally different from the imperialistic diplomacy of the capitalist states.

In addition to this innovation in nomenclature, the organizational structure of the Commissariat was considerably expanded during the course of the year. The new constitution of 1918 provided a strong executive for each department in the person of the Commissar. Accordingly the Commissar was fully empowered to make and execute decisions in the name of his Commissariat. A Collegium, which included the Commissar and his ranking assistants, headed each People's Commissariat. This body advised the Commissar and served as a forum for the discussion of important issues. However, the Commissar could make decisions unilaterally, although he was bound to inform the Collegium of them. The Collegium had the right to appeal his decisions to the Council of People's Commissars, but the execution of his orders proceeded during the course of an appeal.[86] This formal structure of authority was severely modified, however, by the prominence of the Bolshevik party in higher government circles. Thus Chicherin, the most powerful man in the Narkomindel according to its organizational chart, was outranked by several of his subordinates in terms of party power and prestige.

The first Collegium of the NKID, set up sometime in the latter half of 1918, included Commissar Chicherin, Deputy Commissar Karakhan and two other members, Lev B. Kamenev and Petr Ivanovich Stuchka. A few months later, in April 1919, Litvinov was added to the group.[87] Immediately below the Collegium, a Secretariat functioned to provide technical services as well as communications and overall coordination for the Commissariat.

As the volume of work at the Commissariat increased, several new departments were established to augment the original seventeen subdivisions of the Narkomindel. By July of 1918 there were five additional sections:

The Department for Neutral States (soon to be merged with the Department of the West),
The Department for Central Europe,
The Ukrainian Department (existing only until Soviet power was established in the Ukraine),
The Rumanian Department (subsequently joined to the Ukrainian Department and finally abolished),
The Department of Diplomatic Couriers.[88]

The new divisions fell into three rough categories: sections for handling the Commissariat's technical and internal business; sections for relations with small states bordering directly on the RSFSR; and sections for relations with the Western powers. The mere fact that there were only two (and subsequently just one) departments for analyzing and dealing with the whole Western world, including all the great powers except Japan, while there were separate departments for both the Ukraine and Rumania, highlights the contemporary Soviet perspective on international relations. During this period the RSFSR had few official contacts with the great capitalist powers and the Bolsheviks were still firmly convinced that a revolution in the industrial heartland of Europe would eliminate the imperialist threat. In contrast, the problems of Bessarabia, Balkan communism and the civil war in the Ukraine forced the Soviet leaders to give much closer attention to their western border regions.

It is surprising that not all the directorships of these important departments went to Bolsheviks. The Department of the East, an area where the Bolsheviks had great hopes for revolutions of national liberation, was chaired by A.N. Voznesenskii, one of the rare holdovers from the former Ministry.[89] The Department of the West, however, was headed by Karl Radek. Here the emphasis was clearly on revolution, since Radek was a former member of the German Socialist Party and was currently in contact with the most revolutionary elements of the German left. The Economic and Legal Department was first administered by a certain comrade Lutskii, but he was soon succeeded by Professor A.A. Nemirovskii.[90] Dr S.I. Gillerson, a Bolshevik physician, took charge of the section for prisoner of war affairs, but the whole department was soon separated from the Commissariat.[91] Finally, Chicherin's protégé, F.N. Petrov, administered two departments, the Department of Personnel and the Department of (internal) Economy, which were subsequently merged, along with the Department of Monetary Grants and Transfers, to form the new Department of Finance and Personnel.[92]

The Treaty of Brest-Litovsk prohibited the Soviet government from engaging in revolutionary propaganda against the Central powers, so the NKID Bureau of International Revolutionary Propaganda was disbanded. It was soon replaced, however, by the Bureau of Foreign Political Propaganda, under the same leadership — Boris Reinshtein, John Reed and Albert Rhys Williams — and with about the same duties.[93] In addition, a Department of Soviet Propaganda of the All-Russian Central Executive Committee of Soviets was set up under the control of the Narkomindel.[94] This department took charge of the Russian Telegraphic Agency (RTA or *Rosta*) which had offices in a number of foreign countries. The Foreign Affairs Commissariat was also responsible for the censoring of foreign press dispatches from Russia. This task was carried out by the Press Department under the control of Fedor Aronovich Rotshtein (Theodore Rothstein). The president of the United Press Association commented that the censors were tactful and understanding. The work was not done in secret and, he claims that in the 1920s a dispatch already passed and filed was never subsequently altered. Apparently if a correspondent could substantiate them, statements of fact almost always passed, and expressions of opinion derogatory to the RSFSR could be debated with the censor. Some would pass, some would not.[95]

The Commissariat was also given more authority over the issuance of passports and visas. On 24 April 1919 a Sovnarkom decree deprived the Commissariat for Internal Affairs of the power to issue passports for foreign travel to both Russian nationals and foreigners.

Now only the NKID had that right. However, in order to obtain a passport, an applicant still had to receive clearance from the Commissariat of Internal Affairs or, in some cases, from the Commissariat of Military and Naval Affairs. It is likely that this measure was taken not just to streamline bureaucratic procedures, but rather to bring any and all travelers in Russia into direct contact with the Narkomindel. In this period of relative isolation the Soviet regime attempted to use every possible method of establishing de facto relations with foreign countries, in the face of a determined campaign of non-recognition by the great powers.

Besides its propagandistic activities, the Commissariat of Foreign Affairs now also began a serious publishing program. In addition to the secret treaties of the Entente which were translated and printed in a number of languages, the Narkomindel also sponsored two periodicals. *Vestnik narodnogo komissariata po inostrannym delam* commenced publication on 20 June 1919. It contained articles on foreign policy and recent diplomatic history and it reprinted public documents. Major policy issues were discussed in long country-by-country surveys and important articles from the foreign press were often reproduced. The contributors included well-known leaders (e.g. Chicherin, Ioffe, Radek) and scholars (e.g. Professor Mikhail Pokrovskii) as well as less famous Commissariat staff workers (e.g. Boris Shtein, Andrei Sabanin and Professor E.A. Adamov) whose articles appeared frequently. *Vestnik NKID,* which was often revolutionary in tone, was replaced in 1922 by the semi-scholarly journal *Mezhdunarodnaia zhizn'*.[96] The Commissariat's Information Bureau also issued a frequently, though irregularly, appearing pamphlet entitled *Biulleten.* This was an information bulletin intended for the NKID staff which contained current surveys of international relations arranged by countries. Its 'news' section consisted of a collation of Western press reports, since the Narkomindel did not as yet have an extensive foreign reporting network of its own. This journal appeared from 22 February 1920 to 13 March 1922.

In addition to its central offices in Moscow, the People's Commissariat for Foreign Affairs maintained establishments at a number of locations throughout Russia. Besides the RSFSR, there were several other Soviet successor states on the territory of the former Russian Empire. Between 1918 and 1923, as the Red armies achieved victories on the various fronts of the civil war and as foreign intervention was liquidated, the Ukrainian, Belorussian, Georgian,

Armenian and Azerbaidzhanian Soviet Socialist Republics came into existence, as well as the Far Eastern Republic and the two Asian Soviet People's Republics (Bukhara and Khorezm). Each of these states set up a foreign affairs commissariat and proceeded to engage in diplomatic relations, though mostly among themselves or with the RSFSR. The Ukrainian Soviet Republic, the most prestigious of the group, had established diplomatic missions in a few Western capitals. On the whole, however, all the Soviet republics maintained a common foreign policy which was formulated in the Kremlin and executed by the NKID. To ensure proper coordination, the Narkomindel attached its representatives to the foreign offices of each of these sister states.[97]

In addition to these smaller Soviet republics, a number of local Soviets of Workers, Soldiers and Peasants Deputies, especially those located in cities distant from Petrograd or in non-Russian areas, had set up their own sections for dealing with foreign states and nationals. Chicherin moved to bring them under NKID control on 22 February 1918. In a circular telegram he welcomed their spontaneous development but instructed them to keep in close touch with the central Commissariat. They were ordered to send frequent reports on local conditions and any foreign activities in their areas, and to follow the Narkomindel's instructions. Chicherin was especially concerned that the independent actions of some Soviets in the Far East might provide an excuse for Japanese intervention.[98] Soon, because the White armies and foreign intervention began to encircle the RSFSR, there were few problems with the international sections of distant Soviets, most of which were cut off from Moscow and overrun by hostile forces.

The Narkomindel also opened its first two branch offices during this period, one in Petrograd, after the central offices had moved to Moscow, and the other in Tashkent. They were to facilitate transactions between foreign visitors on one side and Soviet citizens and governmental organs on the other.[99]

While the organizational structure of the NKID was experiencing great expansion at both its central and local offices in Russia, the same cannot be said for its foreign missions. Few countries maintained formal relations with the first communist state and the list of those which did was rapidly growing shorter. Of course, while the Brest-Litovsk negotiations lasted, the Soviet Republic possessed an international platform for voicing its positions. The Russian delega-

tion to the peace conference was characterized by an eclectic admixture of revolutionary adventurism and traditional diplomacy. At the
core of the mission dispatched to the Brest-Litovsk armistice talks in
December 1917 were four capable NKID officials — Ioffe,
Kamenev, Karakhan and Sokol'nikov. For reasons of domestic
politics Anastasia Bitsenko, the famous SR terrorist, was added to
the group, and for obvious propagandistic considerations it also included a soldier, a sailor, a worker and a peasant. In addition, nine
former tsarist officers accompanied the delegation as technical
staff.[100] The well-known Soviet historian Pokrovskii, as well as Trotskii and Chicherin, participated in the subsequent peace negotiations.

When the conference ended, however, the Narkomindel had to rely once again on its few embassies in order to express its views
abroad. Vorovskii remained in Stockholm as the Soviet representative (*Polpred*) for all of Scandinavia, with Iakov Zakharovich
Surits at Copenhagen as his resident agent in Denmark. Litvinov still
spoke for the RSFSR in London. In July of 1918 Lenin had attempted to appoint Litvinov as Soviet representative to the United States,
but the American State Department refused to issue him a visa.
When Germany recognized the Soviet Republic under the terms of
the Treaty of Brest-Litovsk, Ioffe became the Soviet representative
in Berlin and Viacheslav Menzhinskii took up the post of Consul-
General there. Ian Antonovich Berzin went to Switzerland at about
the same time, replacing Zalkind. N.Z. Bravin, the former tsarist
Consul in Brijand, Persia, having telegraphed his willingness to serve
the revolutionary regime, served temporarily as the Soviet representative in Teheran from the beginning of 1918. The Shah's government permitted Bravin to establish a mission in Iran, but the Persians
continued to recognize tsarist Ambassador Von Etter. Bravin was
replaced in August by a Bolshevik emissary, Ivan Osipovich
Kolomiitsev, though he was no more successful than his predecessor
in gaining official recognition from the Iranian authorities. In addition to these regular diplomatic missions, bureaus for prisoner of
war repatriation were established under NKID auspices in Germany,
Austria, and Hungary.

The Plenipotentiary Representative and his chief assistants were
usually Russian Bolsheviks, but many of the people needed to fulfill
technical duties were citizens of the country to which the mission was
accredited. The Press Bureau of the Berlin embassy, for example,

was staffed with about twenty young Germans, mostly Spartakists (i.e. communists).[101] In these early days Narkomindel missions relied on native communists, where possible, for the screening of locally hired employees.

Even where politically reliable local assistance was available, these first embassies of the Soviet state experienced great difficulty in carrying out their tasks. Apparently as late as July of 1918 there were no standard office procedures. This may have reflected Chicherin's ideas on office routine and bureaucratic procedure. Georgii Solomon, a self-styled efficiency expert sent to the Berlin embassy, reported that Ioffe and Krasin readily admitted the state of total disorder in which their mission existed. Important documents were often mislaid and then the whole building had to be searched for them. Solomon blamed these conditions on the lack of trained, experienced and capable personnel.[102] Such inefficiency could be very costly. In all probability, Ioffe failed to provide his government with adequate information about the deteriorating situation in Germany during 1918. Had the Russians realized the precariousness of the German army's position in France and the shakiness of the German home front, they would never have signed the supplementary treaty to the Peace of Brest-Litovsk which forced Moscow to pay a huge additional indemnity.[103]

Communications between Narkomindel headquarters and its missions were seldom adequate. Soviet embassies at this time typically operated on the basis of infrequent and sketchy instructions from Moscow. Ivan Maiskii has recounted the telling example of Litvinov's experience in London:

> After sustained pressure on my side, in March 1918, I was at length informed by Moscow that N.K.I.D. was sending me the first diplomatic courier. It is easy to imagine how impatiently I awaited his arrival! . . . The courier arrived with a large bag covered all over with diplomatic labels. . . . Even greater was my excitement as I started to open this precious receptacle which I expected to contain all the instructions and orders I needed. Imagine my dismay on finding a pile of the latest Moscow papers but not a single directive! True enough, G.V. Chicherin, who was then Deputy People's Commissar for Foreign Affairs, had included a little letter addressed to me in the bundle of newspapers. But this letter was in the most general terms and gave me no definite instructions whatever on the matters in which I was particularly interested.[104]

The Soviet consular service was also organized at this time. The 'Decree of the Council of People's Commissars regarding the

Organization of Consulates' (18 October 1918) provided for the combining of diplomatic with consular activities, thus attempting to bypass the problem of non-recognition by entrusting diplomatic functions to consuls.[105] The decree ascribed all the usual duties to Soviet consuls: the protection of the economic and legal interests of Soviet citizens and their organizations while operating abroad, the protection of the legal and economic interests of the RSFSR, and the exclusive right to represent all the agencies of the Soviet government in their dealings with foreign governments and nationals, except in cases involving political and military considerations which would be handled by specifically diplomatic agents of the NKID.[106] A Consul or Consul-General headed each Consulate, with a Deputy-Consul as his assistant. Fully staffed offices in the world's larger cities often included several technical specialists expert in some particular branch of trade, industry or agriculture. Aleksandr Barmin, the consul in Resht, Persia, had a staff consisting of two Russian secretaries, two Persian clerks, and a Deputy-Consul at the nearby port of Enzeli.[107] The Consuls were placed under the control of the chief diplomatic representative, the *Polpred,* in countries maintaining official relations with the RSFSR. Thus, a *Polpred* could direct the Consul's work, closely supervise his performance, suspend the execution of his instructions and even add to or delete members from his staff.[108] Consuls were also supposed to assist the Soviet diplomatic mission, in the country to which they were accredited, with intelligence-gathering functions and generally to act as embassy information officers.[109] Some of the Consuls-General, especially in Asiatic Russia or wherever the military situation was uncertain, were Red Army officers whose duties were, at times, primarily military. Barmin led the local militia in eastern Bukhara and a Soviet Consul in Turkestan, Khassis, commanded a Red Army division there.[110]

By the end of 1918 the Narkomindel, under Chicherin's energetic leadership, possessed the minimum attributes of a foreign service, and some semblance of order had been imposed upon its previously jumbled ranks. The NKID had found a permanent home in Moscow and it now had at least a few foreign missions in operation. The new year, however, would see this progress halted and even reversed, for the advent of 1919 saw the intensification of civil war and foreign intervention. Diplomats were now forced to give place to soldiers and revolutionary agitators in the struggle to preserve the Soviet state.

NOTES

Publisher's note: In these and all notes to chapters some works are cited only with brief details. For full details the reader is referred to 'Secondary Works' which forms part of the 'Select Bibliography' at the end of the volume.

1. L. Trotskii, *Moia zhizn': opyt avtobiografii* (Berlin, 1930), vol. II, pp. 59-60. Also see A.A. Ioffe, 'Pervoe proletarskoe pravitel'stvo', *Kommunisticheskii internatsional,* 1919, no. 6, col. 777. Cf. V.D. Bonch-Bruevich, *Vospominaniia o lenine* (Moscow, 1969), p. 129, and N.K. Krupskaia, *Vospominaniia o lenine* (Moscow, 1968), p. 337.

2. On the founding of Soviet institutions see M.P. Iroshnikov, *Sozdanie sovetskogo tsentral'nogo gosudarstvennogo apparata: sovet narodnykh komissarov i narodnye komissariaty, oktiabr' 1917g. — ianvar' 1918g.* (Moscow and Leningrad, 1966); E.N. Gorodetskii, *Rozhdenie sovetskogo gosudarstva, 1917-1918gg.* (Moscow, 1965); *Problemy gosudarstvennogo stroitel'stva v pervye gody sovetskoi vlasti* (Leningrad, 1973); and Walter Pietsch, *Revolution und Staat: Institutionen als Träger der Macht in Sowjetrussland, 1917-1922* (Köln, 1969).

3. *Sobranie uzakonenii i rasporiazhenii rabochego i krest'ianskogo pravitel'stva: sbornik dekretov, 1917-1918 gg.* (Moscow, 1920), 1917, no. 1, article 1.

4. The archives of the NKID, which could conceivably contain more information on this topic, are not open to Western scholars. However, even Soviet writers (e.g. Iroshnikov, Vygodskii), whose works contain archival references, have failed to unearth any further considerations concerning the founding of the Narkomindel.

5. See *Lenin v bor'be za revoliutsionnyi internatsional* (Moscow, 1970), pp. 397-98.

6. Lenin, *PSS,* vol. XXXVII, p. 153.

7. Trotskii, *Moia zhizn'*, vol. II, pp. 62-3.

8. Ibid., p. 64. Trotskii's account is confirmed by S.S. Pestkovskii, future Soviet ambassador to Mexico, who quotes the Bolshevik leader as saying, 'I have accepted the post of Commissar of Foreign Affairs just because I wanted to have more leisure for party affairs. My job is a small one: to publish the secret documents and to close the shop.' Pestkovskii, 'Ob oktiabr'skikh dniakh v pitere', *Proletarskaia revoliutsiia,* 1922, no. 10, p. 99. Cf. Max Eastman, *Since Lenin Died* (London, 1925), p. 16.

9. Trotskii, *Moia zhizn'*, vol. II, p. 64.

10. Ibid.

11. Louise Bryant, *Six Red Months in Russia* (New York, 1918), p. 145.

12. M.P. Iroshnikov, 'Iz istorii organizatsii narodnogo komissariata inostrannykh del', *Istoriia SSSR,* 1964, no. 1, p. 109.

13. I. Zalkind, *'NKID v semnadtsatom godu', Mezhdunarodnaia zhizn',* 1927, no. 10, p. 12; and I.I. Mints, ed., *Dokumenty velikoi proletarskoi revoliutsii* ([Moscow], 1938), vol. I, p. 50.

14. Iroshnikov, 'Iz istorii', p. 109; and S. Zarnitskii and A. Sergeev, *Chicherin,* 2nd edn. (Moscow, 1975), pp. 69ff.

15. Pestkovskii, 'Ob oktiabr'skikh dniakh', p. 60; *Novaia zhizn',* 28 October 1917; and B. Kantorovich, 'Organizatsionnoe razvitie NKID', *Mezhdunarodnaia*

zhizn', 1922, no. 15, p. 51.

16. Zalkind, 'NKID v semnadtsatom godu', p. 13; and *Novaia zhizn'*, 9 November 1917.

17. During the course of the war the Bolsheviks had totally refused to support the war effort, even to the extent of defending Russian soil from foreign invasion. They felt that military defeats would foster the development of a revolutionary situation and that any cooperation with the imperialist war-mongers was unthinkable for a genuine socialist. This policy came to be known as revolutionary 'defeatism'. See Merle Fainsod, *International Socialism and the World War* (Cambridge, 1935); and Georges Haupt, *Socialism and the Great War* (London, 1972).

18. Iroshnikov, 'Iz istorii', p. 107-8; and Wade, *The Russian Search for Peace*, pp. 1-50.

19. The strikers' manifesto was published in *Volia naroda*, 10 November 1917.

20. *Pravda*, 4 November 1917; Zalkind, 'NKID v semnadtsatom godu', pp. 13-14; Kantorovich, 'Organizatsionnoe razvitie', pp. 51-52; V. Korostovetz, *Seed and Harvest* (London, 1931), pp. 301-2; and D.R. Francis, *Russia from the American Embassy* (New York, 1921), p. 187.

21. Trotskii, *Sochineniia* (Moscow, n.d.), vol. III, part II, p. 110.

22. *Pravda*, 10 November 1917; and *Sobranie uzakonenii*, 1917, no. 4, article 63.

23. *Dokumenty velikoi proletarskoi revoliutsii*, p. 246.

24. Zarnitskii and Sergeev, *Chicherin*, pp. 71-72.

25. Kantorovich, 'Organizatsionnoe razvitie', p. 51.

26. Lenin, *PSS*, vol . XLV, p. 361.

27. Zalkind, 'NKID v semnadtsatom godu', p. 17.

28. *Den'*, 15 November 1917.

29. *Desiat' let sovetskoi diplomatii (akty i dokumenty)* (Moscow, 1927), p. 5.

30. See, for example, Iván Völgyes, 'Hungarian Prisoners of War in Russia, 1916-1919', *Cahiers du Monde Russe et Soviétique*, 1973, XIV, 1-2, pp. 54-85.

31. E.H. Carr, *The Bolshevik Revolution, 1917-1923* (Baltimore, 1966), vol. III, pp. 27-28; George F. Kennan, *Soviet-American Relations 1917-1920*, vol. I, *Russia Leaves the War* (New York, 1967), p. 359; John W. Wheeler-Bennett, *Brest-Litovsk: The Forgotten Peace, March 1918* (London, 1966), p. 90; A.S. Iakushevskii, *Propagandistskaia rabota bol'shevikov sredi voisk interventov v 1918-1920gg.* (Moscow, 1974), pp. 68-9; and Warren Lerner, *Karl Radek: The Last Internationalist* (Stanford, 1970), p. 66.

32. Vygodskii, *U istokov*, pp. 32-33; A.S. Bakhov, 'Organy vneshnikh snoshenii', in: *Istoriia sovetskogo gosudarstva i prava*, vol. I, *Stanovlenie sovetskogo gosudarstva i prava (1917-1922gg.)* (Moscow, 1968), p. 234.

33. Vygodskii, *U istokov*, pp. 31-33; L.I. Trofimova, 'Pervye shagi sovetskoi diplomatii', *Novaia i noveishaia istoriia*, 1971, no. 6, p. 42; and V. Bonch-Bruevich, *Na boevyakh fevral'skoi i oktiabr'skoi revoliutsii* (Moscow, 1930), pp. 139-40.

34. *Desiat' let sovetskoi diplomatii*, p. 5.

35. *Dokumenty vneshnei politiki SSSR* (Moscow, 1957), vol. I, p. 41 [hereafter, *DVP*].

36. S.Iu. Vygodskii, *V.I. Lenin — rukovoditel' vneshnei politiki sovetskogo gosudarstva (1917-1923gg.)* (Leningrad, 1960), p. 47. At a few Russian embassies some minor staff members expressed their willingness to serve the Soviet regime, but were prevented from doing so by the anti-Bolshevik diplomats who controlled each mission. See, for example, M.I. Kazanin, *Zapiski sekretaria missii: stranichka istorii pervykh*

let sovetskoi diplomatii (Moscow, 1963), pp. 50-51.

37.   *DVP*, vol. I, pp. 43-44.

38.   See John M. Thompson, *Russia, Bolshevism and the Versailles Peace* (Princeton, 1966), pp. 66-78.

39.   Ibid.; Nabokoff, *Ordeal of A Diplomat*, passim; Abrikossow, *Memoirs*, ch. IX; and George A. Lensen, *Japanese Recognition of the USSR: Soviet-Japanese Relations, 1921-1930* (Tokyo and Tallahassee, 1970), p. 207.

40.   Actually, the Russian embassies had been actively opposing the Bolsheviks even before the October revolution. For example, Konstantin Nabokov, the Chargé in London, had prompted the British authorities to arrest G.V. Chicherin in August of 1917 on charges of pro-German activities. When the imprisoned Chicherin was subsequently named Deputy Commissar of Foreign Affairs, Nabokov unsuccessfully tried to prevent his release. See Richard K. Debo, 'The Making of a Bolshevik: Georgii Chicherin in England, 1914-1918', *Slavic Review*, 1966, XXV, 4, p. 659. Also see A. Popov, 'Diplomatiia vremennogo pravitel'stva v bor'be s revoliutsiei', *Krasnyi arkhiv*, 1927, XX, 1, pp. 3-38.

41.   See Richard Kent Debo, 'Litvinov and Kamenev—Ambassadors Extraordinary: The Problem of Soviet Representation Abroad', *Slavic Review*, 1975, XXXIV, 3, pp. 463-82; and Richard H. Ullman, *Anglo-Soviet Relations, 1917-1921*, vol. I, *Intervention and the War* (Princeton, 1968), p. 60. Since Litvinov could not secure control of the Russian Embassy, he rented other offices and opened the 'Russian Peoples Embassy'.

42.   Debo, 'Litvinov and Kamenev', p. 469; Nan Milton, *John Maclean* ([London], 1973), pp. 154-57; and P. Simonov, 'Tri s polovinoi goda sovetskogo diplomaticheskogo predstavitel'stva', *Mezhdunarodnaia zhizn'*, 1922, no. 5, p. 64.

43.   Quoted in Trofimova, 'Pervye shagi', p. 43.

44.   Angelica Balabanoff, *My Life as a Rebel* (Bloomington, 1973 [1938]), p. 179.

45.   Kennan, *Russia Leaves the War*, pp. 405 and 408-9; and cf. Robert A. Rosenstone, *Romantic Revolutionary* (New York, 1975), p. 314.

46.   Senn, *Diplomacy and Revolution*, pp. 42-45.

47.   Ibid., pp. 51-7; Zalkind, 'N.K.I.D. v semnadtsatom godu', pp. 15-25; and Debo, 'Litvinov and Kamenev', pp. 469-81.

48.   B.N. Ponomaryov, *History of Soviet Foreign Policy, 1917-1945* (Moscow, 1969), p. 47; also see the letter by Martens to Bakhmet'ev asserting the claims of the former, 10 April 1919, Hoover Institution Archive, Ts, Russia, R969L.

49.   Simonov, 'Tri s polovinoi', p. 64.

50.   George W. Buchanan, *My Mission to Russia and Other Diplomatic Memories* (London, 1923), vol. II, p. 213.

51.   Kennan, *Russia Leaves the War*, p. 379; and Buchanan, *My Mission to Russia*, vol. II, pp. 244-45.

52.   Kennan, *Russia Leaves the War*, pp. 381-83. Also see R.H.B. Lockhart, *Memoirs of a British Agent* (London, 1932); Jacques Sadoul, *Notes sur la Révolution Bolchevique* (Paris, 1920); and William Hard, *Raymond Robins' Own Story* (New York, 1920).

53.   Wade, *Russian Search for Peace*, pp. 142ff.

54.   *Desiat' let sovetskoi diplomatii*, p. 5.

55.   M. Tanin, *Desiat' let vneshnei politiki SSSR (1917-1927)* (Moscow-Leningrad, 1927), pp. 3-20.

56. *Sbornik sekretnykh dokumentov iz arkhiva byvshego ministerstva inostrannykh del* (Moscow, 1917-1918). Also see M.P. Iroshnikov, *Tainoe stanovitsia iavnym: ob izdanii sekretnykh dogovorov tsarskogo i vremennogo pravitel'stva* (Moscow, 1970).

57. *DVP*, vol. I, p. 21.

58. *Sbornik zakonov i rasporiazhenii rabochego i krest'ianskogo pravitel'stva s 1-go ianvaria 1917g. po 1-oe aprelia 1918g.* (Moscow, 1918), issue 2, no. 13, pp. 21-2.

59. V. Narischkine-Witte [Naryshkin-Vitte], *A Petrograd pendant la Révolution* (Paris, 1925), pp. 189-95.

60. Trotskii, *Sochineniia,* vol. III, part II, p. 99.

61. Carr, *Bolshevik Revolution,* vol. III, pp. 41ff.

62. G.V. Chicherin's report to the Fifth Congress of Soviets on 4 July 1918 makes it clear that the Kremlin's view of the international situation had changed. The Soviet Union would have to seek temporary accommodation with the capitalist world and exploit the rivalries among the imperialist powers in order to gain time for the maturation of the global revolution. Thus, diplomacy had become a respectable tool for Soviet power. Chicherin, *Stat'i i rechi po voprosam mezhdunarodnoi politiki* (Moscow, 1961), pp. 37-62. Also see Lenin, *PSS,* vol. XXXVI, pp. 327-45.

63. Germany, Auswärtiges Amt, Akten betreffend zur deutschen Auswärtigen Politik, Die diplomatische und konsularische Vertretung Russlands im Auslande, Russland no. 87, vol. XIX, German Minister von Lucius, Stockholm to Reichkanzler, 12 March 1918 [hereafter AA, Die dip. und kons. Vertretung Russlands].

64. Francis, *Russia From the American Embassy,* pp. 210-11; *Papers Relating to the Foreign Relations of the United States, 1918, Russia,* vol. I (Washington, 1931), p. 363; Kennan, *Russia Leaves the War,* p. 403; and Bryant, *Six Red Months in Russia,* pp. 200-1.

65. For fuller descriptions of Chicherin's career see Richard K. Debo, 'George Chicherin: Soviet Russia's Second Foreign Commissar', Ph.D. dissertation, University of Nebraska, 1964; Debo, 'Making of a Bolshevik', pp. 651-62; and 'Deiateli soiuza sovetskikh sotsialisticheskikh respublik i oktiab'rskoi revoliutsii: avtobiografii i biografii', *Entskilopedicheskii slovar' russkogo bibliograficheskogo instituta granat* (Moscow, 1929), vol. XLI, part III, cols. 215-29. Also see Theodore H. Von Laue, 'Soviet Diplomacy: G.V. Chicherin, Peoples Commissar for Foreign Affairs, 1918-1930', in Gordon A. Craig and Felix Gilbert, eds., *The Diplomats, 1919-1939* (New York, 1965), pp. 234-81; Louis Fischer, *Men and Politics: Europe Between the Two World Wars* (New York, 1966), pp. 140-47; and Alexander Meyendorff, 'My Cousin, Foreign Commissar Chicherin', *The Russian Review,* 1971, XXX, 2, pp.. 173-78. For recent Soviet treatments of the Foreign Commissar see I. Gorokhov, L. Zamiatin and I. Zemskov, *G.V. Chicherin — diplomat leninskoi shkoly* (Moscow, 1974); Zarnitskii and Sergeev, *Chicherin;* L.I. Trofimova, 'Vstupitel'naia stat'ia', in: Chicherin, *Stat'i i rechi,* pp. 3-20; L.I. Trofimova, 'Stranitsa diplomaticheskoi deiatel'nosti G.V. Chicherina', *Voprosy istorii,* 1973, no. 2, pp. 114-23; A. Gromyko, 'Diplomat leninskoi shkoly', *Izvestiia,* 5 December 1962; and E.M. Chossudovsky, *Chicherin and the Evolution of Soviet Foreign Policy and Diplomacy* (Geneva, 1973). Also see Satho Tchimichkian, 'Extraits de la correspondance Mihail Kuzmin-Georgij Čičerin', *Cahiers du Monde Russe et Soviétique,* 1974, XV, 1-2, pp. 147-81; and G. Kizel'shtein, 'Muchitel'no zhazhdu vysokoi tseli: iz arkhiva G.V. Chicherina', *Ogonek,* 1963, no. 48, p. 18.

66. Chicherin's potential as a diplomat apparently impressed Lenin as early as 1907. Having become acquainted with the future Foreign Commissar in Paris at that time, Lenin is alleged to have said that Chicherin possessed 'some indispensable qualities that could help him to become an excellent diplomat'. Aline, *Lenine à Paris,* (Paris, 1929), p. 55.

67. *Leninskii sbornik* (Moscow and Leningrad, 1929), vol. XI, p. 19; *Protokoly tsentral'nogo komiteta RSDRP (Avgust 1917-Fevral' 1918)* (Moscow, 1929), p. 165; and Ivan Zalkind, 'Iz pervykh mesiatsev narodnogo komissariata po inostrannym delam', *Mezhdunarodnaia zhizn',* 1922, no. 15, p. 61.

68. *Desiat' let sovetskoi diplomatii,* p. 7.

69. Trotskii, *Moia zhizn',* vol. II, p. 72.

70. *Desiat' let sovetskoi diplomatii,* p. 7.

71. Memoir of De Witt Clinton Poole. Columbia University Oral History Project, Columbia University, vol. II, p. 191.

72. G.V. Chicherin, 'Lenin i vneshniaia politika', in: F.A. Rotshtein, ed., *Mirovaia politika v 1924g.: sbornik statei* (Moscow, 1925), p. 3.

73. Lockhart, *British Agent,* p. 253.

74. Maisky, *Journey into the Past,* p. 71.

75. *Leninskii sbornik,* vol. XXXVI, pp. 54-5. Also see Winfried Baumgart, *Deutsche Ostpolitik, 1918: Von Brest-Litowsk bis zum Ende des Ersten Weltkrieges* (Vienna and Munich, 1966), pp. 41-42 and 271.

76. Grigory Bessedovsky [Grigorii Z. Besedovskii], *Revelations of a Soviet Diplomat* (London, 1931), pp. 93-94; and Katsuji Fuse, *Rono Rokoku Yori Kaerite* [Home From Workers' and Peasants' Russia] (Tokyo, 1921), pp. 16-18 and 244.

77. Fischer, *Men and Politics,* p. 141.

78. Arthur U. Pope, *Maxim Litvinoff* (New York, 1943), p. 147.

79. S. Dmitrievsky, *Dans les coulisses du Kremlin* (Paris, 1933), p. 183.

80. Kantorovich, 'Organizatsionnoe razvitie NKID', pp. 51-55.

81. Nabokoff, *Ordeal of a Diplomat,* pp. 263-64.

82. Trotskii, *Sochineniia,* vol. III, part II, p. 99.

83. *Desiat' let sovetskoi diplomatii,* p. 6.

84. John Reed, 'Foreign Affairs', *The Liberator,* 1918, vol. I, p. 28; and Ia. S. Ganetskii, *O lenine: otryvki iz vospominanii* (Moscow, 1933), pp. 72-75.

85. *Izvestiia,* 4 June 1918, reprinted in L.A. Modzhorian and V.K. Sobakin, eds., *Mezhdunarodnoe pravo v izbrannykh dokumentakh* (Moscow, 1957), vol. II, p. 5.

86. *Sobranie uzakonenii i rasporiazhenii rabochego i krest'ianskogo pravitel'stva* (Moscow, 1918), sections 37-42.

87. *Desiat' let sovetskoi diplomatii,* pp. 9 and 10; and Kantorovich, 'Organizatsionnoe razvitie NKID', p. 53. Cf. Edward L. Crowley, ed., *The Soviet Diplomatic Corps, 1917-1967* (Metuchen, 1970), pp. 4-6. The latter is somewhat inconsistent with the records published by the NKID.

88. *Desiat' let sovetskoi diplomatii,* p. 8. The Narkomindel experimented briefly with a different arrangement in the spring of 1918. The Eastern and Western Departments were temporarily abolished in favor of a Chancellery of the Deputy Commissar for Western Affairs and a similar Deputy's Chancellery for Eastern Affairs. Each chancellery then encompassed a number of national or regional area desks. This system apparently did not function well and so regional departments were soon recreated. See A.S. Bakhov, *Na zare sovetskoi diplomatii* (Moscow, 1966), pp. 91-92;

and Vygodskii, *U istokov,* pp. 33-34. Cf. *Spravochnik tsentral'nykh i mestnykh uchrezhdenii RSFSR partiinykh organizatsii i professional'nykh soiuzov* (Moscow, 1920), pp. 155-58.

89.   Kantorovich, 'Organizatsionnoe razvitie NKID', p. 52.
90.   Ibid.
91.   Ibid.
92.   *Desiat' let sovetskoi diplomatii,* pp. 8-9.
93.   Wheeler-Bennett, *Brest-Litovsk,* p. 261, n. 1.
94.   *Sobranie uzakonenii,* 1918, no. 90, article 923.
95.   Karl A. Bickel, 'How the Outside World Gets Its Information Concerning Events in Russia', in: *The Internal and External Problems of Russia: Proceedings of General Conference, August 1 and 2, 1930* (Williamstown, 1930), pp. 12-14; and Paul Scheffer, *Seven Years in Soviet Russia* (New York, 1932), p. viii.
96.   *Mezhdunarodnaia zhizn',* the official Russian language journal of the Narkomindel was published from 1922 to 1930. A journal of the same title began publication in several languages in 1954 under the auspices of Znanie.
97.   For discussions of the diplomatic role of these other Soviet republics see Bakhov, *Na zare,* pp. 101-45; Vernon V. Aspaturian, *The Union Republics and Soviet Diplomacy: A Study of Soviet Federalism in the Service of Soviet Foreign Policy* (Geneva and Paris, 1960); and Vasyl Markus, *L'Ukraine Soviétique dans les Relations Internationales et son statut en Droit International, 1918-1923* (Paris, 1959). Also see Kazanin, *Zapiski sekretaria missii,* pp. 23-24 and 156 for a disucssion of the use of 'buffer' republics in Soviet diplomacy.
98.   *DVP,* vol. I, pp. 109-11.
99.   *Desiat' let sovetskoi diplomatii,* p. 9.
100. Wheeler-Bennett, *Brest-Litovsk,* pp. 84ff. Also see D.G. Fokke, 'Na stsene i za kulisami brestskoi tragikomedii', in: V. Gessen, ed., *Arkhiv russkoi revoliutsii* (The Hague and Paris, 1970), vol. XX, pp. 5-208.
101. Georgii A. Solomon, *Among the Red Autocrats: My Experience in the Service of the Soviets* (New York, 1935), p. 24.
102. Ibid., pp. 18-23. The chaos at the Berlin embassy was apparently typical of early Soviet missions. Alfred Senn notes that the members of the Soviet embassy in Switzerland 'had no firm conception of hierarchical organization', *Diplomacy and Revolution,* p. 98.
103. Wheeler-Bennett, *Brest-Litovsk,* pp. 346-47.
104. Maisky, *Journey into the Past,* p. 63. Litvinov notes that he was angry at the time, but learned later that Lenin was so preoccupied with the gravest matters that he could not direct the normal activities of Soviet missions abroad. Cf. Kazanin, *Zapiski sekretaria missii,* p. 141.
105. *Sobranie uzakonenii,* 1918, no. 78, article 823.
106. Ibid., section 3.
107. Alexander Barmine, *One Who Survived* (New York, 1945), p. 141.
108. *Sobranie uzakonenii,* 1918, no. 78, article 823, sections 8 and 9.
109. Ibid., section 4, paragraph v.
110. Barmine, *One Who Survived,* p. 107.

2

THE ECLIPSE OF DIPLOMACY, 1918-1921

By the summer of 1918 the People's Commissariat of Foreign Affairs had elaborated an organizational structure sufficient to manage the foreign relations of the young Soviet state and had also established a few more-or-less official and well functioning foreign missions. This rapid expansion was soon to be reversed when, in the grip of civil war and foreign intervention, the RSFSR found its opportunities for diplomatic contacts with the outside world rapidly dwindling.

The Allied powers, and especially the United States, had greeted the February revolution and the liberal government which it brought to power with some enthusiasm. Now the Allied cause could represent itself as a united front of liberal-democractic peoples arrayed against the autocratic central empires. However, the progressive radicalization of the Russian political scene, culminating in the Bolshevik victory, gave pause to the statesmen of the Western alliance. Yet, as much as they despised the political and social ideas of Marxism-Leninism, the precarious military situation on the western front dictated to the Entente governments the necessity of maintaining relations with the Soviet regime in an effort to revitalize the eastern front and thereby prevent the transfer of huge German armies to France. Under these circumstances the Allied states decided to maintain unofficial or semi-official contacts with the Soviet republic for the dual purpose of encouraging renewed military campaigns against the Central Powers and attempting to assess the domestic and international significance of the Bolshevik takeover.

This Allied policy of maintaining cautious, limited contacts with the new regime in Petrograd gradually evolved toward open hostility as the seriousness of Lenin's peace initiative and the radicalism of Bolshevik social and economic policies were more clearly perceived in the Western capitals. A series of decrees promulgated by the Council of People's Commissars beginning in December of 1917 provided for the nationalization of banks and of many industries and further legitimatized the already existing de facto workers' control of most factories. A decree of 29 December 1917 unconditionally annulled all foreign loans and stopped immediately any payment of interest or dividends on stocks or bonds, and prohibited trading in them.[1] These measures provoked considerable distress in capitalist circles and carried little appeal for politicians such as Lloyd George, Clemenceau or Wilson who had been schooled in the traditions of nineteenth-century liberalism.[2] Bolshevik domestic policy and ideology were probably even more repulsive to the Allied leadership than Soviet economic practices. The dissolving of the Constituent Assembly and the use of political terror in Russia violated the democratic principles for which the World War was supposedly being fought. The fiery sermons delivered by Lenin and his comrades advocating international proletarian revolution provided an even more direct challenge to the democracies.

It was the Bolsheviks' foreign policy, though, rather than their economic, revolutionary or domestic political activities which finally led to a complete rupture of relations with the Entente. While there was still hope for further military cooperation with the RSFSR, Paris and London found it possible, at least temporarily, to tolerate the communists' revolutionary rhetoric and nationalization schemes. However, after Soviet threats of a separate peace took on concrete form in the Treaty of Brest-Litovsk on 3 March 1918, the Western powers became increasingly hostile.[3] There were a few realistic statesmen in the Allied camp, such as George Buchanan, the British Ambassador in Petrograd, who advocated accepting the loss of the Russian alliance with good grace, but the intransigent attitude of the French (especially Clemenceau) and the Italians made that sensible policy impossible.[4]

The Allies' growing disillusionment with Soviet domestic and foreign policies coincided with the advent of serious internal opposition to the Bolshevik regime. After the October insurrection and the subsequent dissolution of the Constituent Assembly, the other two major Russian revolutionary parties, the Mensheviks and the Socialist Revolutionaries (SRs) had refused to cooperate with the Bolshevik-dominated Soviet government. They considered the uprising premature and they resented Lenin's dictatorial methods. Only the radical Left-SRs had been willing to form a coalition with the Bolsheviks. But even this alliance proved short-lived. The Left-SRs, together with important segments of the Bolshevik party itself, favored a declaration of revolutionary war against the Germans in preference to signing the harsh, and to their minds, compromising, Peace of Brest-Litovsk. When Lenin's superior realism carried the issue in favor of approving the treaty, the Left-SRs went into active opposition. Their Commissars resigned from the Sovnarkom and on 6 July 1918, in a deliberate attempt to sabotage the Brest-Litovsk treaty, Left-SR terrorists assassinated the German Ambassador. In the following month Right-SR agents made an attempt on Lenin's life and succeeded in murdering Mikhail Uritskii, the head of the Petrograd *Cheka*.

At about the same time an even more serious threat to the Soviet Republic was developing in the distant provinces to the south and east. In the extremely fragmented political situation of 1917 relatively small exertions of force had succeeded in toppling unpopular governments in the February and October revolutions. Now, however, the very existence of a radical Marxist-Leninist regime served to unite a diverse opposition of army officers, monarchists, conservatives, liberals, right-wing SRs and some Mensheviks. 'White' (i.e. anti-Red) armies, politically heterogeneous but sharing a common hatred of the communists, began to form in south Russia and in Siberia. Actual civil war was touched off in May of 1918 when a misunderstanding developed between Soviet authorities and Czechoslovak prisoner of war units, who had been rearmed to fight for national independence against the Central Powers. The Czechs seized a number of Siberian towns and took control of the Trans-Siberian Railway.[5] In addition, numerous minority populations inhabiting the border lands of the defunct tsarist empire (the Ukrainians, Latvians, Georgians, etc.) fielded national militias in an effort to gain political independence from the Russian state. Although these disparate forces seldom cooperated and occasionally even fought among themselves, they constituted an extremely grave danger to the RSFSR.

The Allied statesmen, already predisposed to favor any opposition to Lenin's regime, seized this apparent opportunity to produce a more acceptable government for Russia. Relations between the RSFSR and the Western capitals deteriorated rapidly. At the beginning of the year, when the Soviet government transferred its seat from Petrograd to Moscow, the foreign diplomatic corps chose to move en masse to Vologda rather than to take up residence in the new capital, ostensibly for reasons of safety. The Bolsheviks sent Karl Radek after them to urge their departure for Moscow, but on 18 July 1918 the foreign diplomats left Vologda for distant Archangelsk which was soon to be occupied by Allied troops. Moscow thus lost its last feeble contact with the official representatives of the Western states. This was a blow to the Bolsheviks; it further deepened their isolation and it seemed to presage a full-scale military assault on the Soviet regime by the imperialist powers. The Commissariat of Foreign Affairs issued a proclamation expressing the hope that this removal would not effect a break in diplomatic relations.[6]

The Allies did not limit their participation in the Russian civil war to gestures. After a long series of debates on ends and means, the Entente powers decided on a policy of direct military intervention in Russia. The initial landing at Murmansk in March of 1918 involved only a small number of troops and was authorized specifically to protect war material from German raids. But soon much larger contingents of British soldiers arrived in the north, while French and British military and naval units were dispatched to South Russia, and American and Japanese armies began to swarm into Siberia from the Pacific coast. At first, while the German menace was still alive, the Soviet government was not entirely unhappy with the limited Allied landings. However, with the subsiding of any threat from the German army, the increased flow of foreign soldiers onto Russian soil, coupled with the tendency of Allied commanders to cooperate with White forces, led the Bolsheviks to denounce the intervention as an illegal invasion. Trotskii declared that the Soviets could '. . .not regard this intervention of the Allied imperialists in any other light than as a hostile attempt against the freedom and independence of Soviet Russia'.[7] In further protest, Chicherin issued an order for the expulsion of French Ambassador Noulens.[8]

By the time the foreign dipolmats evacuated Vologda in July, relations with the West were already very strained. Only the unofficial agents of the Allies, Lockhart, Sadoul and Raymond Robins, remained in contact with the Bolsheviks, and even these ties disappeared shortly as the undeclared war between the Entente and the RSFSR escalated. Relations with Great Britain came to a complete break in early September of 1918. On 31 August a pro-Bolshevik mob, enraged over the shootings of Lenin and Uritskii, invaded the British consulate in Petrograd and the English Naval Attaché, Captain Cromie, was killed in the ensuing gun battle. Then on 3 September the chief British political agent in Russia, Bruce Lockhart, was arrested for attempting to subvert the loyalty of a Lettish rifles unit in the Red Army.[9] In response, Litvinov was arrested in London and subsequently deported on the grounds that he had used sealed diplomatic pouches to ship revolutionary materials into Great Britain.[10] Following the departure of Lockhart, the remaining unofficial agents and consular representatives of the other Allied powers and of the neutral states began to make their exits as well. The Dutch recalled their mission, and Rosen, the Soviet representative assigned to Holland, was refused permission to enter the country. Sweden requested Vorovskii's recall and both Norway and Denmark broke all governmental relations with the Soviet Republic.[11] In December of 1918 the Russian Red Cross mission was expelled from Warsaw, and four of its five members assassinated.

The Soviet government tried to establish diplomatic relations with the United States by appointing Ludwig K. Martens as its representative in New York City in January 1919, but it was rebuffed here as well. The State Department honored the credentials of Provisional Government Ambassador Boris Bakhmet'ev until his resignation in 1922 and thereafter it recognized another Provisional Government appointee, Financial Attaché Serge Ughet, as chief of the Russian Embassy.[12] Martens proceeded to establish a sizable Soviet mission in New York city despite this lack of official recognition.[13] The unsanctioned Bolshevik legation busily set about soliciting foreign trade and issuing information bulletins to combat the anti-Soviet version of Russian events which dominated the Western press. Martens and his associates were constantly harassed, however, by the local police, the US Department of Justice, and investigating committees of the New York State Assembly and the US Senate.[14] After a series of legal battles, Martens was deported in February 1921.[15] Secretary of State Colby expressed the prevailing American attitude in an exchange with the Italian Ambassador:

> . . .the existing regime in Russia is based upon the negation of every principle of honor and good faith, and every usage and convention, underlying the whole structure of international law; the negation, in short, of every principle upon which it is possible to base harmonious and trustful relations, whether of nations or individuals. . . . In the view of this Government, there cannot be any common ground upon which it can stand with a Power whose conceptions of international relations are so entirely alien to its own, so utterly repugnant to its moral sense.[16]

This series of political disasters for Bolshevik foreign policy was capped by the defection of Germany from the Moscow diplomatic scene. On 6 July 1918 Left-SR terrorists assassinated the German Ambassador, Count Mirbach-Harff, in a deliberate attempt to pro-

voke a renewal of hostilities with Germany. Karl Helfferich replaced
Mirbach, arriving in Moscow in late July, but he was ordered back to
Berlin by his government almost immediately. Soon after the ambassador's departure the entire embassy was moved to Pskov,
behind German lines. Only Consul-General Hauschild remained in
the Bolshevik capital.[17] In August supplementary agreements to the
Brest-Litovsk Treaty were concluded in Berlin by Admiral von
Hintze, German Secretary of State for Foreign Affairs and Ioffe, the
Soviet representative. Further territorial sacrifices and the payment
of a large indemnity were the new price which the Soviets had to pay
for peace.[18] Subsequently, when the inevitability of defeat in the west
became obvious in Berlin, German policy toward Russia shifted
from exploitation to isolation. The Germans decided to sever relations with the RSFSR in hopes of appeasing the Allies.

To provide some justification for this break, the Prussian police
undertook to see that one of the large packing crates consigned to the
Soviet Embassy in Berlin would 'accidentally' break open. On 5
November 1918 Foreign Minister Solf reported to the German
cabinet that this mishap had indeed occurred and that the carton had
proved to be filled with inflammatory and seditious materials. Ioffe
and his entire staff were expelled on this basis.[19] The Social-
Democratic government which was formed in Berlin just a few days
later, after the fall of the Kaiser, made no move to restore relations
with Moscow. Thus, by early 1919 Soviet Russia was almost completely cut off from the outside world. The only foreign representation remaining in Moscow was the Danish Red Cross Mission which
had agreed to oversee the interests of the Scandinavian, European,
and American states in Russia.[20]

The only significant exceptions to this isolation occurred in Soviet
relations with countries in Asia. The line between traditional
diplomacy and revolutionary initiative was frequently blurred in
Moscow's dealings with its southern neighbors, since most of these
states were in revolt against British domination. The situation in this
region was further complicated by the existence of powerful White
armies there which made communications difficult. By collaborating
with various native nationalist movements on Russia's southern
flank, the Bolsheviks hoped both to isolate the White forces and to
strike a blow against British imperialism. Therefore, after some
agonizing over the fate of Turkish communists, the Soviet leadership
decided to support the nationalist government of Kemal Pasha in

Turkey, dispatching A.A. Kistiakovskii as their representative in
Ankara in 1919.[21] Establishing normal diplomatic relations with Iran
proved a more difficult task than was the case with Turkey. Ivan
Kolomiitsev had already set up a Soviet mission in Teheran in 1918,
but the Persian government refused to recognize it and maintained a
generally hostile attitude toward the Bolsheviks. The Soviet mission
was attacked in November by elements of the Iranian Cossack
Brigade and Kolomiitsev was forced to flee to Baku. When he tried
to return the following year, he was captured and killed by White
forces.[22] Thereafter the Bolsheviks followed a more militant policy
toward Iran. They seized the Persian port of Enzeli and threw their
support behind the radical, separatist Soviet Republic of Ghilan.[23]

In contrast, the Soviet government readily established good relations with Afghanistan. There the new Amir, Amanullah, was intent
upon eliminating British influence in his country. The Bolsheviks
were obvious allies. Amanullah therefore welcomed political and
economic assistance from Moscow. N.Z. Bravin arrived to set up a
Soviet mission in Kabul in the autumn of 1919, but he was soon
replaced by a higher ranking Bolshevik envoy, Iakov Surits.[24] The
chaotic situation in China prevented the establishment of similar
relations with that country. The nominal government in Peking,
under heavy pressure from the Western Powers, refused to recognize
the Soviet regime. However, in 1920 the Chinese government
withdrew its recognition of the Provisional Government's diplomats
and permitted an 'unofficial' delegation from the Bolshevik puppet
Far Eastern Republic to enter Peking. This mission, led by Ignatii
Iurin, accomplished little, but it did open a channel for communication with the Peking government and with the Japanese military
authorities in China.[25] Except for these few ties with Asian states,
Moscow was essentially cut off from the main stream of world
politics during the years of civil war and foreign intervention.

This dramatic rupture of diplomatic relations with the European
powers naturally had a profound impact on the People's Commissariat of Foreign Affairs. The size of the Narkomindel was
diminished, both in terms of the overall number of personnel
employed and of the number of sections into which the Commissariat was divided. All the departments were reduced in size as
well. The simplified structure of the Narkomindel now contained only
nine significant departments. The Chancellery, or administrative office,
provided secretarial and technical assistance to the Commissar

and his Deputy. The Department of Finance and Personnel handled the Narkomindel's business affairs, while the Sub-division of Monetary Transfers and Loans supervised movements of capital and transactions concerning pre-revolutionary loans. The Economic-Material Department was principally concerned with economic relations between the RSFSR and other countries. The Economic-Legal Department was charged with rendering opinions on technical economic and legal questions and with formulating treaties and agreements. The principal diplomatic work was carried out by the Department of the West, subdivided into sections for the Central Powers and for the Entente and Scandinavian states, and by the Department of the East. The Press Department monitored the Soviet image as reflected in the world's press and prepared news releases for both Soviet and foreign correspondents. The Department of Diplomatic Couriers and the Section for Visas and Passports completed the organizational structure of the Commissariat.[26]

An early official history of the Narkomindel admitted that, '. . .the isolation of the Soviet republics reached its high point [in 1918-1919]. The radio remained almost the only means of communication with the outside world.'[27] During this period Lenin, Chicherin and their colleagues literally flooded the telegraph lines and airwaves with innumerable proposals and appeals for peace. Diplomacy of the most public sort was the only avenue left open to them.

DIPLOMACY AND PARA-DIPLOMACY

In this situation Bolshevik diplomacy was forced to show considerable imagination and adaptability in defending the interests of the Soviet state. Pressing need, coupled with frenetic experimentation, soon produced a substitute, albeit inadequate, for Russia's shattered foreign relations — para-diplomacy. This concept involved the calculated use of non-diplomatic personnel, agencies and situations for covertly diplomatic purposes. In 1918 the Soviet government began to lay the groundwork for a set of para-diplomatic organizations which were to fill the gap made by the Western powers' policy of non-recognition during the worst period of isolation and foreign intervention. Officially non-political agencies engaged in relief work, prisoner of war affairs and foreign trade, proved the most useful in this connection.

The People's Commissariat of Foreign Affairs was charged with overall responsibility for prisoner of war affairs, but most of the work in foreign countries had to be done by the Red Cross Society, in the absence of official NKID representatives. Through a series of Sovnarkom decrees the Russian Red Cross Society was 'sovietized' and the Narkomindel proclaimed the willingness of the government to recognize all existing international Red Cross treaties and conventions. A special interdepartmental unit of government, the Central Collegium on Prisoners of War and Refugees (or *Tsentroplenbezh*), was created to coordinate these activities.[28] Over and above humanitarian motives, the purpose of these steps was to ensure open channels of communication between the Narkomindel and various foreign governments despite the lack of formal diplomatic recognition.

The usefulness of such 'Red Cross diplomacy' is well illustrated in the case of Soviet relations with Poland. Julian Marchlewski, a Polish socialist and also an NKID official, was sent as the representative of the Russian Red Cross Society to negotiate with the agents of its Polish counterpart late in 1919. His credentials declared that;

> Comrade Markhlevskii, the representative of the Russian Red Cross Society for the purpose of negotiations with the Polish Red Cross Society, is at the same time empowered by the Russian Soviet Government to conduct negotiations with a representative of the Polish Government concerning all questions which did or should arise between the Polish Republic and the Russian Socialist Federated Soviet Republic, to make inquiries of the representatives of the Polish Republic and to ascertain the attitude of its Government on such questions, as well as to answer similar inquiries made by the representatives of the Polish Republic, to ascertain in concert with them the possibility of a coordinated solution to these questions, and to establish in general, as well as in particular, the basis for an agreement which could ensure peaceful relations between the Polish Republic and the Russian Socialist Federated Soviet Republic. [Dated] 4 October 1919 [Signed] G.V. Chicherin.[29]

Operating under this inoffensive Red Cross cover, Marchlewski was able to reach an agreement with the Poles on the positioning of their respective military forces which freed a number of desperately needed Red Army units for the battles against the White contingents of Kolchak and Denikin.[30]

Prisoner of war and refugee work was also used to repair in part the broken links with England. Following the Allied landings at Archangelsk in August 1918, the Bolsheviks had taken as hostages several West European (and especially British) nationals. As their number grew, the British government was finally forced to abandon its policy of attempting to ignore Moscow and open talks on the matter. In November 1919 a British agent named James O'Grady was dispatched to Copenhagen for meetings with Litvinov. These negotiations over the prisoner of war and hostage issues dragged on until 12 February 1920 and thus provided the RSFSR with a line of communications — though a precarious one — to the major imperialist power, even during the period of armed intervention.[31] Ties with Germany were restored in much the same way. Viktor L. Kopp arrived in Berlin in November of 1919 as an unofficial agent for prisoner of war affairs, but he soon began to engage in both diplomatic and foreign trade activities.[32]

Similar para-diplomatic Red Cross missions were maintained in Sweden, Norway, Denmark and Hungary. France, too, admitted a Soviet Red Cross mission in January of 1919 which tried to negotiate with the government in Paris, but the French, correctly sensing the actual purpose of these representatives, soon expelled them.[33] To circumvent this difficulty, the Russians creatively used their Red Cross mission in Copenhagen to transmit diplomatic messages to the Quai d'Orsay via the local French Consul.[34] Relations with the International Red Cross did not always run smoothly since the Bolsheviks tended to suspect even the most charitable relief organizations of actively supporting the White counter-revolution.[35] These difficulties hampered the effectiveness of the Russian Red Cross Society.

Science was also pressed into the cause of Soviet diplomacy. On 20 August 1918 the Sovnarkom empowered the Bureau of Science and Technology, a part of the Supreme Council of National Economy, to establish relations with scientific societies and institutions abroad.[36] In taking this initiative the Bolsheviks intended to open new avenues of approach to the capitalist powers. Commissar of Education, Anatolii Lunacharskii, later admitted that the Academy of Sciences and other Russian scientific institutions had been used by the Soviet government to establish diplomatic contacts and to facilitate peace negotiations during the period of civil war and foreign intervention.[37]

Another method of circumventing non-recognition involved the use of trade representatives for diplomatic purposes. By early 1920, when it had become clear that neither the White armies nor the Allied blockade and intervention could topple Soviet power, the

Western states decided to resume trade relations with Russia, although they still refused to accord diplomatic recognition to the Bolshevik regime.[38] Accordingly, the Allied Supreme Council approved trade with 'the Russian people' through the All-Russian Central Union of Consumers' Societies (*Tsentrosoiuz*), a non-governmental cooperative society. The Supreme Council warned the Bolsheviks, however, that 'these arrangements imply no change in the policy [i.e. of non-recognition] of the Allied governments towards the Soviet government'.[39] The cooperative movement seemed to the Allied statesmen an ideal vehicle for establishing commercial relationships in Russia while still avoiding contact with the loathsome Bolsheviks, since the leaders of *Tsentrosoiuz* were non-communist or, in some cases, even militantly anti-communist; but the Kremlin was not to be outwitted in the game of para-diplomacy. In response, the Sovnarkom simply coöpted *Tsentrosoiuz*.[40] When the Allies received the names of the *Tsentrosoiuz* delegation which was to be sent to London for trade negotiations, they were shocked to discover the list was headed by Deputy Foreign Commissar Litvinov and Commissar of Foreign Trade Leonid Krasin. Although the British again refused to admit Litvinov, they had been outmaneuvered by the Russians and were forced to receive the rest of the Soviet cooperative delegation.[41]

Trade missions and *Tsentrosoiuz* commissions served as the opening wedge for Bolshevik diplomacy in a number of instances. Krasin, the head of the Soviet Trade Delegation in London, thus became the de facto Russian ambassador to Great Britain.[42] The Soviets used this precedent in an attempt to achieve similar para-diplomatic relations with other countries. In a note of 23 September 1920 to the Norwegian Ministry of Trade, Litvinov pointed out that '. . .the British draft agreement provided for some diplomatic privileges for trade plenipotentiaries. It gave them the right to protect their nationals: issue visas, notarize documents and perform other consular functions'.[43] Similarly, the Soviet Trade Delegation to Czechoslovakia was instructed by Chicherin to use the prisoner of war issue to establish a mission in Bulgaria, '. . .which would have full official status with diplomatic immunities, right of couriers, use of cipher, telegraph and radio'. The Commissar continued, 'We are interested in an effective renewal of relations, although it might bear the name of the Mission for the Affairs of the POW.'[44]

In 1920 trade delegations set up under the authority of

Tsentrosoiuz were established in Estonia, Lithuania and Latvia. Italy, Austria, Turkey, Germany, Finland, Sweden, Persia, Norway and China were added to the list the following year. In fact, it had been representatives of *Tsentrosoiuz* who had appeared before the Allied Supreme Council in Paris in 1920, although official Soviet diplomats were barred from these proceedings, and — acting in concert with Lloyd George — had arranged for both the lifting of the Allied blockade of Russia and the beginning of limited trade carried out through the Russian cooperative societies. Many Western governments, however, either refused to admit even such 'non-political' Soviet emissaries or else consented merely to treat them as private persons engaged in economic or humanitarian activity. The Narkomindel found that it was not always easy to use this back door to diplomatic recognition.

Karl Radek proved to be the most colorful and unusual member of Moscow's para-diplomatic corps. He slipped across the German border in disguise in order to attend the All-German Congress of Workers' and Soldiers' Councils held in Berlin in December of 1918. He was arrested by the German authorities on 12 February 1919 in connection with the so-called Spartakus uprising. Germany had broken relations with the RSFSR, but not specifically with the Soviet Ukraine. In an attempt to liberate Radek, Khristian Rakovskii, the head of the Ukrainian Soviet Republic, appointed him as representative of the Ukrainian SSR to Berlin. The Germans refused to recognize his authority, but Radek's 'cell' (really an apartment in Berlin) soon was filled with visitors who ran the political gamut from communist activists, through Weimar politicians, to Reichswehr officers. Radek thus served as a para-diplomatic representative of the Soviet Republic, though in the absence of communication with Moscow, his role in the development of Soviet-German relations was limited.[45]

While the novel techniques of para-diplomacy achieved limited results, the Bolsheviks' major initiatives in the realm of traditional diplomacy ended in failure. Desperate for peace, the Soviet government dispatched Litvinov to Stockholm in December of 1918 to approach the representatives of the Allied states resident in Sweden. On 24 December he addressed a direct peace appeal to President Wilson of the United States. In response, William Buckler, a State Department official, was sent to talk with Litvinov. The Bolshevik diplomat proved amazingly conciliatory on the questions of repayment of tsarist debts and of the cessation of revolutionary propaganda. Buckler returned a favorable report and, on this basis, the Allied Council of Ten, despite some French and Italian opposition, proposed a conference at Prinkipo of all the belligerent Russian groups for the purpose of achieving a peace settlement. The Soviets immediately accepted the invitation but the whole proposal collapsed under adamant White resistance.[46]

In the sequel to the abortive Prinkipo Conference, Wilson and Lloyd George, the two least bellicose statesmen in the Allied camp, sent a junior American diplomat, William Bullitt, to meet with Soviet officials and discuss possible peace terms. The Bolshevik leaders outlined reasonable terms to Bullitt: an immediate armistice, an end to foreign intervention and the Soviet assumption of Russia's foreign debts. However, by the time Bullitt returned to Paris the political climate had altered radically. Even Wilson and Lloyd George had begun to bend before the unremitting anti-Bolshevism of the French, the Italians and Winston Churchill. Wilson feared that, at this juncture, a compromise peace with Soviet Russia might further embitter his relations with the United States Senate, while Lloyd George worried that, in order to oust him, his political rivals in England would pounce on the issue of any concessions made to Moscow. Both in America and in Great Britain hostility toward the Bolsheviks was rampant not only among conservatives but also in some liberal and moderate socialist circles which objected to Soviet authoritarianism and which hoped for some Kadet or Menshevik alternative to the communists.[47] It was also at this time that Admiral Kolchak's White forces began an offensive which promised to eliminate the Bolshevik problem entirely. Under these circumstances, the Bullitt affair was allowed to drop quietly.[48] In Paris the Allied statesmen and diplomats labored to reconstruct an order on the continent quite at odds with the Soviet view of Europe's future. The result of their work, the Treaty of Versailles, restructured Europe so as to isolate, if not actually to strangle, revolutionary Russia.[49] There would be no help via diplomatic channels for the beleaguered Bolsheviks.

THE REVOLUTIONARY ALTERNATIVE

The natural response for the Soviet regime in this situation was to rely almost completely on its alternative, non-diplomatic approach to the capitalist world — revolution. Trotskii reflected the feeling of most Bolsheviks when he told the Second Congress of Soviets in November 1917 that 'if the peoples of Europe do not arise and crush imperialism, we shall be crushed — this is beyond doubt. Either the Russian revolution will raise the whirlwind of struggle in the west, or the capitalists of all countries will stifle our struggle.'[50] Developments in the next three years seemed to confirm Trotskii's prophecy. The civil war and foreign intervention evidenced the desire of the Russian right and the capitalist powers to join in smashing the Bolshevik experiment. But at the same time, chances for a world-wide, or at least pan-European, revolution never looked brighter. The four eastern bulwarks of reaction, the Hohenzollern, Romanov, Habsburg and Ottoman empires, all lay in ruins. Although reformist Social-Democrats were temporarily in control of Germany, the more radical Independent Socialists soon abandoned the governing coalition and drifted toward the genuinely militant Spartakus Bund and the Shop Stewards movement. Even the victorious Allied countries were not immune to the unrest. French soldiers and sailors, both in France and in the expeditionary force in south Russia, had mutinied against their officers. Industrial disturbances spread throughout France and Italy. In 1919 Great Britain experienced a rash of strikes and the formation of radical Councils of Action, ominously similar to the Russian Soviets. Everywhere hunger, war-weariness and a reaction against the bourgeois politicians and reformist socialists who had supported the war gave promise that the anticipated revolutionary wave might not be far away.

Although 1919 was the darkest year for Soviet foreign policy, it was also the most encouraging from a revolutionary standpoint. In November of 1918 a Soviet-style republic had been proclaimed in Bavaria under the leadership of Kurt Eisner, while Workers' and Soldiers' Councils began to spring up all over Germany. Then 1919 opened with the misnamed Spartakus Uprising in Berlin, a semi-spontaneous outburst of workers, loosely organized by the Revolutionary Shop Stewards and later joined by the communists. Just three months later another nation was added to the growing list of Soviet republics — Béla Kun led a coalition of communists and socialists in forming a Hungarian government which maintained friendly relations with Moscow. In mid-June another workers' insurrection occurred in Vienna. The Bolsheviks excitedly awaited the proclamation of Soviet power in Paris and London. In an attempt to coordinate and promote all of these insurrectionary activities the Russian communists sponsored the founding in 1919 of a new association of revolutionary parties, the Communist International. Lenin hoped to seize the leadership of the working class movement from the reform-minded socialists of the Second International and to prefigure the future international socialist brotherhood which would replace the oppressive capitalist governments.[51]

With all normal diplomatic channels closed and with the Kremlin strongly emphasizing revolution over peaceful co-existence in its relations with the capitalist world, the functions of the People's Commissariat of Foreign Affairs were restricted to what might be called revolutionary diplomacy and the diplomacy of revolution. Revolutionary diplomacy involved the use of unorthodox techniques, such as appeals to the peoples of the Western states rather than to their governments, to achieve ordinary diplomatic goals. The diplomacy of revolution, in contrast, implied the use of diplomatic personnel and privileges to foment revolution in foreign lands. The NKID utilized both approaches with varying success during this period. For example, Trotskii's call for peace on 30 December 1917, addressed to both the governments and peoples of the belligerent states, constituted a breach of diplomatic etiquette and laid bare the revolutionary threat behind Bolshevik diplomacy.[52]

The scene at the arrival of the Soviet delegation to the Brest-Litovsk conference epitomized this juxtaposition of diplomacy with revolutionary agitation. Before going in to meet the diplomats from the Central Powers, the Bolsheviks distributed revolutionary leaflets to the troops of the German army honor guard. With little official diplomacy to conduct, Commissar Chicherin spent much of his time broadcasting lengthy appeals to the world's workers and peasants.[53] As Chicherin put it, '. . .we write fewer notes to governments and more appeals to the working classes'.[54] The toiling masses of Persia were summoned to strike out against imperialism while the Western European proletariat was urged to protest their governments' anti-Soviet campaign.[55]

During the Russo-Polish War of 1920 both traditional and revolutionary diplomacy were employed. A campaign was launched with the aim of persuading Polish and Western workers to oppose Marshal Pilsudski's war effort.[56] This technique enjoyed some success in that Czech, Danzig and Belgian transport workers refused to ship supplies to the Polish army.[57] At the same time, the Russians approached Western and border-state governments through various diplomatic channels to ensure that they would not come to the aid of the Poles or take any steps against their own workers whose refusal to transship Polish war material was of such great value to the Soviet cause. The treaty signed at this time with Lithuania is a good example of political and military advantages secured through diplomatic means even in the period of isolation.[58]

If diplomacy could employ revolutionary means, the cause of revolution might also advance through diplomatic channels. The Bolsheviks saw a German revolution as the linchpin of the hoped-for European upheaval, so special efforts were made in this direction. The first Soviet representative in Berlin, Adolf Ioffe, openly associated with, and provided funds for, the German radical left.[59] After his expulsion from Germany, Ioffe readily admitted that, 'it is necessary to emphasize most categorically that in the preparation of the German revolution, the Russian Embassy worked all the time in close contact with the German Socialists'.[60] The Narkomindel's role in fostering revolutions was not confined to Germany alone. A Sovnarkom decree of 13 December 1917 allocated two million rubles to the NKID for its work in aiding international revolutionary movements.[61]

Despite all the energies expended and anxieties suffered, all parties — the Bolsheviks, the Whites and the Allies — were to be disappointed in the years 1918 through 1920. For the Bolsheviks, the specter of world revolution, so bright in 1919, proved to be merely a mirage. The Spartakus uprising in Berlin was brutally quashed and the leaders of the recently founded German Communist Party (KPD), Rosa Luxemburg and Karl Liebknecht, were murdered. The German Workers' and Soldiers' Councils meekly relinquished their authority to the Weimar National Assembly which was dominated by reformist socialist (SPD) and bourgeois centrist politicians. In Bavaria Kurt Eisner was assassinated and the Soviet experiment there was abolished by federal troops. The power of the military caste remained unbroken in Germany. The attempted rising in Vienna in the summer of 1919 was quickly crushed, and by August a combination of internal political strife and Rumanian intervention brought down the Hungarian Soviet regime. The other East European revolutions all stopped at the bourgeois liberal-national stage. Although Britain, France, Italy and many other countries seethed with class violence in 1919, the great proletarian revolution failed to materialize. The Bolsheviks had misread the situation. The various European workers' movements and their socialist leaders were too divided to form a massive revolutionary coalition, while the forces of the old order effectively, even ruthlessly, exploited their monopoly of military power to suppress strikes and demonstrations.

Nor were the White forces or the Allied powers any more successful in their aims. Hampered by poor communications and lines of supply, an inadequate strategy and disastrously inept political leadership, the White units were gradually eliminated by the Red Army. Foreign intervention also failed to dislodge Bolshevism. By early 1920, under the mounting pressure of mutinies among their own troops and the disintegration of the White armies, the Allies realized that only escalating the intervention into full scale war could prevent a Bolshevik victory. The climates of opinion in the armies and among the domestic populations of the Allied countries made such a strategy politically impossible. The people wanted an end to the fighting and a return to normalcy.

World revolution failed to come to the aid of the Soviet Republic, but war-weariness and lack of resolution among the Allies did. After the brief but inconclusive interlude of the Russo-Polish war in 1920, which temporarily renewed hopes on each side, it was clear to everyone that both the Bolshevik regime and the capitalist powers would continue to exist in the foreseeable future. An awareness began to grow both in Moscow and the Western capitals that, in the absence of victory, the situation demanded at least a temporary accommodation between the former belligerents. It was this need which called forth the re-emergence of the People's Commissariat of Foreign Affairs.

NOTES

1. *DVP,* vol. I, pp. 97-98.

2. For examples of Western reactions to Soviet financial policies see Ullman, *Intervention and the War*, pp. 69-70; and Louis Fischer, *The Soviets in World Affairs* (Princeton, 1951), vol. II, pp. 577ff.

3. Michael Jabara Carley, 'The Origins of the French Intervention in the Russian Civil War, January-May 1918: A Reappraisal', *The Journal of Modern History*, 1976, XLVIII, 3, pp. 413-39; Eugene P. Trani, 'Woodrow Wilson and the Decision to Intervene in Russia: A Reconsideration', *The Journal of Modern History*, 1976, XLVIII, 3, pp. 440-61; and Fischer, *Soviets in World Affairs*, vol. I, pp. 92ff. Also see Karl Radek, *Der Kampf der Kommunistischen Internationale gegen Versailles und gegen die Offensive des Kapitals* (Hamburg, 1923), p. 22.

4. Kennan, *Russia Leaves the War*, p. 133; Buchanan, *My Mission to Russia*, vol. II, pp. 225-26; and Thompson, *Russia, Bolshevism, and the Versailles Peace*, pp. 50-61.

5. Foreign Commissar Chicherin accused the Czech Legion of cooperating with the Whites. Iu. V. Kliuchnikov and A. Sabanin, eds., *Mezhdunarodnaia politika noveishego vremeni v dogovorakh, notakh, i deklaratsiiakh* (Moscow, 1925-26), vol. II, pp. 144-6.

6. *DVP*, vol. I, pp. 407-8.

7. Lev Trotskii, *Kak vooruzhalas' revoliutsiia* (Moscow, 1923-25), vol. I, p. 199.

8. James T. Bunyan, ed., *Intervention, Civil War and Communism in Russia, April-December 1918: Documents and Materials* (Baltimore, 1936), p. 72.

9. Ullman, *Intervention and the War*, pp. 285-96; and Richard K. Debo, 'Lockhart Plot or Dzerzhinskii Plot', *The Journal of Modern History*, 1971, XLIII, 3, pp. 415-39.

10. *Foreign Relations of the United States, 1918: Russia*, vol. I, p. 723; and *Kommunisticheskii internatsional*, 1929, no. 9-10, p. 189. Litvinov strongly denied this use of the pouches. *Foreign Relations of the United States, 1919: Russia*, p. 16.

11. Georgii Chicherin, *Two Years of Foreign Policy: The Relations of the R.S.F.S.R. with Foreign Nations, from November 7, 1917 to November 7, 1919* (New York, 1920), pp. 27-29.

12. US Department of State, decimal file, no. 701.611/711, Robert F. Kelley to Laura B. Pfeiffer, 13 November 1930 [hereafter USDS . . .].

13. Ibid., 701.611/315, L. Martens to Robert Lansing, 22 April 1919.

14. See, for example, *Bolshevik Propaganda: Hearings before a Subcommittee of the Committee on the Judiciary, United States Senate, pursuant to S. Res. 439 and 469, 65th Congress, 3rd Session, February 11-March 10, 1919* (Washington, 1919); and Thomas W. Hardwick, *The Status and Activities of L.C. Martens, Representative of the Russian Socialist Federal Soviet Republic, As shown in the evidence before the subcommittee of the Committee on Foreign Relations of the United States Senate* (n.p. [1920]).

15. For Soviet accounts of Martens' diplomatic activity see Liudmila Gvishiani, *Sovetskaia rossiia i SShA (1917-1920)* (Moscow, 1970); Georgii E. Evgen'ev and B. Shapik, *Revoliutsioner, diplomat, uchenyi (o L. K. Martens)* (Moscow, 1960); and I. Andropov, 'Lenin's Ambassador in America (Ludwig Martens)', *New Times*, 1970, no. 17, pp. 28-32.

16. *Foreign Relations of the United States, 1920*, vol. III, pp. 466-68. Note of 10 August 1920.

17. Baumgart, *Deutsche Ostpolitik*, pp. 245-47. Cf. Gustav Hilger and Alfred G.

Meyer, *The Incompatible Allies: A Memoir-History of German-Soviet Relations, 1918-1941* (New York, 1953), p. 18.

18. Hans W. Gatzke, 'Dokumentation zu den deutsch-russischen Beziehungen im Jahre 1918', *Vierteljahrshefte für Zeitgeschichte*, 1955, vol. III, pp. 67-98; Baumgart, *Deutsche Ostpolitik*, pp. 258-303; and Wheeler-Bennett, *Brest-Litovsk*, pp. 28-29.

19. Baumgart, *Deutsche Ostpolitik*, pp. 358-60; and Wheeler-Bennett, *Brest-Litovsk*, pp. 359-60. The Austrian social democratic press later claimed that these allegedly inflammatory materials . . .were neither written nor printed, nor packed, nor dispatched from Russia. They were in fact inserted into the diplomatic bag by the German police. . . .' *Klassenkampf* (Vienna), 1 December 1927.

20. *Otchet narodnogo komissariata po inostrannym delam sed'momu s"ezdu sovetov* (Moscow, 1919), p. 15.

21. See Harish Kapur, *Soviet Russia and Asia, 1917-1927: A Study of Soviet Policy towards Turkey, Iran and Afghanistan* (Geneva, 1966), pp. 89-114. Cf. S.I. Kuznetsova, *Ustanovlenie sovetsko-turetskikh otnoshenii* (Moscow, 1961), pp. 5-36.

22. *Desiat' let sovetskoi diplomatii*, p. 9; Kapur, *Soviet Russia and Asia*, p. 158; and B.Z. Shumiatskii, *Na postu sovetskoi diplomatii* (Moscow, 1960), pp. 42-45.

23. Kapur, *Soviet Russia and Asia*, pp. 160-77; Schapour Ravasani, *Sowjetrepublik Gilan: Die sozialistische Bewegung im Iran seit Ende des 19. Jhdt. bis 1922* (Berlin, n.d.), ch. IV; and George Lenczowski, *Russia and the West in Iran, 1918-1948* (Ithaca, 1949), pp. 48-60.

24. Kapur, *Soviet Russia and Asia*, pp. 216-22; Ludwig W. Adamec, *Afghanistan's Foreign Affairs to the Mid-Twentieth Century: Relations with the USSR, Germany and Britain* (Tucson, 1974), pp. 51-57; F.M. Bailey, *Mission to Tashkent* (London, 1946), pp. 174-76; and L.B. Teplinskii, *50 let sovetsko-afganskikh otnoshenii* (Moscow, 1971), pp. 10-34. Bravin may have been the first Soviet diplomatic defector. After his replacement as Soviet representative in Kabul by Surits in November of 1919, Bravin resigned from the NKID and took Afghan citizenship. He was murdered in January 1921 by an unknown assassin on the eve of his departure for India.

25. The Far Eastern Republic was nominally an independent, non-communist government, but in practice its policies were formulated in Moscow. For a detailed account of the Iurin mission see Sow-Theng Leong, *Sino-Soviet Diplomatic Relations, 1917-1925* (Honolulu, 1976), pp. 152-206; and Kazanin, *Zapiski sekreteria missii*, passim.

26. *Spravochnik tsentral'nykh i mestnykh uchrezhdenii R.S.F.S.R.*, pp. 155-58.

27. *Desiat' let sovetskoi diplomatii*, p. 10.

28. *Vestnik NKID*, 1919, no. 1, pp. 86-88; and *Desiat' let sovetskoi diplomatii*, p. 10. Also see Fritz T. Epstein, 'Aussenpolitik in Revolution und Bürgerkrieg, 1917-1920', in: Dietrich Geyer, ed., *Osteuropa-Handbuch: Sowjetunion, Aussenpolitik 1917-1955* (Cologne and Vienna, 1972), pp. 89-92 and 100-2.

29. Fischer, *The Soviets in World Affairs*, vol. I, photostat facing p. 239.

30. Tanin, *Desiat' let vneshnei politiki SSSR*, p. 82; Karl Radek, *Vneshniaia politika sovetskoi rossii* (Moscow, 1923), p. 56; and Piotr S. Wandycz, *Soviet-Polish Relations, 1917-1921* (Cambridge, 1969), p. 128 ff.

31. *Godovoi otchet N.K.I.D. k VII s"ezdu sovetov (1919-1920)*, p. 15; Tanin, *Desiat' let vneshnei politiki SSSR*, p. 75; and Richard H. Ullman, *Anglo-Soviet Relations, 1917-1921*, vol. II, *Britain and the Russian Civil War* (Princeton, 1968), pp. 340-44.

32. Solomon, *Among the Red Autocrats*, p. 161. Also see Gerald Freund, *Unholy Alliance: Russian-German Relations from the Treaty of Brest-Litovsk to the Treaty of Berlin* (New York, 1957), pp. 51-72; and Günter Rosenfeld, *Sowjetrussland und Deutschland, 1917-1922* (Berlin, 1960), pp. 350-68. In partial recognition of his actual duties, Kopp was subsequently named Trade Representative (*Torgpred*) in Berlin. *DVP*, vol. II, pp. 459-62.

33. Kazimierz Grzybowski, *Soviet Public International Law: Doctrines and Diplomatic Practice* (Leyden, 1970), pp. 290-91; and Wandycz, *Soviet-Polish Relations*, p. 329, n. 88.

34. *DVP*, vol. III, p. 69.

35. For example, see the letter of 11 September 1918 from Chicherin to Allen Wardwell of the American Red Cross accusing him of anti-Soviet propaganda (i.e. magnifying alleged Bolshevik atrocities and ignoring the crimes of the Whites and of the imperialist invaders). Hoover Archive, Ts, Russia, C533.

36. *Organizatsiia nauki v pervye gody sovetskoi vlasti, 1917-1925* (Leningrad, 1968), p. 82.

37. A.V. Kol'tsov, *Lenin i stanovlenie akademii nauk kak tsentra sovetskoi nauki* (Leningrad, 1969), p. 115. On international contacts by Soviet scientists in these early days see E.D. Lebedkina, 'Mezhdunarodnye sviazi sovetskikh uchenykh v 1917-1924gg.', *Voprosy istorii*, 1971, no. 2, pp. 44-54.

38. See Norbert H. Gaworek, 'From Blockade to Trade: Allied Economic Warfare Against Soviet Russia, June 1919 to January 1920', *Jahrbücher für Geschichte Osteuropas*, 1975, XXIII, 1, pp. 39-69.

39. *Documents on British Foreign Policy, 1919-1939*, 1st series (London, 1947-63), vol. II, nos. 71/3, pp. 867-75, nos. 74/2, pp. 894-96, and nos. 76/1, pp. 911-12.

40. Lenin, *PSS*, vol. XL, pp. 53 and 74-5; and Simon Liberman, *Building Lenin's Russia* (Chicago, 1945), p. 109.

41. Richard H. Ullman, *Anglo-Soviet Relations, 1917-1921*, vol. III, *The Anglo-Soviet Accord* (Princeton, 1972), pp. 36-45.

42. Ibid., ch. III; S.V. Zarnitskii and L.I. Trofimova, *Sovetskoi strany diplomat* (Moscow, 1968), pp. 81-113; and R. Karpova, *L.B. Krasin: sovetskii diplomat* (Moscow, 1962), pp. 73ff.

43. *DVP*, vol. III, p. 207.

44. Ibid., vol. IV, pp. 220-21.

45. Hilger and Meyer, *Incompatible Allies*, pp. 189-91; and Lerner, *Karl Radek*, pp. 84-88. Also see Karl Radek, 'Noiabr' (stranichka iz vospominanii)', *Krasnaia nov'* 1926, no. 10, pp. 155-68; and Marie-Luise Goldbach, *Karl Radek und die deutsch-sowjetischen Beziehungen, 1918-1923* (Bonn-Bad Godesberg, 1973), pp. 44-49.

46. Arno J. Mayer, *Politics and Diplomacy of Peace Making* (New York, 1969), pp. 410-49; and Thompson, *Russia, Bolshevism, and the Versailles Peace*, pp. 82-130. Also see *DVP*, vol. II, pp. 57-60.

47. On the various currents of anti-Bolshevism in Britain and the United States see Alex P. Schmid, *Churchills privater Krieg: Intervention und Konterrevolution im russischen Bürgerkrieg, November 1918-März 1920* (Zurich, 1974), passim; Peter G. Filene, *Americans and the Soviet Experiment 1917-1933* (Cambridge, 1967), ch. II and VI; and Christopher Lasch, *The American Liberals and the Russian Revolution* (New York, 1972), ch. V.

48. William C. Bullitt, *The Bullitt Mission to Russia* (New York, 1919); Beatrice

Farnsworth, *William C. Bullitt and the Soviet Union* (Bloomington, 1967), ch. II; Mayer, *Politics and Diplomacy,* pp. 450-87; Thompson, *Russia, Bolshevism, and the Versailles Peace,* pp. 131-77; and A.D. Skaba, *Parizhskaia mirnaia konferentsiia i inostrannaia interventsiia v strane sovetov (ianvar'-iiun' 1919 goda)* (Kiev, 1971), pp. 101-16.

49. Mayer, *Politics and Diplomacy,* pp. 3-30; and Fritz T. Epstein, *Germany and the East: Selected Essays* (Bloomington, 1973), p. 97.

50. *Vtoroi vserossiiskii s''ezd sovetov* (Moscow, 1928), pp. 86-87.

51. See Albert S. Lindemann, *The 'Red Years': European Socialism vs. Bolshevism, 1919-1921* (Berkeley and Los Angeles, 1974); and Branko Lazitch and Milorad Drachkovitch, *Lenin and the Comintern* (Stanford, 1972), vol. I.

52. Trotskii told an interviewer that he considered '. . .diplomatic intercourse necessary not only with governments, but also with revolutionary socialist parties bent on the overthrow of existing governments', *Izvestiia,* 16 December 1917.

53. For example, *DVP,* vol. II, pp. 131-35, 135-40, and 208-13.

54. Chicherin, *Two Years,* p. 31.

55. Kliuchnikov and Sabanin, *Mezhdunarodnaia politika noveishego vremeni,* vol. II, pp. 384 and 420.

56. *DVP,* vol. II, pp. 507-9 and 576-87. Also see L.J. Macfarlane, 'Hands Off Russia: British Labour and the Russo-Polish War, 1920', *Past and Present,* 1967, no. 38, pp. 126-52.

57. Piotr S. Wandycz, *France and Her Eastern Allies, 1919-1925* (Minneapolis, 1962), pp. 151-53; *DVP,* vol. II, pp. 483-84, 550, and 553-54; and Freund, *Unholy Alliance,* pp. 69-72.

58. *DVP,* vol. II, pp. 438 and 482, and vol. III, pp. 28-40, 60, and 86-89.

59. Baumgart, *Deutsche Ostpolitik,* pp. 334-63; and Wheeler-Bennett, *Brest-Litovsk,* pp. 349-60.

60. Ibid., p. 350, n. 2.

61. Jane Degras, ed., *Soviet Documents on Foreign Policy* (London and New York, 1951), vol. I, p. 22.

3

THE REVIVAL
OF DIPLOMACY

The year 1921 marked a turning point in the history of Soviet foreign policy. Both the Kremlin leadership and the Western statesmen undertook basic reassessments of their previous views concerning the position of the only socialist state within the international system. The Russian communists were not yet prepared to abandon their faith in the inevitability of a world revolution, but they were forced to realize that it might require time to mature and that, meanwhile, the Soviet state would have to make some temporary accommodations with the imperialist powers.[1]

Such compromises were made all the more necessary by the serious domestic problems facing Lenin and his party. Seven years of world war, revolution and civil war had left Russia an economic ruin. Large sections of the countryside were in revolt, the peasants were refusing to deliver their grain, thousands of urban workers were on strike, and finally, the Kronstadt sailors, heroes of the October revolution, had risen in armed revolt against the regime. Lenin's answer was a comprehensive program of retreat from the excesses of revolutionary idealism and a consolidation of the Bolsheviks' positions by all possible means. The economic aspect of this policy, which called for national rebuilding with the cooperation of the native and foreign bourgeois, was titled the New Economic Policy (NEP).

The NEP had important implications for Soviet foreign policy. Peace was a prime requisite of a program aimed at rebuilding the country's industrial sector while simultaneously raising the general standard of living. Wars or even an impressive defense establishment were simply too expensive. The New Economic Policy further required not merely peace but the active assistance of foreign capitalists. Over half of the plants and factories in Russia were standing idle because their capital equipment was worn out or in disrepair. Nothing could be done without machines and tools from the advanced industrial countries. Foreign loans and, above all, foreign trade were also essential in order to finance this program.

Obviously the NEP called for the implementation of a radically different foreign policy. Just as the New Economic Policy signaled a retreat from the extremes of War Communism, so also a new emphasis on traditional diplomacy marked a departure from the previous reliance on revolution as the principal means of dealing with the great powers. Peaceful co-existence emerged as a primary tenet of Soviet foreign policy. This view implied the expectation of a long period of peace, the relative absence of revolutionary opportunities, the maintenance of good diplomatic relations with the powers, and a vast expansion of trade with the capitalist states.[2]

The capitalist powers were likewise forced to re-evaluate their attitudes toward the socialist experiment at this time. The policy of unrelenting hostility to the Soviet Republic had proven a failure. After the collapse of the various White armies, the Western leaders would no longer hold out in the hope of being able to deal with a different Russian government soon. Armed intervention on the part of the Entente had to be curtailed under heavy domestic pressures to demobilize. With the end of the inconclusive Russo-Polish War, it became apparent to even the most anti-communist statesmen that the RSFSR would remain the government of Russia in the foreseeable future and that the Bolsheviks could no longer be ignored. Thus, both sides were prepared for a change, albeit cautious and slow, in their mutual relationship.

Even during the darkest days of civil war and foreign intervention the Soviet state had managed to preserve a few channels of contact with the outside world. Viktor Kopp, who had been sent to Berlin to handle prisoner of war affairs, had remained in Germany and had gradually assumed the role of a general political and commercial representative.[3] The Russian commercial delegation in Copenhagen, nominally representing the All-Russian Central Council of Cooperatives, was in fact a covert diplomatic bureau, established to explore ways to open official relations with the Entente states.[4] These missions, together with the meager para-diplomatic establishments, were supplemented when in 1920 Soviet diplomacy experienced its first major successes. The defeat of the White forces and the subsequent repulsing of Marshal Pilsudski's Polish armies apparently convinced the border states of the need to establish formal relations with Bolshevik Russia. The initial breach in the wall of isolation surrounding the Soviet Republic came with the signing of the Treaty of Tartu (Dorpat) with Estonia on 2 February 1920. This document ended hostilities between the two countries, and it contained a mutual promise to abstain from intervention in each other's internal affairs. Each party agreed not to recognize regimes pretending to the other's sovereignty and to foreswear aggression against the other.[5] Similar agreements were signed with Lithuania and Latvia in July and August of the same year.[6] In October the Finns officially recognized the RSFSR, and in the same month an armistice ended the Russo-Polish War, leading to an exchange of diplomats between Moscow and Warsaw under the terms of the Peace of Riga.[7] By the opening of 1921 the Commissariat of Foreign Affairs had posted its diplomats to Latvia, Lithuania, Estonia, Afghanistan, Turkey, Khiva, Bukhara and Georgia. Persia and Poland were soon added to the list. In addition, the Soviet Republic was represented by trade, prisoner of war or other special missions in Britain, Austria, Hungary, Mongolia, Finland, Denmark, Sweden, Norway and Czechoslovakia.[8]

The normalization of relations between the RSFSR and the outside world had thus begun before the advent of the NEP, but industrial recovery required that this trend be greatly accelerated. The primary goal set for the Narkomindel was the establishment of formal diplomatic relations with the great industrial powers — Britain, France, Germany and the United States. From this first step it was hoped that a thriving foreign trade and perhaps even generous foreign loans would materialize. During the period from 1921 to 1924 the Bolshevik regime realized most of its diplomatic goals, although it was ultimately frustrated in its attempts to secure long-term foreign financial support for its reconstruction program.

In 1921 the Narkomindel endeavored to transform its para-diplomatic agencies into regular diplomatic missions wherever possible. Negotiations in Berlin between the German and Russian prisoner of war affairs bureaus resulted in a provisional German-Soviet trade agreement on 6 May 1921. Under its terms, the local Soviet prisoner of war bureau was expanded and took on consular and political functions and Nikolai Krestinskii was dispatched to Berlin as the trade representative of the RSFSR.[9] Trade was also used as an opening wedge with Great Britain. The Kremlin leaders considered their relations with Great Britain to be especially important, since they regarded England as the fulcrum of the imperialist system. The failure of White and interventionist forces to overthrow Bolshevism, combined with England's desperate need to recapture Russian

markets, finally forced Lloyd George's government to reach an accommodation with the Soviet regime. The Anglo-Soviet Trade
Agreement of 16 March 1921 provided not only economic benefits,
but de facto recognition as well. Leonid Krasin was accredited as
Soviet representative in London.[10] This was a great triumph for the
Narkomindel. Acceptance by the British served as a benchmark of
Soviet respectability and signaled the re-emergence of Russia as a
major participant in European diplomacy. Following Britain's lead,
the other European states began to normalize relations with the
RSFSR. The Swedes signed a trade pact with *Tsentrosoiuz* in
February, while L.M. Mikhailov arrived as Soviet representative in
Oslo after the negotiation of a similar treaty with Norway. In
December formal diplomatic relations were re-established between
Moscow and Vienna, with Aleksandr Shlikhter as Soviet *Polpred*. At
about the same time V.V. Vorovskii took up residence as Soviet
trade representative in Rome.[11] A trade agreement was finally con-
cluded with Czechoslovakia in June, although Konstantin Iurenev
had headed a Soviet commerical delegation in Prague since 1919.

Soviet diplomacy achieved similar successes in Asia, too. Despite
some trepidation in Kabul over the sovietization of Bukhara, the
Soviet-Afghan Treaty of Friendship was signed in February
whereupon F.F. Raskol'nikov replaced Iakov Surits as ambassador
to Afghanistan.[12] Relations were also normalized with Iran. Having
abandoned the mercurial Ghilan Soviet regime, the Bolsheviks signed the Soviet-Persian treaty in February and appointed Fedor Rotshtein as *Polpred* in Teheran.[13] Relations between Soviet Russia and
Turkey were formalized in March of 1921,[14] while the NKID sent
Aleksandr Paikes to Peking in November to discuss the fate of the
Chinese Eastern Railroad.[15] Thus, by the end of 1921 the RSFSR had
definitively broken out of its former isolation and had established a
large number of new diplomatic missions.

The Bolsheviks also attempted to make use of several international
conferences as an additional method of gaining acceptance in the
comity of nations. A decree of the Supreme Allied Council in Cannes
on 6 January 1922 authorized the attendance of Soviet diplomats at
the forthcoming Genoa Conference on the reconstruction of Europe.
Although this is precisely what the Narkomindel had been striving
for, the invitation, '. . .came to many in the West as well as in the
RSFSR as a thunderbolt from a clear sky'.[16] To coordinate the efforts of the East European countries at Genoa, Latvia, Estonia and

Poland convened a pre-conference in which the Soviet Republic also participated. When the Genoa Conference failed to complete all of the business on its agenda, a further conclave was scheduled at the Hague, where Litvinov led the Soviet delegation. A Soviet delegation also participated in the Lausanne Conference in the winter of 1922-23, where Commissar Chicherin jousted with Lord Curzon over British penetration in the Near East. In addition, the new Soviet trade representative at Rome, Nikolai Iordanskii, was admitted to the later stages of the Lausanne Conference and signed a multilateral agreement on the Straits question.[17]

The greatest Soviet diplomatic victory achieved during this period came in conjunction with the Genoa Conference. Germany and Russia shared a number of common interests at this juncture. Each was hostile to the Versailles settlement dictated by the victorious Allied powers. Both suffered from a profound sense of isolation, as they were excluded by the dominant political community. It was only natural that the two outcast nations of Europe should come together to further their respective political, economic and military positions. The Narkomindel's Genoa delegation, headed by Chicherin, stopped in Berlin on its way to the conference. During a series of meetings with German officials a treaty which provided for a degree of political and economic cooperation (and cleared the way for military collaboration) was drafted. At the last moment Walther Rathenau, the German Foreign Minister, refused to sign the agreement, fearing it would handicap his country at Genoa. However, when the Western powers seemed to be ignoring the Weimar contingent, the Germans panicked. They met with the Russian negotiating team and quickly revived the project which had been discussed earlier in Berlin. Allied policy had driven Germany and Russia together. The Rapallo Treaty, signed on 16 April 1922, represented a great victory for Soviet diplomacy. Moscow had served notice to the Western powers that the Soviet state could be ignored only at their own peril.[18]

A second major diplomatic breakthrough for the Soviet Union occurred in the early months of 1924. Under the direction of Lord Curzon the British Foreign Office had pursued an anti-Bolshevik foreign policy, but in late 1923 the Conservatives were swept from office by the Labour party. The Labourites hoped to solve England's unemployment crisis, at least in part, through expanded trade with Russia, and they were not prepared to let the question of pre-war tsarist debts stand in the way. Thus, in February of 1924 Great

Britain granted de jure recognition to the USSR.[19] Britain's defection from the anti-Soviet front served as a signal to the other powers. In rapid succession Italy, Norway, Austria, Greece, China, Sweden, Denmark, Mexico and even France followed suit. Only the United States held out against the trend.[20] But even in America the USSR was able to open a Soviet Information Bureau in Washington, under the direction of Boris E. Skvirskii, which operated until 1933 when it was replaced by a properly accredited embassy. In lieu of formal diplomatic representation, the Information Bureau could at least perform the intelligence gathering and propaganda functions of a regular mission.[21] By 1925 the Soviet Union had become an officially recognized member of the international community with a rapidly expanding network of formal diplomatic missions spread around the globe.

THE COMMISSARIAT EXPANDS

This tremendous expansion of Russian diplomatic contacts with the outside world had a profound impact on the Commissariat of Foreign Affairs. Entire staffs had to be created for the new embassies, the Commissariat's policy sections had to be greatly expanded, and new procedures were needed to handle the increased flow of business efficiently. From around 250 workers in 1918 the Narkomindel's central office jumped to over 1,300 in 1921.[22] As an emergency measure to improve internal efficiency the service departments were combined into a single Chancellery Department to which all of the Commissariat's administrative, organizational, technical and economic work was assigned. The departments of Finance, Personnel, Internal Economy, Visas and Passports and Diplomatic Couriers were abolished in January of 1921 by this amalgamation. The NKID Secretariat, most of its functions having been assumed by the Chancellery Department, now became the Secretariat of the Collegium. It was responsible for the most delicate and sensitive matters, and three new subsections were added to it — the Telegraphic Section, the Cipher Section and the Political Archives section. In addition, two special agencies were created to facilitate the well-being of foreign missions on Soviet soil. The Building and Technical [Services] Bureau was responsible for securing and maintaining housing for the newly enlarged foreign diplomatic corps, while the Bureau of Foreigners' Accounts handled the financial transactions of the embassies in Moscow.[23]

The Sovnarkom decree of 6 June 1921 entitled the 'Statute of the People's Commissariat of Foreign Affairs' gave the Narkomindel its first thorough reorganization. The Commissariat's central machinery now included a Department of the West, subdivided into branches covering Central Europe, the Anglo-American and Romance countries, and the Baltic and Scandinavian states; and a Department of the East, comprised of sub-departments for the Near East, Middle East and Far East. These political departments were to maintain diplomatic relations with the countries in their geographic areas, collect and interpret data concerning those states, oversee all contacts by Soviet governmental agencies with such countries, and maintain close liaison with the diplomatic representatives of those nations accredited to the RSFSR.[24]

The Chancellery Department was responsible for the overall coordination of the work of the Commissariat, and for performing tasks in the administrative, organizational, financial, technical and housekeeping realms. The Chancellery consisted of the Administrative and Organizational Section, the Sub-Department of Finance, the Communications Section, the Cipher Section, the Sub-Department for Diplomatic Couriers, the Sub-Department for Passports and Visas, a Housekeeping Sub-Department and a unit of guards.[25] The Economic and Legal Department was charged with preparing and examining proposed treaties, rendering opinions on questions of international law, supervising Soviet consulates abroad and foreign consulates in the Republic, and resolving problems concerning the rights and duties of Soviet citizens traveling in other countries and foreigners in Russia. Sections for Civil Law, Public Law, Commercial Law, Consular Affairs, Frontier Affairs, Codification, and Communications and Transport comprised this division.[26] The Department of Press and Information prepared all news releases, edited the many NKID publications, and supervised the work of the Russian Telegraphic Agency in other countries.[27] The Collegium also created in August of 1921 a Central Bureau for the Servicing of Foreigners which was to aid foreign diplomats and businessmen in the difficult task of acquiring the necessities of life (food, shelter, fuel, etc.) in Moscow.[28]

The NKID Secretariat had already been transformed into the

Secretariat of the Collegium, consisting of the secretaries of the Collegium members and also of representatives from the General Archives, Current Political Archives and Protocol sections.[29] In December of 1921 the membership of the Collegium of the Commissariat was revised and expanded. It now included Commissar Chicherin, who was responsible for overall policy, relations with Asian countries and public relations; Deputy-Commissar Litvinov, whose province encompassed relations with Western states as well as economic and legal matters; V.P. Menzhinskii, who was in charge of affairs concerning the border states; and P.P. Gorbunov of the Chancellery Department. Soon two deputy members, S.S. Piliavskii and Iakov Davtian, were added.[30] The composition of this body appears to have been rather fluid since its membership was listed as Chicherin, Litvinov, Karakhan, and Ganetskii in November of 1922.[31] Within the next few months Viktor Kopp, Fedor Rotshtein and Khristian Rakovskii also joined the Collegium.

The foreign missions of the RSFSR also received a more precise definition according to the 'General Rules Regarding Soviet Organs Abroad' (26 May 1921).[32] This statute defined three types of Soviet missions abroad: (1) *Polpredstva* (plenipotentiary representations) corresponding to embassies and legations; (2) consular representations; and (3) *Torgpredstva* (trade representations) for which the Narkomindel shared responsibility with the Commissariat of Foreign Trade. The law also provided for the existence of special delegations, missions, commissions, envoys, etc. which might become necessary from time to time. Within the overall Soviet mission in a foreign capital, particular departments might assume the functions of other sub-sections and in countries lacking de jure relations with the Soviet Republic, any existing Soviet agencies were placed under the direct authority of the NKID. This represented an institutionalization of the para-diplomatic strategy. Any Soviet mercantile, humanitarian, cultural or scientific organization located abroad thus assumed quasi-diplomatic status, even (or especially) in countries not recognizing the Bolshevik regime. Foreigners or their governments wishing to patronize such agencies were thereby forced to deal with the Narkomindel. The *Polpred* was designated the only official representative of the RSFSR in the country to which he was assigned and, as such, held a position superior to the heads of all other Soviet agencies within the mission. He even had the authority to suspend their decisions or policies pending a ruling by the Council of Commissars, though it was not intended that the *Polpred* meddle in the day to day functioning of the other agencies. The statute also designated the ambassador as the only channel of communication with the Soviet administration.[33]

The plenipotentiary representatives of the RSFSR were officially appointed to their posts by the Presidium of the Central Executive Committee of the Soviet, which was thus assigned the function of a head of state. Special envoys, commissioned to negotiate treaties or undertake other important and delicate missions, received their authority from the Sovnarkom. Lower diplomatic officials, chargés, d'affaires, counsellors, secretaries, attachés, etc., were appointed directly by the Commissariat of Foreign Affairs. Military and naval attachés and trade representatives were commissioned conjointly by the Narkomindel and the pertinent martial or commercial commissariat.[34]

In an attempt to convert some of its para-diplomatic ties to foreign governments into normal diplomatic channels, a Sovnarkom decree of 13 May 1922 ruled that all communications between any branch of the Soviet government and foreign states must be diverted through the proper Narkomindel offices.[35] The Council of Commissars was thereby seeking to speed the process of attaining de jure recognition for the RSFSR from all the powers who had any kind of dealings with the Soviet Republic.

The next major changes in the legal position and organizational structure of the People's Commissariat of Foreign Affairs occurred in 1923 in connection with the formation of the Union of Soviet Socialist Republics by the Russian, Ukrainian, Belorussian, and Transcaucasian Soviet Socialist Republics. Under the new constitution the formulation of foreign policy and its execution by diplomatic means was specifically reserved to the federal authorities and in particular to the Congress of Soviets and its Central Executive Committee.[36] The Narkomindel of the RSFSR was transformed into the All-Union Commissariat of Foreign Affairs and its chief, Chicherin, received a seat on the federal Council of Commissars. Both the duties of the new All-Union NKID and its central organizational structure remained essentially unchanged.[37] Only the NKID Secretariat was extensively reorganized. It regained its independence from the Collegium and also reclaimed several functions which it had previously relinquished to the Chancellery. The Secretariat was now responsible for taking the minutes of Collegium meetings, overseeing the internal execution of Commissariat orders, handling correspondence for the Collegium and administering its own subsections (the three archival offices, the Protocol Section, the Cipher and Secret Section and the staffs of the Collegium members).[38]

The Treaty of Union among the Soviet Republics (30 December 1922) brought foreign affairs completely under the competence of the All-Union government and required the cessation of independent diplomatic activities on the part of the individual Republics by the middle of 1923.[39] The Ukrainians, led by Khristian Rakovskii, resisted this amalgamation, but their objections were disregarded.[40] Rakovskii was replaced as Commissar of the Ukrainian NKID by the more compliant V.I. Iakovlev who declared that:

> The foreign policy of the Ukraine has not and cannot have any interests other than those common with Russia, which is just such a proletarian state as the Ukraine. The heroic struggle of Russia, in complete alliance with the Ukraine, on all fronts against domestic and foreign imperialists, is now giving place to an equally united diplomatic front. The Ukraine is independent in her foreign policy where her own specific interests are concerned. But, in questions which are of common political and economic interest to all Soviet republics, the Russian as well as Ukrainian Commissariats for Foreign Affairs act as the united federal power.[41]

Rakovskii was appointed Second Deputy Commissar of the NKID as a concession to Ukrainian nationalist sentiment and a Ukrainian was made First Counsellor of Embassy in each of the countries where the Ukrainian SSR had formerly maintained its own missions.[42] In the same way, when the Far Eastern Republic was absorbed into the RSFSR and when the Central Asian Republics joined the USSR, their small diplomatic establishments were incorporated into the NKID.[43]

The foreign offices of the smaller Soviet republics had served Moscow well during the period of isolation. For example, when the Bolsheviks wanted to dissuade Kemalist Turkey from establishing closer ties with Britain and France in 1921, they dispatched General Mikhail Frunze, the Commander-in-Chief of the Ukrainian armed forces, to Ankara. Officially, Frunze represented the Ukrainian Soviet Republic, and his mission was to negotiate a Turko-Ukrainian friendship treaty. In reality, however, he conducted high-level military negotiations concerning possible support from the RSFSR for the Turks in their war with Greece.[44] Similarly, the Moscow authorities utilized a representative of the Turkistan SSR, E.A.

Babushkin, to establish a mission in Teheran in 1918 when Iranian-Soviet relations were strained.[45] It was also diplomats of the Turkistan SSR who took the initiative in normalizing relations between Moscow and Kabul by informing the Afghans that the Bolsheviks had annulled the old Anglo-Russian agreements for the exploitation of Afghanistan and that they wished to develop mutual relations on a peaceful and equitable basis.[46] In much the same way, the Soviet regime had used the foreign office of the Far Eastern Republic as a vehicle for conducting talks with the Peking government in China and with the Japanese military authorities there. The situation had changed by 1923, though. By that time the Soviet diplomatic position was much stronger. The Bolsheviks felt secure enough to demand direct, formal diplomatic recognition from the capitalist powers. Moscow no longer needed to employ diplomats of the smaller Soviet republics as intermediaries, so these republican foreign services were sharply curtailed.

The Narkomindel statute of 12 November 1923 gave the Commissariat the right to maintain an authorized representative at each of the republican Sovnarkoms. This representative was selected by the NKID and confirmed by both the Federation and the Republic. He became an ex-officio member of the republican Sovnarkom, with either a regular or a consultative vote.[47] It was the duty of these officers to keep the Commissariat informed of the republican level problems which might have international ramifications, supervise the execution of treaty terms relating to the Republic, issue passports and visas, maintain contact with the foreign consulates in the Republic, and explain the policies and actions of the Narkomindel to the republican officials.[48]

The creation of an All-Union Commissariat of Foreign Affairs had little effect on the structure or nature of the Narkomindel's foreign missions. Some of the Republics, other than the RSFSR, had operated embassies in a few foreign capitals. The duties, personnel and premises of these missions were now taken over by the regular embassies of the Soviet Union. Although the decree of 26 May 1921 concerning the organization of Soviet missions abroad was not specifically reiterated as an All-Union statute in 1923, it continued to set the standard for the structure and functioning of Soviet embassies. Just as before, top level diplomatic personnel (Commissars, ambassadors, etc.) were directly appointed by the Central Executive Committee, or its Presidium, of the All-Union Congress of Soviets.

Officials of slightly lesser rank received their commissions from the Sovnarkom, while chargés, and all employees beneath them were assigned to their positions by the Commissariat itself.[49]

From its revolutionary origins in 1917, the tiny staff and primitive organization of the Narkomindel had now been expanded into a large and structurally complex government bureaucracy. According to one set of Soviet figures, the NKID in 1924 employed 804 people in its Moscow central offices, 1,098 in its missions abroad, and an additional 231 in the authorized representations and the consulates throughout Russia.[50] This growth obviously mirrors the change in emphasis from an approach to the outside world stressing immediate social revolution as its paramount consideration to a foreign policy based on achieving at least temporary accommodation with the European powers in order to protect the national interests of the Soviet state. By 1924 the Narkomindel had acquired all the usual attributes of a diplomatic service and had evolved an organizational structure which would remain reasonably stable throughout the decade.

THE STRUCTURE OF THE NARKOMINDEL THROUGH 1930

The period from 1924 through 1930 was not marked by the same kind of drastic reorganization in the structure of the People's Commissariat of Foreign Affairs which characterized the years between 1917 and 1924. By 1925 the Soviet Union had achieved de jure recognition from all of the great powers, except the United States, and the continued existence of the Bolshevik regime as the government of Russia was no longer in doubt. Although Soviet relations with the other major states, most notably Great Britain, were disturbed by several serious crises later in the decade, the USSR had become a recognized member of the community of nations. There were no cataclysmic international events in the latter half of the 1920s which could rival the beginning of the civil war and foreign intervention in 1918 or its termination in 1920 in their profound impact upon the organization and personnel composition of the NKID. The organization of the Commissariat established in 1923 remained basically undisturbed except for a few minor reforms designed to improve its working efficiency.

In 1926 the Western and Eastern Departments were abolished and their regional sub-sections were raised to full departmental status. The new geographical area departments now included:

The Department of Anglo-American and Latin States (covering England, the USA, France and Italy),
The Scandinavian Department (for Denmark, Norway, and Sweden),
The Department for the Baltic States and Poland (for Finland, Danzig, Poland, Latvia, Lithuania and Estonia),
The Central European Department (with responsibility for Germany, Austria, Hungary, Czechoslovakia, Holland and Switzerland),
The Balkan Department (for Greece, Yugoslavia, Albania and Rumania),
The Near Eastern Department (for Arabia, Iran and Turkey),
The Middle Eastern Department (covering India, Afghanistan and Central Asia),
The Far Eastern Department (for Japan, Mongolia, China, Tibet and the Tannu-Tuva Republic).[51]

This reorganization was, in all probability, motivated by the mounting work load on these sub-departments as the diplomatic contacts of the Soviet state steadily increased. In 1927, apparently as an economy measure, the Balkan Department was abolished and its duties distributed between the Central European and Anglo-Romance divisions.[52]

The Commissariat's relationship to the foreign press corps in Moscow also changed appreciably. The Narkomindel lost its control over the Russian Telegraphic Agency and in 1930 it also seems to have relinquished its foreign press censorship functions. Up to that time Fedor Rotshtein of the Press Department had been charged with the supervision of foreign correspondents in Russia, but in 1930 he was replaced by Zh. L. Arens of the political police.[53]

The censorship also became considerably more rigid at this time. Writing in 1930, one foreign newspaperman noted that,

> for over a year now, news work in Russia had deteriorated steadily, reaching the point where foreign correspondents had to toe the line like the humblest of their Soviet brethren. The time was gone when a foreign reporter in Moscow could bargain with the Press bureau, appeal to Chicherin, or squeeze in a carefully veiled lead.[54]

Changes in political and economic policies doubtless account for the increasing severity of censorship. The quest for foreign loans and technology was an important feature of the NEP, so it was imperative to create the best possible impression abroad. In the late 1920s, however, Soviet economic policy turned toward autarky, thus eliminating the need to pamper the foreign press. In addition, the Stalinist *apparat* was reaching out in this period to control various areas of Soviet national life which had previously escaped its influence; relations with the foreign press was one such area. Foreign reporters now found the gentle supervision of the Narkomindel replaced by the harsh domination of the GPU and party apparatus.[55]

The Soviet authorities also moved to redefine the rights to foreign representation of the Union Republics and to broaden the powers of the Narkomindel's Authorized Representatives to the Republics. Now all of the Republics acquired the right to participate in the selection of counsellors, secretaries and attachés of Soviet embassies located in countries in which they had some special (usually economic) interest. This step was taken to compensate for the loss of the Republic's own diplomatic organs after the formation of the Union in 1923. The NKID Authorized Representatives assigned to each of the Union Republics were now dually responsible to the Commissariat and to the highest republican authority. This gave the Republics at least a minimum of authority over the actions of Narkomindel personnel operating on their territory. These representatives, however, were given the power to select their own staffs, with Commissariat approval.[56]

The Sovnarkom and Central Executive Committee of the Soviet also increased and defined more clearly the powers of Soviet ambassadors. A decree of 27 June 1927 clearly established the *Polpred* as the chief executive of the entire Soviet mission in a foreign capital. He could suspend the decisions, not only of fellow diplomats, but also of other Soviet functionaries (e.g. trade representatives, military attachés, police officials) within the mission.[57] This decree also reflected the improved diplomatic position of the USSR. In the days when Moscow relied on various para-diplomatic expedients, Russian missions abroad were small, irregular, even chaotic. By the middle of the decade, in contrast, the Soviet Union was represented in many foreign capitals not only by an official diplomatic legation, but also by trade delegations, military missions and — covertly — by intelligence, political police and revolutionary agents as well. It was essential, therefore, that one official, the *Polpred,* control and coordinate the diverse sections of a Soviet mission.

The Consular Service received a new statute on 27 October 1927 which was much more detailed than its predecessor but which did not change the basic consular functions significantly.[58] Even though, with the loss of most of its economic functions after 1921, the Consular Service tended to become less and less distinguished from the diplomat sections of the NKID, the two remained separate legal entities. This separation, if only as a legal fiction, had important advantages for the Narkomindel. Even the breaking of diplomatic relations with another country, with the consequent closing of the Soviet embassy, did not necessarily entail the recall of the consular agents. This actually happened in China which severed relations with the USSR in 1926 but did not oust the last Soviet Consul until 1929.[59]

The matter of diplomatic ranks also received attention during this period. The abolition of formal diplomatic ranks had proved inconvenient in practice. Foreign governments often used the Soviet representative's lack of formal rank to discriminate against him. For example, the Poles refused the Soviet *Polpred* in Warsaw the right to present his credentials to the head of the Polish state on the grounds that his 'rank' did not entitle him to this privilege.[60] It was necessary, therefore, in a number of cases to circumvent the 1918 provision for the equality of diplomats. Sometimes a *Polpred's* credentials would indicate a specific rank for the official even though he did not actually bear that title.[61] Thus, in 1924 Moscow agreed to exchange representatives of full ambassadorial rank with China and in 1928 the USSR sent an 'Ambassador' to Afghanistan.[62]

The tremendous expansion of the Narkomindel, especially in terms of number of personnel employed, which had occurred between 1921 and 1924 was now halted and even slightly reversed. In 1923 the NKID had boasted over 1,300 diplomats, officials and functionaries, but by 1927 the Commissariat employed only about 1,200 people.[63] Improvements in organization, better training of personnel, and more rational procedures allowed the Commissariat to carry out its tasks somewhat more efficiently and with fewer employees. The Sovnarkom was also pressing all the commissariats and other government agencies to reduce the size of their staffs as a budgetary measure. Nevertheless, the Narkomindel retained a reputation of being generally over-staffed. For instance, in 1923 the Soviet delegation in Persia apparently numbered over forty members while the British Embassy in Teheran performed its functions with a staff of only five or six men.[64] Besides simple inefficiency, of course, the size of Soviet missions was swollen by foreign trade, economic assistance, journalistic, GPU, and other types of essentially non-diplomatic personnel.

The Soviet foreign service suffered a rash of defections during the middle and late 1920s. This was a period of uncomfortable transition for many of the Narkomindel's diplomats. Stalin and his henchmen were then completing their conquest of power. This development was unpleasant even for many Commissariat employees who were not particularly interested in party politics. The Old Bolshevik leaders had been cosmopolitans of largely middle class origins, but the new Stalinist cadres which were coming to dominate Soviet politics sprang from lower, coarser stock. They had little sympathy for the essentially bourgeois life style of the diplomats; rather, many of the *apparatchiki* tended to view the Narkomindel staff with suspicion and hostility — all the more so since the Commissariat included veterans of the Imperial Foreign Service as well as former Mensheviks, Kadets and other supposedly 'class hostile' elements. In other areas, most notably science and engineering, the Stalinists had already begun to purge such 'undesirables'.[65]

To make matters worse, the NKID was caught up in the bruising debate over economic strategies that marked the transition from the NEP to the first five year plan. In that peace was a prime requisite for the success of the NEP, the Commissariat of Foreign Affairs had discharged its obligations by securing a legitimate place for the USSR in the international state system (though the war-scare of 1927 demonstrated the fragile character of Russia's hard won diplomatic position). But the NEP also required foreign loans, trade and technical assistance. Here Soviet diplomacy had been only partially successful at best. The European and American capitalists had not seized the investment opportunities offered by Moscow with the alacrity Lenin predicted. This failure to secure the necessary credits and aid from abroad contributed, at least in part, to the decision to rely almost entirely on domestic sources of investment and production as embodied in the five year plans. The tendency toward autarky implied by these plans cannot have been popular among Narkomindel officials, since it lessened the importance of diplomacy in the campaign to build communism in Russia and since it complicated their dealings with the capitalist states. Thus, some combination of disgust over the trend in domestic politics, sensitive reaction to criticisms of the Commissariat's failure to carry out the international aspects of the NEP, and disagreement with the Politburo's foreign and economic policies provoked numerous Soviet diplomats to abandon their posts during these years.

Diplomatic defections became a serious problem in the second half of the decade. Sergo Ordzhonikidze told the delegates at the sixteenth party congress that party members serving in Russian missions abroad had embezzled state funds and absconded in the following numbers: 38 in 1926, 26 in 1927, 32 in 1928, 65 in 1929 and 43 in the first half of 1930.[66] The list of defectors included the First Counsellor of Embassy in Paris, Grigorii Besedovskii; Sergei Dmitrievskii, a Counsellor in Stockholm; Georgii Solomon, a Soviet Consul in Germany; an Attaché in Iran, Grigorii Agabekov, and Boris Bazhanov, a diplomatic and security agent in Central Asia. Dmitrievskii, to take one example, apparently defected when he was recalled to Moscow because he feared that the failure of the Soviet embassy in Stockholm to make satisfactory economic and political progress with the Swedish government would be blamed on him.[67]

This rash of defections provoked measures from both the government and the party to tighten discipline in the embassies. One Soviet diplomat, Aleksandr Barmin, who was himself later to defect, has left a record of such an attempt by a team of investigators.

A number of non-Party specialists serving on trade missions abroad recalled to Moscow at this time [ca. 1930], refused to return. Many of them took posts with foreign firms. Going back to Russia meant giving up a life of comfort and also rendering an account of their behavior while abroad. These considerations played a greater part in leading most of them to act as they did than any spirit of political opposition. The Central Committee [of the Party] decided to start a *chistka* [a cleansing or purge] of all foreign embassies and trade missions.

The cleansing commission made the rounds of all the capitals of Europe, interrogating without mercy the staffs of the Soviet missions. Its arrival from Moscow brought fear into all hearts. Private life, amusements, past records, personal origins, contracts — everything was raked up. At the meeting at which we were introduced to this commission, an old, harsh, and domineering member of it began to berate us as though we had all been corrupted by the bourgeois influences around us. I lost my temper and answered him in an angry tone and without mincing my words. The result was unexpected. Shortly afterward I was recommended by the Central Committee in Moscow for election as secretary of our Communist cell and was, it is needless to say, elected. Of a hundred Communists who were summoned before the commission, only sixteen escaped reprimand, exclusion from the Party, or recall.

To keep us free from bourgeois influences, it was recommended that our col-

ony read *L'Humanité,* the French Communist paper. The White Russian [i.e. anti-Bolshevik] papers *Poslednia Novosti* and *Vozrozhdenie* were absolutely forbidden
.... Almost all the colony members, except for a few timid souls, continued to buy the papers and read them in secret.[68]

Security was also tightened by making the selection process for assignment abroad more rigorous. By 1930 the dossier of every diplomat who was a candidate for a foreign post had to be examined and passed by the Narkomindel, the political police, and the foreign cadres section of the party Central Committee.[69]

Besides these 'cleansing' operations, Soviet diplomats also had to worry about violence directed against them by anti-Bolshevik Russian émigré organizations. The Soviet Vice-Consul in Canton, A.I. Khassis, and the *Polpred* in Warsaw, P.L. Voikov, were murdered in 1927, and two diplomatic couriers, Teodor Nette and I. Makhmastal, were killed the preceding year.[70] Narkomindel missions in Peking, Berlin, Königsberg, Warsaw and Lemberg experienced attacks by mobs or terrorist groups. V.V. Vorovskii, the Soviet trade representative in Rome, was shot while at Lausanne in 1923. The previous year Vorovskii had informed Moscow 'We live in a state of siege, our gates are barred, and we do not go out needlessly.'[71] Ambassador Valerian Dovgalevskii wrote along the same lines from Paris in 1929: 'We have information that the White Guards are organizing an assault. Parisian philistines get restless, excesses may follow. I get menacing letters.'[72] The first regularly accredited Soviet ambassador to the United States, Aleksandr Troianovskii, received similarly intimidating mail. Not long after taking up his duties in Washington he received this anonymous threat:

Detroit, Mich.
Feb. 28 1935

To
A Murderer of the Ukrainians:

Here is one American who is becoming fed-up with the horors, mass assassinations, foul schemings, and all-round barbarisms of the damned gang of cutthroats that are strangling the people of Russia.

This country cannot feel itself other than besmirched by the presence here of you and your loathsome crew. The sooner you leave these shores behind you the better for America.

May the day come quickly when humans of your kind are herded onto anything that will float and taken beyond the sight of our great country. You befoul the very atmosphere of the land. Get back to the God-damned place from whence you came. And get there PRONTO. . .if you know what that means. America has had quite enough of your vile propaganda. . .your lies. . .your schemings.

The writer of this is leaving on Sunday for Washington. He will be there until he personally observes your departure for New York, to take ship out of this country. You and your crew are GOING, perhaps, sooner than you expect. There are ways and means of REACHING you if we find you in Washington After March 15th. It will be wiser to take this HINT and GO while you can. . .on your feet. And when you GO be sure that no successor comes after you.

> May you die in agony.
> [signed]   AMERICAN

The Blood Stained Ambassador and Propaganda Chief of the World's Most Infamous Gang of Murderers, now for a SHORT time resident in the city of Washington. D.C.[73]

The Estonian police uncovered a Russian monarchist plot to assassinate Soviet diplomats in Tallin in 1927, and in 1930 a bomb was found in the house of V.A. Antonov-Ovseenko, the Russian Ambassador to Poland. In response, many of the Narkomindel's representatives carried pistols whenever abroad. The climate of fear generated by these attacks made the work of the NKID foreign missions considerably more difficult.

PERSONALITIES AND POLICY IN THE NARKOMINDEL

Like most large bureaucratic institutions, the Commissariat of Foreign Affairs soon generated an internal political system of its own, complete with struggles for power and personal rivalries. The continuing struggle for influence and prestige between Commissar Chicherin and his deputy, Maksim Litvinov, formed the central feature of NKID politics, around which all of the other major figures in the organization tended to polarize. Chicherin was a quiet, intellectual, eccentric and, above all, extremely sensitive man. Litvinov, in contrast, was an aggressive, outspoken and ambitious individual.[74]

Their rivalry involved substantive disagreements on major foreign policy issues as well as personal antipathy. The question of Russia's

Far Eastern policy was such an issue. Litvinov, though not responsible for that geographic area, continually intrigued against Lev Karakhan, the Soviet ambassador to Peking and a Chicherin supporter, who favored an aggressive policy in Asia. In particular Karakhan advocated increased support for the nationalist forces in south China, even though that course would bring Russia into conflict with Japanese imperialism in China. The Deputy Commissar gave his backing to Viktor Kopp, the *Polpred* in Tokyo, who pressed for a policy of caution and the maintenance of good relations with Japan.[75] Chicherin was also a Germanophile. He shared a close friendship with the German Ambassador Brockdorff-Rantzau, and he saw a significant community of interest between Moscow and Berlin. At the same time, the Foreign Commissar harbored extreme hostility toward the Versailles settlement and therefore toward Great Britain and the League of Nations, which he regarded as the chief defenders of that settlement. Litvinov took the opposite view. He tended to be pro-British and much less favorably inclined toward Germany than his chief.[76]

Each man strove to minimize the influence of the other. Litvinov was especially aggressive in his struggle with the Foreign Commissar. When Chicherin continued to campaign for peace with Warsaw, even after the outbreak of the Russo-Polish War in 1920, Litvinov enlisted the support of Trotskii to hinder Chicherin.[77] Similarly, Litvinov launched numerous assaults against Chicherin while the latter was attending the Lausanne conference and Litvinov remained in Moscow as acting Commissar.[78] Litvinov even went openly over his superior's head to criticize Chicherin before the Politburo.[79] Aleksandr Barmin recorded this impression of the Commissar reciprocating his opponent's public attacks:

> He [Chicherin] had a broad grin on his face: he had just been elected to the Central Committee of the Party. It was probably the last great pleasure of his life. The Litvinov group had fought bitterly against him for control of the Foreign Office, and had set themselves to bring to nothing every decision he made. Chicherin declared finally that he found it quite impossible to work with Litvinov and openly called him his 'antipode' at the Central Committee Conference.[80]

According to Georgii Solomon, another defector, Litvinov at times openly tried to sabotage Chicherin's administration. Solomon claimed that in October 1918 Litvinov failed to send several crucial messages which the Commissar had dictated concerning Russo-

German relations.[81]

The fact that the relative status of the combatants did not parallel their official ranks probably exacerbated the conflict. As Commissar, Chicherin should have enjoyed a commanding position within the Narkomindel. Unfortunately several of his nominal subordinates outranked him in party status and thus in actual political influence. Chicherin was only a recently converted ex-Menshevik, while a number of his staff were old Bolsheviks of some prestige who held high party offices in addition to their NKID assignments. A contemporary American observer accurately summed up the situation.

> Litvinov, more than Tchicherin has been Lenin's spokesman to the outside world in the past three years [1920-1922?]. Litvinov is closer to Lenin; he knows how Lenin will react on most situations, while Tchicherin is usually in doubt. This knowledge gives Litvinov power to make immediate decisions. Litvinov has worked with Lenin since the Communist party was created, while Tchicherin actually only came into the Communist ranks after the revolution — he was formerly connected with another group and his allegiance is naturally a little more conservative.[82]

One of Litvinov's biographers hypothesizes that the selection of Litvinov as Chicherin's deputy, with the almost predictable resulting conflict, may have been a deliberate attempt on the part of the Bolshevik leadership to counterbalance the ambitions and weaknesses of each man through the establishment of this rivalry.[83] Lack of evidence makes it impossible to substantiate this claim, but an American diplomat then in Moscow who knew the situation well, came to the same conclusion.[84]

Litvinov ultimately won his struggle to command the NKID. Commissar Chicherin, never an especially healthy individual, was increasingly plagued by his many illnesses, real and imagined. In addition, the special ties between the two 'outcast' nations of post-war Europe, Russia and Germany, which characterized the Chicherin era of Soviet diplomacy, had begun to weaken. The successful diplomatic campaigns which both the Narkomindel and Auswärtiges Amt had conducted in order to overcome their isolation by the Entente powers had, by their very triumphs, lessened the value of the Moscow-Berlin connection. The Germans were now no longer tied to the Russians as their only associate against the hostile Versailles powers. The Locarno Agreements signed in late 1925 provided security for the Weimar Republic, and the subsequent admission of

Germany to the League of Nations brought its painful isolation to an end. The Soviet Union, for its part, also displayed considerable independence from its German partner, especially in courting the favor of their mutual enemy, Poland. Relations between Moscow and Berlin remained correct, but the *Schicksalsgemeinschaft* was a thing of the past.[85] It is difficult to tell whether Chicherin's ill health, the change in policy toward Germany, or perhaps even the Deputy-Commissar's political influence, played the most significant role in the Foreign Commissar's eclipse. There is no evidence to show that the growing ascendency of Litvinov and the eventual retirement of Chicherin caused the gradual shift of Russian policy from the Rapallo tradition to the search for collective security. It is more likely that external developments — namely, the cooling of German ardor for the alliance, the rise of Hitler and the increasing political possibility of Soviet ties with the Western states — account for this change.

Suffering from diabetes and polyneuritis, Chicherin took a leave of absence from his duties in 1928 and traveled to Germany for treatment. Chicherin not only lost control of the NKID while abroad; he was not even well informed about all aspects of Soviet foreign policy.[86] Although defeated, he was not disgraced. On the tenth anniversary of his joining the Narkomindel both *Pravda* and *Izvestiia* printed lauditory articles on the accomplishments of the Foreign Commissar.[87] Chicherin returned to Russia in 1930 and resigned his post. Thereafter, he lived in seclusion in Moscow until his death in 1936. Meanwhile, Litvinov had assumed an increasingly important role in directing the NKID until by 1928 he had become the de facto Commissar.[88] He was formally appointed People's Commissar of Foreign Affairs on 21 July 1930.

Besides this primary rivalry between Chicherin and Litvinov, the Narkomindel was rent by numerous other antagonisms, all of which served to lessen its effectiveness.[89] Aleksandr Orlov, who served as an Assistant Prosecutor for the Supreme Court in 1923, dealt with numerous denunciations of Soviet diplomatic personnel for corruption, embezzlement and even treason. Such accusations often 'consisted largely of unsubstantiated charges which antagonistic bureaucrats, instigated by their quarreling wives, had made against each other'.[90] Personal rivalries, factionalism and intrigues were, of course, not unique to the Narkomindel. In fact, compared to the dissension prevalent in some other commissariats, the discord within the Foreign Commissariat was moderate indeed.[91]

NOTES

1. Lenin, *PSS,* vol. XLII, p. 22.

2. E.M. Chossudovskii credits Lenin with developing the basic concept of peaceful coexistence and Commissar Chicherin with formulating the phrase *mirnoye sosushchestvovanie.* See Chossudovsky, *Chicherin and the Evolution,* p. 19; and *DVP,* vol. II, p. 639. Cf. Dale Terence Lahey, 'Soviet Ideological Development of Coexistence: 1917-1927', *Canadian Slavonic Papers,* 1964, VI, pp. 80-94.

3. Hilger and Meyer, *The Incompatible Allies,* pp. 24-26; AA, Die dip. und kons. Vertretungen Russlands, Politik 9, Russland, letter from the German foreign office to Die Actiengesellschaft H.F. Eckert, 18 May 1920; and *DVP,* vol. III, pp. 14-16.

4. Karpova, *L.B. Krassin,* p. 54.

5. *DVP,* vol. II, pp. 339-55.

6. Ibid., pp. 28-41 and 101-16.

7. Ibid., pp. 265-80; 245-55; and 618-57.

8. *Godovoi otchet N.K.I.D. (1920-1921),* p. 160; Grzybowski, *Soviet Public International Law,* p. 296; and also. see a list of Soviet representatives compiled by *ROSTA* (Vienna), 23 November 1921, in the clippings archive of the Institut für Weltwirtschaft of Kiel Univeristy.

9. *DVP,* vol. IV, pp. 99-104; *Vestnik NKID,* 1921, nos. 5-6, p. 124; and Hilger and Meyer, *Incompatible Allies,* pp. 65-67. Also see Horst Günther Linke, *Deutsch-sowjetische Beziehungen bis Rapallo* (Cologne, 1970), pp. 125-39; and I.K. Kobliakov, 'Bor'ba sovetskogo gosudarstva za normalizatsiiu otnoshenii s germaniei v 1919-1921 gg.', *Istoriia SSSR,* 1971, no. 2, pp. 17-31. The German *Reichswehr* and the Red Army were also in the process of establishing close military ties. See John Erickson, *The Soviet High Command: A Military-Political History, 1918-1941* (London, 1962), ch. VI, IX and XI.

10. *DVP,* vol. III, pp. 607-14; Tanin, *Desiat' let vneshnei politiki,* pp. 89-90; and *Godovoi otchet za 1923 god k II s"ezdu sovetov* (Moscow, 1924), p. 153. Also see M.V. Glenny, 'The Anglo-Soviet Trade Agreement, March 1921', *The Journal of Contemporary History,* 1970, V, 2, pp. 63-82; Ullman, *Anglo-Soviet Accord,* ch. X; and Judit Garamvölgyi, *Aus den Anfängen sowjetischer Aussenpolitik: Das britisch-sowjetrussische Handelsabkommen von 1921* (Cologne, 1967), ch. VI. Cf. I.M. Maiskii, 'Anglo-sovetskoe torgovoe soglashenie 1921 goda', *Voprosy istorii,* 1957, no. 5, pp. 60-77; and O.F. Solov'ev, 'Iz istorii bor'by sovetskogo pravitel'stva za mirnoe sosushchestvovanie s angliei', *Voprosy istorii,* 1965, no. 2, pp. 54-64.

11. See V.A. Buriakov, 'Missiia V.V. Vorovskogo v italii v 1921 godu', *Voprosy*

istorii, 1971, no. 11, pp. 131-42.

12.   *DVP*, vol. III, pp. 550-53; Tanin, *Desiat' let vneshnei politiki*, pp. 91-92; Kapur, *Soviet Russia and Asia*, pp. 222-30; Adamec, *Afghanistan's Foreign Affairs*, pp. 56ff.; and Teplinskii, *50 let sovetsko-afganskikh otnoshenii*, ch. 1.

13.   Kapur, *Soviet Russia and Asia*, pp. 178-88; A.N. Kheifets, *Sovetskaia diplomatiia i narody vostoka, 1921-1927* (Moscow, 1968), pp. 55-63; and I.A. Iusupov, *Ustanovlenie i razvitie sovetsko-iranskikh otnoshenii (1917-1927 gg.)* (Tashkent, 1969).

14.   Kapur, *Soviet Russia and Asia*, pp. 92-114; Kuznetsova, *Ustanovlenie sovetsko-turetskikh otnoshenii*, pp. 37-59; and Tanin, *Desiat' let vneshnei politiki*, p. 94.

15.   *Godovoi otchet NKID (1920-1921)*, pp. 8-9; and Leong, *Sino-Soviet Diplomatic Relations*, pp. 198ff.

16.   *Mezhdunarodnaia politika RSFSR v 1922 g.*, p. 3. Also see N.N. Liubimov and A.N. Erlikh, *Genuezskaia konferentsiia (vospominaniia uchastnikov)* (Moscow, 1963); and Carr, *Bolshevik Revolution*, vol. III, ch. XXIX.

17.   Tanin, *Desiat' let vneshnei politiki*, pp. 116-20; Carr, *Bolshevik Revolution*, vol. III, pp. 479-83; and Harold Nicolson, *Curzon: The Last Phase, 1919-1925: A Study in Post War Diplomacy* (New York, 1939), pp. 309-13 and passim. For a full list of the international conferences in which the RSFSR participated, see Sterling Hale Fuller, 'The Foreign Policy of the Soviet Union in the League and United Nations', Ph.D. thesis, University of Texas, 1952, pp. 412-13.

18.   Linke, *Deutsch-sowjetische Beziehungen*, pp. 175-214; A. Akhtamzian, *Rapall'skaia politika: sovetsko-germanskie diplomaticheskie otnosheniia v 1922-1932 godakh* (Moscow, 1974), pp. 49-80; and Hilger and Meyer, *Incompatible Allies*, pp. 76-83.

19.   Gabriel Gorodetsky, *The Precarious Truce: Anglo-Soviet Relations, 1924-27* (Cambridge, 1977), pp. 1 ˈ3; and Daniel F. Calhoun, *The TUC and the Russians, 1923-28* (Cambridge, 1976), pp. 1-48.

20.   Robert Paul Browder, *The Origins of Soviet-American Diplomacy* (Princeton, 1953), pp. 3-24.

21.   V.K. Furaev, 'Informatsionnoe biuro sovetskogo soiuza v vashingtone (1923-1933gg.)', *Problemy otechestvennoi i vseobshchei istorii*, 1973, no. 2, pp. 70-77.

22.   *Desiat' let sovetskoi diplomatii*, pp. 12 and 18; and *Godovoi otchet NKID (1920-1921)*, p. 155. Subsequently a series of campaigns to reduce the number of employees in the Soviet bureaucracy trimmed this figure first to 650 and then to 458. By the opening of 1923 the Commissariat employed a total of just 1,007 staff members at its central, 'local', and foreign offices combined.

23.   *Ibid.*, pp. 154-55 and 166.

24.   *Ibid.*, p. 158; and Kantorovich, 'Organizatsionnoe razvitie NKID', p. 54. On NKID organization also see Andrė Sabanine, 'L'Organisation du Service diplomatique et consulaire de la RSFSR', *Bulletin de L'Institut Intermediaire International*, 1923, VIII, pp. 213-16.

25.   *Godovoi otchet NKID (1920-1921)*, pp. 158-59; and Kantorovich, 'Organizatsionnoe razvitie NKID', p. 54.

26.   *Desiat' let sovetskoi diplomatii*, p. 19.

27.   *Godovoi otchet NKID (1920-1921)*, p. 54.

28.   *Ibid.*, pp. 156 and 183-84.

29. Kantorovich, 'Organizatsionnoe razvitie NKID', p. 54.

30. *Godovoi otchet NKID (1920-1921)*, pp. 157-58; and Bessedovsky, *Revelations of a Soviet Diplomat*, p. 127.

31. Kantorovich, 'Organizatsionnoe razvitie NKID', p. 54.

32. *Sobranie uzakonenii*, 1921, no. 49, article 261.

33. Ibid., paragraphs 5-11.

34. *Sobranie uzakonenii*, 1921, no. 49, article 261, and 1922, no. 11, article 105.

35. *Vestnik NKID*, 1922, no. 8, p. 52.

36. *Annuaire diplomatique du Commissariat du Peuple pour les Affaires Étrangères pour l'année 1927* (Moscow, 1927) p. 131.

37. *Vestnik tsentral'nogo ispolnitel'nogo komiteta, soveta narodnykh komissarov i soveta truda i oborony SSSR: postanovleniia i rasporiazheniia pravitel'stva* (Moscow, 1923), article 300, ch. I and II, paragraphs 1-2; and *Sobranie uzakonenii*, 1923, vol. II, no. 107.

38. *Vestnik VTsIK*, 1923, article 300, ch. III, paragraphs 3 and 4 and ch. IV, paragraph 5; *Godovoi otchet za 1924 god k III s''ezdu sovetov SSSR* (Moscow, 1925), appendix, p. 10; and *Desiat' let sovetskoi diplomatii*, p. 19.

39. *Izvestiia*, 13 August 1922.

40. Aspaturian, *The Union Republics*, p. 37; and Francis Conte, 'Autour de la polémique Rakovskij — Staline sur la question nationale, 1921-1923', *Cahiers du Monde Russe et Soviétique*, 1975, XVI, 1, pp. 111-17.

41. *Izvestiia*, 13 August 1922.

42. Aspaturian, *The Union Republics*, p. 38.

43. Ibid., p. 40.

44. Kuznetsova, *Ustanovlenie sovetsko-turetskikh otnoshenii*, pp. 69-71; S.I. Aralov, *Vospominaniia sovetskogo diplomata, 1922-1923* (Moscow, 1960), pp. 33-34; and Kapur, *Soviet Russia in Asia*, pp. 109-13.

45. M.V. Popov, *Missiia E.A. Babushkina v irane* (Moscow, 1974), ch. II.

46. *Sovetsko-afganskie otnosheniia 1919-1969gg.: dokumenty i materialy* (Moscow, 1971), p. 7.

47. Aspaturian, *The Union Republics*, pp. 41-42.

48. *Vestnik VTsIK*, 1923, article 300, ch. V, paragraphs 11 and 12.

49. *Annuaire diplomatique*, 1927, pp. 202ff.; and Grzybowski, *Soviet Public International Law*, pp. 285-86 and 348, n. 15.

50. Alexei F. Neymann, 'The Formation and Administration of Soviet Foreign Policy', in: Samuel N. Harper, ed., *The Soviet Union and World Problems* (Chicago, 1935), p. 228.

51. See *Annuaire diplomatique* for 1925, pp. 147-48; 1926, pp. 178-79; 1927, pp. 207-8; and 1928, pp. 194-96. Cf. Crowley, ed., *Soviet Diplomatic Corps*, pp. 14-15.

52. *Desiat' let sovetskoi diplomatii*, p. 23.

53. Sylvia R. Margulies, *The Pilgrimage to Russia: The Soviet Union and the Treatment of Foreigners, 1924-1937* (Madison, 1968), p. 72; and Paul Scheffer, *Seven Years in Soviet Russia* (London, 1931), pp. vii-x. Note, however, that Arens had previously worked in the Narkomindel Press Department himself.

54. William Reswick, *I Dreamt Revolution* (Chicago, 1952), p. 287.

55. Ibid., p. 210.

56. *Annuaire diplomatique*, 1927, pp. 198-202.

57. Ibid., pp. 202-4.

58.   Grzybowski, *Soviet Public International Law*, p. 322. Also see *Konsul'skii ustav soiuza SSR* (Moscow, 1926); *Konsul'skii ustav soiuza SSR s postateinymi primechaniiami* (Moscow, 1931); and A.V. Sabanin, *Posol'skoe i konsul'skoe pravo: kratkoe prakticheskoe posobie* (Moscow, 1934).

59.   Grzybowski, *Soviet Public International Law*, p. 326.

60.   Ibid., pp. 294-95.

61.   E.A. Korovin, ed., *Mezhdunarodnoe pravo* (Moscow, 1951), pp. 332-33; and Modzhorian and Sobakin, eds., *Mezhdunarodnoe pravo*, vol. II, p. 5.

62.   *Izvestiia*, 25 December 1928.

63.   *Desiat' let sovetskoi diplomatii*, pp. 23 and 27.

64.   Barmine, *One Who Survived*, pp. 139ff.

65.   See, for example, Kendall E. Bailes, 'The Politics of Technology: Stalin and Technocratic Thinking Among Soviet Engineers', *The American Historical Review*, 1974, LXXIX, 2, pp. 445-69.

66.   *XVI s''ezd vsesoiuznoi kommunisticheskoi partii (bol'shevikov): stenograficheskii otchet* (Moscow, 1931), p. 315. It is not possible to tell whether all of these defectors actually took state funds with them as charged. It is also impossible to ascertain whether those defectors who did take government monies had done so earlier and then defected in order to avoid arrest for this crime, or whether, as seems more likely, many of them decided to leave Soviet service for political reasons and only at that point took state funds to finance their defection.

67.   Edward Savage Crocker, Chargé in Stockholm, to Secretary of State, 18 April 1930, USDS 701.6158/20. Also see John M. Morehead, Ambassador to Sweden, to Secretary of State, 1 May 1930, 701.6158/22.

68.   Barmine, *One Who Survived*, pp. 186-87.

69.   Grigorii S. Agabekov, *O.G.P.U.: The Russian Secret Terror* (New York, 1931), p. 269.

70.   See N.D. Kondrat'ev, *Skvoz' revol'vernyi lai*. . (Moscow, 1962); and V.I. Popov, 'Proval odnoi mezhdunarodnoi provokatsii', in: *Dipkur'ery: ocherki o pervykh sovetskikh diplomaticheskikh kur'erakh* (Moscow, 1973), pp. 171-202.

71.   Dispatch quoted from Arkhiv Vneshnei Politiki SSSR in V. Sokolov, 'Break Through the Diplomatic Blockade (Fiftieth Anniversary of the Period of Recognition of the USSR)', *International Affairs*, 1974, no. 6, pp. 85-86.

72.   Quoted by A. Alexandrov and L. Sergeyeva, '90th Anniversary of Valerian Dovgalevsky's Birth', *International Affairs*, 1976, p. 129.

73.   USDS 701.6111.

74.   Dmitrievsky, *Dans les Coulisses du Kremlin*, p. 207.

75.   Raoul Girardet, 'Litvinov et ses énigmes', in: Jean-Baptiste Duroselle, ed., *Les Relations Germano-Soviétique de 1933 a 1939* (Paris, 1954) pp. 119-20; and Bessedovsky, *Revelations*, pp. 126ff. Also see V. Sokolov, 'Break Through Diplomatic Blockade (A Documentary Survey)', *International Affairs*, 1974, no. 12, p. 100.

76.   Girardet, 'Litvinov et ses énigmes', p. 120; and Hilger and Meyer, *Incompatible Allies*, pp. 111-13.

77.   Isaac Deutscher, *The Prophet Armed: Trotsky, 1879-1921* (New York, 1959), p. 459. Also see Jan M. Meijer, ed., *The Trotsky Papers, 1917-1922*, vol. II, *1920-1922* (The Hague and Paris, 1971), documents 504 and 507.

78.   See various dispatches of German Ambassador Rantzau to the Auswärtiges Amt in the German foreign ɔffice micro-filmed document series, nos. 2860/D552716,

2778-80; 9101/H225068; and K281/K096584-88. Also see Edgar V. D'Abernon, *The Diary of An Ambassador* (Garden City, 1929-31), vol. II, pp. 181-84.

79. B. Bajanov (Bazhanov), *Stalin, der Rote Diktator* (Berlin, 1931), pp. 110-11. Also see Fischer, *Men and Politics*, pp. 127-30.

80. Barmine, *One Who Survived*, p. 119.

81. Georgii Solomon, *Sredi krasnykh vozhdei* (Paris, 1930), pp. 170-83.

82. Louise Bryant, *Mirrors of Moscow* (New York, 1923), p. 199. Simon Liberman, a participant in several foreign trade missions, came to much the same conclusion:

> It should be noted that as a 100 per cent Bolshevik he [Litvinov] was appointed by the government to assist Foreign Commissar Chicherin because the latter was never really forgiven by the Communists for either his former Menshevism or his aristocratic origin. Litvinov was detailed by the party to be its watchdog in Chicherin's commissariat. . . .
>
> In 1920 Litvinov felt that, on the basis of his past experience, he ought to have been the titular foreign commissar. . . .

Liberman, *Building Lenin's Russia*, pp. 111-12.

83. Girardet, 'Litvinov et ses énigmes', pp. 116-17.

84. Poole, 'Reminiscences', vol. II, p. 193.

85. See Jon Jacobson, *Locarno Diplomacy: Germany and the West, 1925-1929* (Princeton, 1972), passim; Lionel Kochan, *The Struggle for Germany* (New York, 1963), pp. 29-53; Harvey L. Dyck, *Weimar Germany and Soviet Russia, 1926-1933: A Study in Diplomatic Instability* (New York, 1966), pp. 109-208; and Josef Korbel, *Poland Between East and West: Soviet and German Diplomacy toward Poland, 1919-1933* (Princeton, 1963), pp. 188-222.

86. Chicherin to Fischer, 14 February 1930, Louis Fischer-Georgii Chicherin Correspondence, Yale University. Also see Debo, 'George Chicherin', pp. 365ff.

87. *Pravda* and *Izvestiia*, 30 May 1928. Thereafter Chicherin was ignored in Soviet literature on foreign policy published between 1930 and the mid-1950s. Since then, however, Soviet commentators once again give his accomplishments fulsome praise. See, for example, the introduction by Deputy Foreign Minister V. Semenov to the 1966 edition of Gorokhov, Zamiatin and Zemskov, *G.V. Chicherin*.

88. Trofimova in Chicherin, *Stat'i i rechi*, pp. 19-20; and Degras, ed., *Soviet Documents*, vol. II, p. 229.

89. For other examples see Girardet, 'Litvinov et ses énigmes', pp. 130-31; Bryant, *Mirrors of Moscow*, pp. 201-3; and Bessedovsky, *Revelations*, p. 98.

90. Alexander Orlov, *The Secret History of Stalin's Crimes* (New York, 1952), pp. 336-37.

91. In discussing 'friction' within the Red Army with S.I. Aralov, a soldier who subsequently became a diplomat, Lenin advised him, 'You ought to follow the example of the People's Commissariat of Foreign Affairs. They have none of it [i.e. factionalism] — it's an excellent Commissariat.' Quoted in S. Aralov, 'On Lenin's Instructions', *International Affairs*, 1960, no. 4, p. 12.

4

NARKOMINDEL PERSONNEL

The problem of staffing a new socialist government was not an issue to which the Bolshevik leaders had devoted much thought prior to October 1917. Lenin's earliest ideas on the problems of administration under socialism were clearly Utopian. He maintained that ordinary workers could easily master the necessary skills and could effectively supervise technical specialists where expertise was required.[1] In *State and Revolution,* written in the summer of 1917, Lenin went on to predict the end of any sort of governmental bureaucracy. Even the simplest scrub woman, he argued, could readily acquire the skills necessary to manage the dictatorship of the proletariat.[2] Bukharin, emphasizing the latent anarchist strain in Marxism, asserted that the workers' revolution would, of necessity, destroy the bourgeois state apparatus and create an entirely new proletarian government which would, in turn, soon wither away.[3]

The evolution of the Commissariat of Foreign Affairs did not substantiate Lenin's and Bukharin's theories on administration. The recruitment of cadres of workers from the nearby Siemens plant and the assignment to the NKID of party members who had little or no competence in foreign affairs may, perhaps, have reflected this thinking. However, as in other spheres of governmental activity, such ideas were progressively abandoned. From the inception of the Commissariat, the Bolsheviks tried to enlist the services of officials from the former Ministry of Foreign Affairs. Within just a few years the Narkomindel could boast of a core of professional diplomats and foreign policy specialists. The Bolsheviks quickly abandoned their Utopian attitudes toward administration. In his last published article, 'Better Less, but Better', Lenin was forced to admit that the average worker had neither the general cultural background nor the specific training necessary for the execution of the complex tasks involved in high level Soviet work.[4] After the first days of the October revolution, workers, peasants and soldiers never played a prominent part in the development of the NKID.

A PROSOPOGRAPHY OF THE NARKOMINDEL STAFF

Since extremely few of the tsarist and Provisional Government diplomats answered Foreign Commissar Trotskii's call to serve the Soviet regime, the Narkomindel had to be created almost ex nihilo. The diplomatic service which emerged was unique both among Soviet Commissariats and among European Foreign offices. The political coloration of the Narkomindel's personnel is striking, though not at all surprising. The most obvious place for the Bolshevik leaders to turn in search of recruits was to their own party and to other Russian and European radical parties in sympathy with their aims. Table 1 illustrates the pre-revolutionary political party affiliations of Soviet diplomats and responsible officials of the NKID central apparatus during the period from 1917 to 1930.[5] Bolsheviks, counting both recent recruits and members of long standing, comprised 63 percent of the Commissariat's high and middle level employees.[6] It seems that the relative size of the Menshevik contingent in the organizatization (only 9 percent of the total) has been

Table 1

Pre-revolutionary (i.e., pre-1917) Political Party
Affiliation of NKID Personnel, 1917-1930

Party	N	%
Old Bolsheviks[7]	231	44
Bolsheviks	102	19.4
Mensheviks	48	9
Other socialists[8]	51	10
Revolutionaries (unspecified affiliation)	30	5.7
Socialist Revolutionaries	30	5.7
Kadets (and other liberals)	18	3
Anarchists	3	0.6
Other parties	3	0.6
No affiliation	9	2
Totals	525	100

generally overestimated.[9] Many of the Narkomindel staff who had previously belonged to non-Bolshevik political movements apparently joined the Communist party after the October revolution. In 1927 the Commissariat reported that 376 of its 483 'responsible workers' (about 78 percent) were party members.[10]

The NKID appears to have been the most completely 'Bolshevized' department of government. The comparison with other commissariats is striking. The Commissariat of Agriculture remained a stronghold of former Socialist Revolutionaries until late in the decade, while in the *Cheka* Left-SRs and other non-party people continued to hold responsible posts.[11] Similarly, even in the central apparatus of the Commissariat of the Workers' and Peasants' Inspectorate (*Rabkrin*) communists made up only 42 percent of the staff.[12] Party members constituted only tiny minorities at the Supreme Economic Council and the Gosplan.[13] In 1924 86 percent of the Commissars, Deputy Commissars and Collegium members in the central government as a whole were communists, while in the Narkomindel all of these posts were occupied by party members.[14] Even by 1929 only one quarter of all Soviet government employees were party members.[15] In the Foreign Commissariat, on the other hand, 51 percent of the 'specialists' and 76 percent of the senior and medium rank officials held party cards.[16] Party membership was one effective tool which the Politburo had at its disposal to ensure that its decisions on foreign affairs were properly executed by the Soviet diplomatic corps. The allocation of so many veteran Bolsheviks to the NKID at a time when their services were badly needed throughout the state apparatus also seems to show that the Bolshevik elite placed high priority on the speedy development of an able and reliable foreign service.

The social origins of Soviet diplomats diverged sharply from what might be expected of the representatives of a 'workers' state' (see Table 2). 'According to calculations made during the 1920's, about 60 percent of the Bolshevik [pre-1917] underground were workers, 8 percent were peasants, and a third were drawn from middle class groups (professional and white-collar workers, intelligentsia, students, etc.)'[17] In contrast, the upper and middle levels of the Commissariat staff were predominantly bourgeois in origin (69.6 percent) with an additional significant admixture of nobles. Commissar Chicherin himself, who could trace his noble lineage back to fifteenth-century Muscovy, is a good example of the aristocratic

Table 2
Social Origins of Narkomindel and CPSU Members[18]

Class	N in NKID (1917-1930)	% in NKID (1917-1930)	% in CPSU in 1927
Workers	39	9	55.7
Peasants	21	5	19
Middle Classes (professionals)	207	48	—
Middle Classes (other)	93	21	—
'White-collar workers'	—	—	25.3
Nobles	75	17	—
Totals	435	100	100

strain in the Narkomindel. Even the cadres of the NKID drawn from the ranks of the Old Bolsheviks tended to be heavily middle class in composition. This reflects both the educational requirements of diplomatic work and the nature of pre-revolutionary Bolshevism which drew its leading cadres principally from the gentry and bourgeois intelligentsia.

Although few members of the fledgling Soviet foreign service had any specific training in the arts of diplomacy, the general level of education within the Narkomindel was very impressive (see Table 3). The overwhelming majority of Commissariat officials (87 percent) had received some instruction beyond the high school level. The list of distinguished institutions attended by future Soviet diplomats includes: in Russia, Moscow University, St Petersburg University, St Petersburg Junker School, Tomsk University, University of Odessa, University of Kiev, Kharkov Technical Institute, and the Psychoneurotic Institute (St Petersburg); in Western Europe, University of Munich, Marburg University, the Academy of Commerce in Mannheim, University of Bern, and the University of Geneva; and in America, Harvard University, Valparaiso University, and Marietta College. Advanced degrees in medicine, law, engineering, and the liberal arts were relatively common among Soviet diplomats during this period. The NKID counted among its ranks

Table 3
Educational Levels of Soviet Diplomats and Responsible NKID Officials[19]

Level	N in NKID (1917-1930)	% in NKID (1917-1930)	% in CPSU 1919	1922	1927
Graduate or professional studies	126	25			
University	243	49	5	0.6	0.8
Technical school	66	13			
Secondary school	33	7	8	6.3	7.9
Primary school	21	4	87	92.7	91.3
Self-educated	3	1			
No education	3	1			
Totals	495	100	100	99.6	100

four scientists, nine physicians, twenty-three lawyers, thirty engineers, sixteen journalists and writers, nineteen professors, teachers, and librarians, and a large number of other miscellaneous professionals. Knowledge of foreign languages was also widespread among NKID members. Besides what they may have learned by formal instruction, these future diplomats often acquired additional language competency when, in the pre-revolutionary era, the tsarist *Okhrana* (political police) forced many of them to flee Russia and settle in Western Europe for a number of years. Some Soviet foreign officers were fluent in as many as seven languages and a knowledge of both German and French was not at all unusual.

These scholarly attainments are especially striking when compared to the educational standards of the party as a whole. At a time when fully 50 percent of the general Russian population over the age of 8 years were illiterate and when the CPSU was experiencing a precipitous decline in the overall educational level of its membership (due to severe casualties in the Civil War and to heavy recruitment among the proletariat and peasantry), the party was making an extremely great investment in the Narkomindel from its tiny pool of well-educated members. For example, Leonid Krasin and Valerian

Dovgalevskii, each of whom served for a time as the Soviet representative in Paris, were talented engineers. Despite the chronic shortage
of qualified and experienced technical personnel after 1917 and the
resulting necessity of employing politically unreliable 'bourgeois
specialists', the regime chose to utilize these two men in diplomatic
work. This obvious commitment to the establishment of an able
diplomatic corps casts some doubt on the assertion of a number of
scholars that the Bolsheviks had little use for diplomacy during this
period, allegedly much preferring to employ insurrectionists and intelligence agents in the execution of their foreign policy.[20]

Despite its otherwise elaborate organizational structure, the Commissariat of Foreign Affairs did not develop adequate institutions
for the training of its personnel in the 1920s. In the early days of
revolutionary enthusiasm immediately following the October 1917
seizure of power, it was thought that an imminent European revolution would eliminate the need for people trained in the arts of
bourgeois diplomacy. With the failure of this expectation, the shortage of qualified foreign service officers became critical.

On-the-job training was at first the only possible remedy, given the
pressing demands placed on the diplomatic corps in its early days.[21]
Many of the more conscientious Narkomindel employees attempted
to make up for their deficiencies through wide reading as well as conversations with more knowledgeable colleagues. When S.I. Aralov
was notified of his appointment as Soviet representative to Turkey,
he immediately began to study the relevant diplomatic archives as
well as books on Turkish foreign policy, history and culture. He also
questioned other NKID staff members who were familiar with the
Near Eastern situation. Finally, Aralov was carefully briefed about
his mission by Chicherin and Lenin.[22] Such attempts at self-
education were not always successful as the following account by a
Soviet diplomat illustrates:

> The whole staff had been warned by Voikov [ambassador to Poland] that if
> they made the slightest mistake they would be sent straight to Moscow. The
> members of the Russian *corps diplomatique* he ordered to learn dancing at
> once! On this occasion he gave a lecture on diplomacy as he understood it. He
> spoke of details which I am sure are unknown to the most hardened foreign
> diplomats. He said, for instance, that the greatest diplomatic victories had been
> won in conservatories. I will not quote the examples he cited in support of this
> astonishing theory; it is enough to say that the most recent cases he cited related
> to the Vienna Conference. The others were drawn from the more scandalous
> history of the eighteenth and even the seventeenth century. Voikov knew these

stories by heart.
Such was the lecture read by a Communist Minister to his subordinates.[23]

Lacking training facilities of its own the Commissariat was forced to rely on the cooperation of other educational institutions. A number of scholarships were provided each term for potential foreign service officers to study at the diplomatic section of the faculty of social sciences of the First Moscow State University.[24] The Narkomindel also joined forces with the War College to create a special faculty of oriental languages, headed by two NKID officers, Vladimir Tsukerman and A.I. Dolivo-Dobrovol'skii, an accomplished linguist who had served formerly in the Imperial Ministry of Foreign Affairs. Nariman Narimanov, the director of the Commissariat's Near Eastern Affairs sub-section, also taught at this school. The diplomatic students and military cadets studied not only oriental languages (Persian, Hindustani, Arabic, Chinese, Japanese, etc.) but also heard lectures on geographic, cultural and political topics.[25] This faculty apparently spawned both the Eastern Department of the Military Academy and the Institute for Eastern Studies (later called the Narimanov Eastern Institute). NKID trainees studied at both of these latter institutions. One Soviet diplomat estimated that by as early as 1925 over three quarters of the Narkomindel's representatives and agents serving in Asia had studied at one of these schools.[26] Toward the end of the decade a few more formal courses were begun within the Commissariat for on-the-job trainees.

It was not until 1935 that the Narkomindel finally established a satisfactory program for preparing foreign service officers by opening the Institute for Training Diplomatic and Consular Workers. The two year course at this Institute prepared candidates for positions in the NKID central apparatus as well as the Soviet missions abroad. Those seeking admission to the program were required to have a univerity degree, to pass entrance examinations in history, politics, geography and mathematics, and to present references from their party organization.[27] At the same time another special school was opened to train clerks, stenographers, typists and other technical personnel for the foreign service.[28] While the majority of novice Soviet diplomats attended the new Institute, those slated for positions in Asia studied at the Oriental Institute in Moscow as before. There the rigorous four year curriculum in foreign languages, economics, geography and politics prepared students for consular and diplomatic posts throughout the Orient.[29]

The officers of the People's Commissariat of Foreign Affairs represented most of the important nationality groups within the old Russian Empire, although the contingent of Great Russians predominated (see Table 4).

At first glance it seems that the Narkomindel's membership more accurately reflected the proportion of each nationality in relation to the total population than did the party at any time during this decade. These figures are deceptive, however. They include many people in the minority nationalities who had only a tangential connection with the Commissariat (e.g. officials serving briefly in the various republican foreign offices). In reality the Soviet diplomatic corps was almost completely dominated by Great Russians, though, upon occasion, diplomats from the minority nationalities played a significant role in Soviet foreign policy. For instance, Kerim A. Khakhimov was the first Soviet representative to Arabia who was permitted to reside in Mecca — because he was Moslem by birth.

The age structure of the Narkomindel closely paralleled that of the Russian Communist Party. Both organizations had an extremely youthful membership. A sampling of communists during the civil war revealed that over 50 percent of them were under thirty years of age while 90 percent were under forty.[30] The average age of all high and medium rank foreign service officers was almost 38 years, while the average age for ambassadors, Collegium members and heads of the major departments was 39.3 years. Soviet diplomats tended to be much younger than their foreign counterparts during this period. This propensity toward youthfulness is explained by the recent origin of the Commissariat itself and by the age structure of the Bolshevik party from which it drew a large proportion of its personnel.

The NKID was also an almost entirely male organization, at least in its upper echelons. Except for Aleksandra Kollontai and a very few other female diplomats, most of the women in the Commissariat were employed in minor technical positions (e.g. typists, translators). During the period from 1917 to 1930 approximately 96 percent of Narkomindel staff in the high and middle grades were men, while only 4 percent were women. These figures are quite similar to the corresponding statistics for the party where in 1922 92.2 percent of the membership consisted of males and 7.8 percent of females.[31] Only a very few segments of the state and party bureaucracy, such as the Commissariat of Enlightenment (education), the Marx-Engels Institute and the *Zhenskii Otdel* (Women's Department) of the

Table 4

Nationality Composition of the NKID, CPSU and General Population, 1917-1930

Nationality[32]	N in Narkomindel 1917-1930	% of Narkomindel 1917-1930	% of Party 1922	% of Party 1927	% of Population 1926
Great Russian	258	42	72	65	52.9
Ukrainian	58	9	5.9	11.7	21.2
White Russian	10	2	1.5	3.2	3.2
Jewish	98	16	5.2	4.3	1.8
German	34	6			
Baltic and Finnish	26	4			
Polish	20	3	3.4	3.6	2.5
Transcaucasian	42	7	2.5	3.5	7.0
Central Asian	36	6			
Foreigners (non-Soviet populations)	32	5			
Other			2.9	3.8	6.4
Polish and Baltic			4.6	2.6	0.7
Minority people of the RSFSR			2.0	2.3	4.3
Totals	614	100	100	100	100

Central Committee, employed many female staff members in responsible positions.[33]

SOURCES OF DIPLOMATIC PERSONNEL

During the first years of its existence the Commissariat of Foreign Affairs gathered its personnel from several distinct sources. The Soviet government made a determined effort to secure the services of the experienced former tsarist diplomats, but most of them, detesting Bolshevism, refused to cooperate. Only a tiny minority of the old Imperial Foreign Ministry staff remained at their posts. Two former consuls, Solov'ev and Ungern-Sternberg, together with several officials from the central ministry apparatus (Florinskii, Sabanin, Kliuchnikov, Voznesenskii, Dolivo-Dobrovol'skii, Murav'ev and Kolchanovskii) provided the NKID with a small nucleus of officials familiar with the mechanics of operating a foreign office. Some of these men were merely opportunists, who hoped to protect their own careers. Others, though anti-Bolshevik, considered it a patriotic duty to continue their work at this time of crisis for Russia. Only a few were convinced Marxists. In an introduction to Solov'ev's autobiography, Theodore Rotshtein, a Narkomindel Collegium member, praised the knowledge and usefulness of these former tsarist diplomats. He characterized Solov'ev and his colleagues as essentially non-political diplomatic technicians. Rotshtein criticized them for their general lack of 'class viewpoint' and for their tendency to ignore the role of class conflict in international affairs.[34]

The use of these well-trained and experienced servitors of the old regime ('bourgeois specialists' in Soviet parlance), whether in diplomacy, the military, science or industry and commerce, caused considerable debate in communist circles. Critics doubted whether communism could be built by such 'former' people, tainted as they were by bourgeois ideology. The recruitment of tsarist military officers into the Red Army was especially controversial.[35] In practice, the Narkomindel, together with the *Cheka,* were notable for the relatively small number of former Imperial and Provisional Government officials in their ranks. In contrast, the Commissariats of Finance, Navy, Workers' and Peasants' Inspectorate, and Communications were largely staffed by veterans of the Imperial regime.[36] From time to time the NKID attempted to attract more of the old tsarist diplomats to its service, but without success.[37] Those few experienced foreign service officials who remained with the NKID played a significant role in that they helped to smooth the transition from the former Ministry to the new Commissariat and to introduce novice Bolshevik diplomats to the mores of bourgeois diplomacy. The already thin ranks of these veteran officials were depleted by the 'cleansing' of 1929-1930 and their remnant was destroyed in the Great Purges of the latter 1930s.

Men of the Russian radical emigration comprised a far more important group in the early Soviet diplomatic corps. Hundreds of revolutionary-minded intellectuals had been forced to leave Russia as tsarism became increasingly repressive under the reigns of Alexander III and Nicholas II. These émigrés, representing every element of the anti-tsarist political spectrum, took up residence in the major cities of Europe, often spending much of their lives abroad. With the victory of the February revolution in 1917 these exiles returned to Russia in great numbers. It is not surprising that many of them found their way into the Narkomindel. They spoke foreign languages, had acceptable European manners, and were familiar with the political and social dynamics of the European states. The career of Valerian Dovgalevskii provides an excellent example. He was arrested for revolutionary activity as a youth, but he escaped to Belgium and subsequently migrated to France. Dovgalevskii's qualifications for diplomatic work are described admiringly by Aleksandr Barmin who served under him in the Paris embassy in the late 1920s.

> Dovgalevsky's personal gifts were daily put to the test. Speaking French perfectly, and familiar with the habits and psychology of the country — he had lived in France as a student — the ambassador distinguished himself by his patience, his courtesy, and a subtlety that lay behind a dignified exterior. He could have passed anywhere for a great French engineer, which indeed by training he was. No one was better suited to carry on the struggle for Soviet influence, and by the time he died at his post the situation had greatly improved.[38]

Many of these former émigrés also had some 'diplomatic' experience. They had been involved in the complicated relationships, and resultant negotiations, among the European socialist parties. Aleksandra Kollontai, the future Soviet ambassador to Sweden, had

served in that country before the October revolution as liaison between the Russian Bolshevik faction and the Swedish socialists.

Chicherin, Litvinov and Ivan Maiskii (the latter was subsequently
Soviet ambassador in London) were each officers of the pre-war
Russian political émigré association in Great Britain. Their organization conducted complicated negotiations not only among various
émigré groups, but also with the British government and the West
European socialist parties. It was this group, exemplified by Trotskii
and Chicherin, who filled all of the key positions and who set the
style of the Commissariat in its early years.

Party and government bureaucrats also contributed to the formation of the Commissariat of Foreign Affairs. Throughout this period
the Communist Party conducted a series of large scale recruiting
drives which greatly enlarged its membership. The Thirteenth Party
Congress, in 1924, resolved that:

> The chief task standing before the party in connection with the incorporation of
> over 200,000 new members [the so-called Lenin Enrollment] consists in ar-
> ranging to draw them into state work. . . . This should not be hampered by the
> lack of training of the new members. . . .[39]

Many party members who possessed no special competence in
diplomatic work flowed into and out of the NKID during these
years. Most of them had some previous experience in another
government department. Few of the people in this group ever achieved high rank within the Narkomindel and most of them worked in
the Commissariat for only a short period of time, engaged mainly in
technical work, soon departing for other party or state assignments.
A few powerful Bolshevik political figures also served briefly with
the NKID, typically performing some temporary assignment of
special importance and then departing. Sergei Kirov, for example,
was appointed as the representative of the RSFSR to Soviet Georgia
in 1920 when the Caucasus were undergoing 'Bolshevization'.
Stalin's ally, G.K. Ordzhonikidze, held the same post the following
year. Similarly, General Frunze was appointed Ambassador to
Turkey of the Ukrainian SSR in 1924 in order to conduct important
military negotiations in Ankara. These bureaucrats and prominent
political figures helped the undermanned Commissariat to perform
its tasks but they do not appear to have significantly affected its
development.

Foreign socialists also provided a small but important contingent on the Narkomindel staff. Many radicals from all over the world flocked to Petrograd after the February revolution. They wanted to experience the revolution first hand and they were eager to help build the new order. A few of these idealistic young men joined the Commissariat of Foreign Affairs. Two Americans, John Reed and Albert Rhys Williams, worked in the Press Bureau, preparing news releases and propaganda for the English-speaking countries. Julian Marchlewski, a Polish communist, played a very significant part in Russo-Polish negotiations in 1919. These foreign radicals were a small group numerically, but they possessed skills and knowledge critically needed by the NKID in the first two or three years of its existence.

The Narkomindel also shared the services of a body of foreign area specialists with several other state and party organizations whose responsibilities required a staff knowledgeable of foreign affairs (the Commissariat of Foreign Trade, the Foreign Affairs Bureau of the party Central Committee, the Soviet international press agency [INOROSTA], the Comintern, etc.). These men, who were well acquainted with foreign conditions, were recruited from the ranks of the Russian radical emigration and from foreign communists. A number of major Soviet officials (e.g. Leonid Krasin, A.A. Troianovskii, Konstantin Umanskii and Nariman Narimanov) show a career pattern of service in several government or party agencies which dealt with the outside world.

PERSONNEL POLICIES

The recruitment of qualified personnel was always a problem for the Commissariat of Foreign Affairs in the period from 1917 to 1930. The Central Labor Board of the government and the Record and Assignment Division of the party Secretariat seem to have been the chief sources of new diplomats and staff members.[40] The Administrative and Organizational Section of the Chancellery, subsequently the Personnel Department, handled personnel matters for the Commissariat. This section was responsible for reviewing all applications for NKID positions, verifying the applicants' statements and consulting with the proper party authorities concerning the candidates' suitability. Applicants for positions of the higher ranks within the Narkomindel had to be recommended and approved by the Collegium. Candidates for posts of secondary importance needed the support of the department in which they sought work as well as the sanction of the Collegium member who headed the Chancellery. The Chancellery staffed the lower echelons on its own authority. Vacancies in the Commissariat's branches in the Republics were filled by the Commissar upon the recommendation of the party Secretariat. In the foreign missions the ambassadors nominated men to fill minor vacancies. These latter appointments were confirmed by the People's Commissar.[41]

Ambassadors (i.e. *Polpredy*) were appointed and subject to recall by the Presidium of the Central Executive Committee of the Congress of Soviets. Diplomatic assignments below the rank of plenipotentiary representative were made by the Council of Commissars while the Narkomindel had the power to appoint chargés d'affaires, temporary substitutes for ambassadors and other miscellaneous diplomatic personnel.[42]

As with other branches of the Soviet government, the Narkomindel appealed to the broad masses of the country, especially those of proletarian origin, to participate in its work. In 1922 the Commissariat publicly proclaimed that:

> The Constitution of Soviet Russia opens all the positions in the government to all the workers without any distinction of nationality, sex, or race, except for those positions which demand essential technical knowledge (such as medicine, engineering, etc.); it imposes no preconditions concerning diplomas, experience, examinations, etc., and establishes the principle that the Russian diplomatic and consular service is accessible to everyone enjoying the rights of Russian citizens — without any other formality than registration in the rolls of the Commissariat. Consequently, no examination or prior experience requirements are known in our service.[43]

In practice, however, the extensive educational and linguistic requirements of diplomacy, coupled with the need for good letters of reference from party organs and the keen scrutiny of all applications for foreign posts exercised by the party Secretariat, tended to block the candidacies of all but well-educated party members. Gaining the imprimatur of the Secretariat and Orgburo could be a particularly difficult hurdle for diplomatic aspirants. In 1921 the posting of G.L. Shklovskii to Berlin required the determined intervention of Lenin himself to overcome the disapproval of the party apparatus.[44]

The staff of the Foreign Commissariat was subdivided into eighteen levels of rank.[45] The highest rank was shared by the Commissar, the members of the Collegium and all of the ambassadors. This lack of status differentiation on the highest level implied a collegial rather than a hierarchical pattern of decision-making among the Narkomindel leaders. This was only natural since party status rather than bureaucratic rank constituted a more accurate indicator of the actual authority configuration within the organization. Salaries were paid according to these grades. The lowest six levels were to receive the basic stipend of approximately 75 rubles per month.[46] Each step beyond the sixth rung meant the addition of 25 percent of the base pay to the employee's salary. Thus, Commissars, Collegium members and most ambassadors received about 280 rubles each month. Exceptions to these rates were made for diplomats posted to foreign missions who received proportionally more or less depending on the cost of living in the countries to which they were assigned.[47] For example, the minimum rate of pay for a Commissariat employee in Estonia was $31 per month, while the same official would earn $100 each month if stationed in Canada.

The Commissariat of Foreign Affairs experienced a rather large turnover in personnel during the first fourteen years of its existence (see Table 5). The great amount of people to serve in the NKID for three years or less is accounted for by the large number of party or governmental officials who served on short-term special missions to foreign countries and by the substantial number of people assigned

Table 5
Stability of NKID Personnel

Length of Assignment to Narkomindel	N of Employees	% of Employees
1 year or less	73	13
2-3 years	135	24
4-5 years	80	14
6-9 years	165	29
10-14 years	115	20
Totals	568	100

to the Commissart in its early years who proved unsuited to diplomatic work and were soon transferred to other tasks. Fully 49 percent of its employees served in the Narkomindel for six years or longer and many of these people remained members of the Commissariat after 1930, the terminal date of this study. Despite some instability in personnel, the NKID was developing a substantial base of truly professional diplomats in the embassies and experienced foreign service officers in its central apparatus.

Soviet foreign missions (i.e. diplomatic, commercial and other personnel combined) were rather large in comparison to those of other countries (see Table 6). These large missions were made up not

Table 6
Size of Soviet Foreign Missions, 1924[48]

Country	Officers on Diplomatic List	Total	Employees Diplomatic & Consular	Trade Delegation
England	4	882	22	860
Germany	11	779	19	750
Latvia	5	397	56	341
Turkey	4	84	46	38
Estonia	4	62	9	53
Austria	8	60	28	32
Poland	4	57	25	32
Persia	8	55	15	40
Sweden	4	53	_____(53)_____	
France	9	31	_____(31)_____	
Denmark	6	26	_____(26)_____	
Norway	4	11	_____(11)_____	
Lithuania	4	8	8	
Mexico	3	4	4	

only of Soviet government officials but also of a substantial number of nationals of the country to which the mission was accredited. The Russians preferred to hire local communists to assist in their embassies. The huge Soviet compound in Berlin included three hundred Russian citizens (all of whom were apparently CPSU members) and four hundred members of the German Communist Party, as well as three hundred Germans with no communist party affiliation.[49] Many observers have speculated that such large staffs were required for covert revolutionary and espionage activities.[50] The actual explanation for such unwieldy establishments may well lie in the generally low level of efficiency prevalent in the Commissariat and the tremendous volume of not only diplomatic but also commercial and cultural matters handled at the Berlin embassy and other major missions.

NOTES

1. Lenin, *PSS*, vol. XXXIV, pp. 287-339; and Merle Fainsod, *How Russia is Ruled* (Cambridge, 1965), pp. 88-89. Cf. Iu. V. Shabanov, *Leninskie printsipy raboty gosudarstvennogo apparata* (Minsk, 1971), pp. 197-207.

2. Lenin, *PSS*, vol. XXX, pp. 99-102.

3. Nikolai Bukharin, 'K teorii imperialisticheskogo gosudarstva', in: *Revoliutsiia prava: sbornik pervyi* (Moscow, 1925). Lenin had initially damned Bukharin's theories as 'semi-anarchistic', but he subsequently adopted Bukharin's ideas in his pamphlet *State and Revolution*.

4. Lenin, *PSS*, vol. XLV, pp. 389-406.

5. This and all subsequent statistical information about the personnel of th Narkomindel was derived from a study of all available biographical information on Soviet diplomats and responsible officials of the Commissariat. The origins of this information and the biases of this sample are discussed in the Bibliographical Essay.

6. The statistics on Narkomindel personnel composition presented throughout this chapter differ slightly in some cases from those given in the author's article, 'The Soviet Diplomatic Corps in the Čičerin Era', *Jahrbücher für Geschichte Osteuropas*, 1975, XXIII, 2, pp. 213-24. The larger and more reliable data base from which the present calculations are drawn acc⊂ s for such differences.

7. 'Old Bolsheviks' re defined here as those members who had joined the party before 1914. 'Bolsheviks a : defined as those members joining the party between 1914 and October 1917.

8 Fc example, *Mezhraiontsy*, Bund members, foreign socialists.

9. See for example, Vernon V. Aspaturian, *Process and Power in Soviet Foreign Policy* (Boston, 1971), p. 627.

10. *Desiat' let sovetskoi diplomatii*, p. 17.

11. Cohen, *Bukharin and the Bolshevik Revolution,* pp. 271 and 422, n. 3; and Lennard D. Gerson, *The Secret Police in Lenin's Russia* (Philadelphia, 1976), pp. 56-57.

12. Philip Scott Spoerry, 'The Central Rabkrin Apparatus: 1917-1925', Ph.D. dissertation, Harvard University, 1967, p. 189.

13. Z.K. Zvezdin, 'Iz istorii deiatel'nost Gosplana v 1921-1924 gg.', *Voprosy istorii KPSS,* 1967, no. 3, pp. 45-56.

14. T.H. Rigby, *Communist Party Membership in the U.S.S.R., 1917-1967* (Princeton, 1968), pp. 420-21. Also see M.P. Iroshnikov, 'O partiinom sostave sovetskogo gosudarstvennogo apparata v 1918 g.', *Voprosy istorii KPSS,* 1974, no. 9, pp. 115-16.

15. Rigby, *Communist Party Membership,* pp. 420-21.

16. *Sostav rukovodiashchikh rabotnikov i spetsialistov soiuza SSR* (Moscow, 1936), pp. 298-301.

17. Ibid., p. 63.

18. 'Workers' includes industrial proletarians, artisans, menials, domestics, guards, etc.; 'Peasants' includes landless or small-holding farmers; 'Middle Class (professional)' includes lawyers, doctors, professors, etc.; 'Middle Class (other)' includes merchants, businessmen, larger farm owners, etc.; and 'White-collar Workers' is a combination of the two preceding categories, excluding large farm owners. The data on the CPSU class composition are drawn from Rigby, *Communist Party Membership,* p. 162.

19. Narkomindel officials are listed at the highest level at which they began studies. Data on educational levels within the party at large were obtained from ibid., pp. 400-2.

20. For example, Von Laue, 'Soviet Diplomacy: G.V. Chicherin', pp. 234ff.

21. Neymann, 'Formulation and Administration of Soviet Foreign Policy', in: Harper, ed., *Soviet Union and World Problems,* p. 230.

22. Aralov, *Vospominaniia sovetskogo diplomata,* pp. 14-17.

23. Bessedovsky, *Revelations of a Soviet Diplomat,* pp. 78-79.

24. Neymann, 'Formulation and Administration', p. 230; and *Desiat' let sovetskoi diplomatii,* pp. 21-22.

25. Neymann, 'Formulation and Administration', p. 230; and Barmine, *One Who Survived,* pp. 85-87.

26. Ibid.

27. *Izvestiia,* 3 April 1935.

28. *Komsomolskaia pravda,* 17 June 1935.

29. *Moscow Daily News,* 5 December 1932.

30. Data concerning the age structure of the CPSU were abstracted from ibid., pp. 353-4.

31. Ibid., p. 360.

32. Statistics for the CPSU and general population nationality composition were drawn from Rigby, *Communist Party Membership,* p. 366.

33. Sheila Fitzpatrick, *The Commissariat of Enlightenment* (London, 1970), p. 19.

34. Iu.Ia. Solov'ev, *Dvadsat' piat' let moei diplomaticheskoi sluzhby, 1893-1918* (Moscow, 1928), p. 4.

35. John Erickson, *The Soviet High Command 1918-1941* (London, 1962), pp. 31-34; and S.A. Fediukin, *Sovetskaia vlast' i burzhuaznye spetsialisty* (Moscow, 1965),

pp. 48-94. On the general problem of 'specialists' in Soviet service also see Nikolai Valentinov, 'Non-Party Specialists and the Coming of the NEP', *The Russian Review*, 1971, XXX, 2, pp. 154-63.

36.   M.P. Iroshnikov, 'K voprosu o slome burzhuaznoi gosudarstvennoi mashiny v Rossii', in: Iu. S. Tokarev, et al., eds., *Problemy gosudarstvennogo stroitel'stva v pervye gody sovetskoi vlasti: sbornik statei* (Leningrad, 1973), pp. 53-54.

37.   Solov'ev, *Dvadsat' piat' let,* p. 395.

38.   Barmine, *One Who Survived,* p. 178. Ivan Maiskii formed a similar impression of Litvinov: 'When I arrived in London [in 1912] he was already an "old inhabitant".

He had been in England since 1908 and in the past four years had mastered the language, established many local connections and acquired a good knowledge of the commercial and political set-up in the capital. . . . Maxim Maximovich was even then versed in the home and foreign policies of Great Britain and had close ties with the leaders of the English Labour movement (which was very useful to him later on when he became People's Commissar of Foreign Affairs). . . .' *Journey into the Past,* pp. 55 and 57.

39.   *Kommunisticheskaia partiia sovetskogo soiuza: v rezoliutsiiakh i resheniiakh s"ezdov, konferentsii i plenumov TsK* (Moscow, 1953), vol. I, p. 824.

40.   *Vestnik NKID,* 1920, no. 4-5, p. 148; and Robert Daniels, *Conscience of the Revolution* (New York, 1969), p. 90.

41.   *Sbornik polozhenii, instruktsii i rasporiazhenii po upravleniiu delami NKID* (Moscow, 1925), pp. 3-7.

42.   *Sobranie uzakonenii,* 1922, no. 11, article 105.

43.   Sabanine, 'L'Organisation du Service diplomatique', p. 215.

44.   Roy A. Medvedev, *Let History Judge: The Origins and Consequences of Stalinism* (New York, 1972), pp. 18-19. The selection process became more rigid and exclusive as time passed. See Viacheslav P. Artem'ev, *Selection and Training of Soviet Personnel for Trade Missions Abroad, and the Soviet Mission in Iran, Two Studies* (New York, 1954), pp. 1-2. Also see USDS, 701.6160d/22, James R. Wilkinson, Consul in Helsingfors, to the Secretary of State, 27 March 1930, 'Concerning Conditions at and Staffs of Soviet Legations', p. 3.

45.   *Sbornik polozhenii,* pp. 3, 15-16 and 85.

46.   This figure was computed by Eugene Magerovsky in his doctoral dissertation, 'The People's Commissariat for Foreign Affairs, 1917-1946', Columbia University, 1975, p. 224.

47.   *Sbornik polozhenii,* pp. 84-85.

48.   Table compiled by the USDS, 701.6100/5, report by Division of Eastern European Affairs, 13 March 1924.

49.   AA, Die dip. und kons. Vertretungen Russlands, vol. VIII, vom Okt. 1927 bis Okt. 1931, report of Der Preussische Minister des Innern to Auswärtiges Amt, 9 January 1930.

50.   The matter of revolutionary and espionage activities is discussed in Chapter 6 of this volume.

5

THE NARKOMINDEL IN
STATE AND PARTY AFFAIRS

The most interesting, but also the most difficult, questions about the Narkomindel concern policy and politics. What role did the NKID play in the formulation of Soviet foreign policy and in what ways was the Commissariat involved in the titanic intra-party political struggles of the 1920s? These problems remain especially murky because of the fragmentary nature of available sources. It is precisely on the sensitive issues of policy and politics that the Soviet regime has been least willing to publish documentary materials and that the commentary of Soviet scholars has been least informative. It is worthwhile, nevertheless, to marshal the available data in order to gain some impression of how the Foreign Commissariat actually functioned within the Soviet system.

THE NARKOMINDEL AND FOREIGN POLICY

The constitutions of the RSFSR and USSR, together with the various Narkomindel statutes not only prescribed the organizational pattern of the NKID but also attempted to define its role in the foreign policy-making process. The 1918 Constitution of the RSFSR ambiguously gave powers of supervision over foreign policy matters to the All-Russian Congress of Soviets, its Central Executive Committee, and the council of People's Commissars (on which sat the Foreign Commissar). The Congress of Soviets was specifically charged with responsibility in the fields of admission of new areas into the Federation, foreign relations, decisions for war and peace, treaty-making and ratification, and the conclusion of economic and financial agreements with foreign states. These same powers were transferred to the All-Union government under the Agreement of Union in 1922. These enactments were supplemented by the 1924 Constitution which provided that the above functions would become the responsibility of the Congress of Soviets of the USSR and its

Central Executive Committee. Whenever the Congress or its Committee was not in session, the Presidium of the Central Executive Committee was authorized to perform a wide range of these duties (including the ratification of treaties) not specifically reserved for the Congress or full Committee. The Constitution of 1924 described the Sovnarkom merely as the executive and administrative agency of the Central Executive Committee.[1]

The 1923 Narkomindel statute charged the Commissariat with conducting the diplomatic relations of the USSR and of its component Republics with foreign states. The NKID was authorized to examine all treaties and then to forward them to either the Central Executive Committee or the Council of Commissars (depending on the nature of the treaty) for ratification.[2] A later decree established the Sovnarkom as the body to which all kinds of treaties and agreements had to be submitted. The Council of Commissars, using the NKID as its administrative agent, was responsible for the negotiation, review and confirmation of all treaties, although it did send some of them to the Congress of Soviets, the Central Executive Committee or its Presidium for formal ratification.[3]

The constitutionally authorized foreign policy apparatus thus provided for a circular flow of information and command. At the top of the process stood the Congress of Soviets which set the general orientation of foreign policy and reviewed the Sovnarkom's past work. The trends established at the Congress were then communicated to the Council of Commissars which translated that general orientation into specific policies and which supervised the execution of those policies by the Commissariat of Foreign Affairs. The Sovnarkom's directives were then passed down to the Narkomindel which devised the best strategies for their execution and actually carried them out. The reverse flow of communication began with reports on conditions in specific foreign countries together with policy reports which the NKID sent to the Sovnarkom. The Council of Commissars evaluated these reports and prepared from them recommendations on the future course of Soviet diplomacy which were, in turn, directed to the Congress of Soviets. Here the whole cycle repeated itself again with the issuing of new general policy guidelines.[4] The most important position in this circuit was that occupied by the Sovnarkom, for it was at this level that the contemporary situation was evaluated in toto and specific policies were fashioned from general directives.

The foregoing description, while including all of the constitutionally created organs charged with elaborating and executing foreign policy, is deficient in that it ignores the most important, though unofficial, agency in that process — the Communist Party of the Soviet Union. In actual practice, the party, or at least its more prominent leaders, played a decisive role in charting Soviet Russia's diplomatic course. Lenin admitted that 'not one important political or organizational question is decided by any one state institution in our republic without guiding instructions from the Central Committee of our Party'.[5] He later reiterated this point with specific reference to the NKID.

> How is it possible to unite the Party institutions with the Soviet [governmental] ones? . . .why really not unite the former and the latter, if it is demanded in the interest of the cause? Has anyone not noticed that in such a People's Commissariat as the Narkomindel this merger is of the utmost usefulness and has been practiced from its very inception? Doesn't the Politburo discuss, from the Party point of view, various small and large questions regarding the 'moves' on our part in reply to 'moves' of foreign states in order to avoid their, well, shall we say, slyness, in order not to speak less properly? Does not this flexible union of Soviet [governmental] institutions and Party [organs] constitute a source of extraordinary strength in our policy?[6]

During the first two years of Soviet power most major questions concerning foreign policy were resolved within the party's Central Committee while the Council of Commissars was responsible for the practical implementation of Central Committee decisions. This procedure was illustrated by Trotskii in a speech at the Second Comintern Congress in 1920.

> Today we have received from the Polish government proposals for the conclusion of peace. Who decides this question? We have Sovnarkom, but it must be subject to a certain control. What control? The control of the working class as a formless chaotic mass? No. The Central Committee of the party has been called together to discuss the proposal and decide whether to answer it.[7]

The debate over whether to adopt the harsh Treaty of Brest-Litovsk provides another example of the role of the party in Soviet foreign affairs. The crucial debates and the decision on this matter took place entirely within the Central Committee.[8] Very soon, however, the smaller and more efficient Politburo replaced the cumbersome Central Committee as the primary decision-making authority. Its early membership included Bukharin, Dzerzhinskii, Kamenev, Krestinskii, Lenin, Rykov, Stalin, Tomskii, Trotskii and

Zinoviev. In practice, the Politburo formulated foreign policy and the Narkomindel carried out its decisions.[9]

The constitutionally sanctioned pattern of foreign policy formulation and implementation was often completely disrupted by the powerful intrusion of the Politburo into the process. For instance, when, in June of 1921 the Soviet leadership was considering the problem of trade relations with Japan, Commissar Chicherin discussed the relevant issues thoroughly with the NKID Collegium and then forwarded his recommendations, not to the Sovnarkom, but directly to Lenin who added his own responses to Chicherin's report and submitted it to the Politburo for decision.[10] The Council of Commissars was brought into the matter only after policy had been formulated. Chicherin apparently composed reports for the Politburo quite frequently on a wide range of foreign policy questions.[11]

In addition to its central position in the foreign policy-making process, the party made its presence felt in the NKID in a number of other ways. A rather large number of the Commissariat's employees were party members. Their appointments were handled jointly by the Narkomindel personnel office and the Records and Assignments Division of the party Secretariat. Party members were organized into cells within each of the Commissariat's branches and missions. This gave the party Secretariat which supervised these cells another source of leverage over the Narkomindel. While the NKID was thus closely tied to the party, the party attempted to maintain its independence from the Commissariat. In order to avoid total dependence on the Commissariat's reports as its sole source of information on world conditions and international politics, the Central Committee maintained a Foreign Bureau which compiled synopses of current events and made policy recommendations in addition to monitoring the performance of the Narkomindel. Several NKID employees had a record of previous service in this Bureau. The Comintern, its agents and its foreign constituent parties also provided reports on conditions abroad. By the late 1920s Stalin's power had grown sufficiently so that he was able to organize a personal secretariat (*osobyi sektor*) which contained a foreign section, directed by Eugene Varga, paralleling both the Central Committee Foreign Bureau and the Commissariat of Foreign Affairs.[12] These various party organs apparently took their duties quite seriously for the Narkomindel occasionally received sharp rebukes when it failed to execute Politburo directives fully.[13]

The party as an institution certainly had an impact on Soviet foreign policy, but the influence of certain individual Bolsheviks was even more important. Current Soviet scholarship, following the popular cult of Leninism, claims for Lenin a completely dominant role in the formation and even in the execution of Russian foreign policy, to the almost total exclusion of all other factors.[14] Western observers have also commented on Lenin's importance in Soviet diplomacy.

> No important decision was adopted before he was consulted, and no move was carried out except under his close watch. In foreign affairs, he helped outline policy, he wrote or edited notes, directed *démarches*, and kept himself *au courant* even of negotiations concerning exchange of prisoners. Between 1917 and 1922 the lines of Soviet foreign policy lay firmly in his hands.[15]

Chicherin himself admitted that he never took important initiatives on his own authority, but always acted in consultation with Lenin.[16] The Commissar described that relationship in a laudatory article written shortly after Lenin's death.

> In the first years of the existence of our republic, I spoke with him [Lenin] by telephone several times a day, often at length, and had frequent personal interviews with him. Often I discussed with him all the details of current diplomatic affairs of any importance. Instantly grasping the substance of each issue and giving it the broadest possible interpretation, Vladimir Ilich always provided in his conversation the most brilliant analysis of the diplomatic situation, and his counsels (often he straightway suggested the text of a reply to a foreign govenment) were models of diplomatic art and flexibility.[17]

This was the case, for example, in 1921 when Chicherin was negotiating a treaty to establish friendly relations between the RSFSR and Turkey. Lenin telephoned the Commissar every night for a detailed report on the day's progress.[18] Lenin's importance in Soviet diplomacy cannot be denied. As the party's leading theoretician, his views, especially as expressed in *Imperialism: The Highest Stage of Capitalism,* helped to shape Bolshevik perceptions of the outside world. He was instrumental in the founding of the Narkomindel and occasionally indulged directly in diplomacy (e.g. the 'Decree on Peace'). Finally, as the strongest figure in both the Politburo and the Sovnarkom, Lenin exercised the greatest influence over all policy questions. However, Soviet diplomatic historians and political commentators tend to overestimate his significance. Lenin's was certainly not the only input into the policy-making process, nor was his voice always decisive.[19]

Lenin was, rather, the most important member of the Soviet foreign affairs elite which also included Trotskii, Kamenev, Chicherin, Sokol'nikov, Krasin, Karakhan, Litvinov and others.[20] All these men were pre-1917 émigrés with substantial knowledge of Western European political, economic and social conditions.[21] Among this group Lenin was the leader, but certainly not the dictator. His authority stemmed, in part, from his position as arbitrator of disputes within the elite.[22] As one witness at Sovnarkom meetings expressed it:

> Lenin was not merely a chairman [of the Sovnarkom] but a recognized chief to whom everyone brought his thorny problems. The commissars quarreled among themselves in their daily work, but here Lenin had the last word; and all alike left these meetings reassured, as though their quarrels had been those of children now pacified by a wise parent.[23]

By 1921 the deteriorating state of Lenin's health was starting to limit his participation in the policy articulating process and he began to delegate more of the work to his comrades. Chicherin noted that Lenin's personal dominance in Soviet foreign policy was beginning to '. . .give way to collective deliberations. . .' involving the Politburo and high Narkomindel officials.[24] The 1920s appear, for the most part, to have been a period characterized by genuine collective leadership in foreign affairs. The elite which formulated Soviet foreign policy at this time formed an interlocking directorate, representing the Politburo and the highest officials of the party Secretariat, the Narkomindel, the Comintern and the Commissariat of Foreign Trade. Stalin interfered relatively little in diplomatic matters, concentrating his efforts on securing absolute control of the party apparatus. Thus, it was only late in the decade that the future dictator began to make his heavy hand felt in diplomatic councils.[25]

The role of the Commissariat of Foreign Affairs in the policy-making process was an ambivalent one in the period from 1917 to 1930. In the past, the view that the NKID was little more than a glorified messenger service and public relations agency for the Politburo has been widely accepted. An American Secretary of State claimed that 'until Molotov's time, Soviet foreign ministers were minor officials, whose function was to deal insincerely with the capitalist powers'.[26] Gustav Hilger, a German diplomat who spent many years in the USSR, held roughly the same opinion.[27] The most extreme statement of this position has come from the pen of a Soviet defector. In his memoirs Grigorii Besedovskii claimed to recall, verbatim, a conversation held eight years previously with a colleague in the Narkomindel of the Ukrainian SSR:

> 'The Moscow Commissariat [NKID],' he told me, 'is just a diplomatic chancellery attached to the Central Committee of the party. All diplomatic notes are drawn up by the Committee, then sent to the Commissariat for their style to be revised, and afterwards sent on to their destinations. As for the Council of Commissars, it is quite extraneous to all that concerns our Commissariat; it merely receives at very long intervals brief informatory statements.'[28]

The essential grain of truth contained in these appraisals is that the Narkomindel was neither constitutionally nor de facto the hub of the decision-making process concerning diplomatic affairs. Few, if any, modern foreign offices fulfill that description. Students of diplomacy in the twentieth century have often remarked on the decline in relative importance of the diplomatic chancelleries and professional foreign services.[29] Modern means of communication, the trend to summit conferences, and the so-called 'new diplomacy' seem to have brought to a close that age in which the Talleyrands, Metternichs, and Palmerstons played such a crucial role. Thus, career diplomats frequently either have been bypassed by their national political leadership or, in some cases, have become little more than glorified messenger boys — executing policies but not making them.

Existing treatments of the Soviet foreign office conform to this general outline in denying any significant part to the People's Commissariat of Foreign Affairs in the process of charting Russia's course.[30] These views err in giving the impression that the Commissariat was merely a technical service for carrying out the instructions of a remote party leadership. In the period following Lenin's death most of the ranking Bosheviks were essentially preoccupied with the succession struggle. In this atmosphere the NKID enjoyed a relatively great degree of freedom, so long as it stayed within the general guidelines of Soviet policy as established by the Politburo. It may well be that Chicherin possessed greater independence than later Russian foreign ministers precisely because he was *not* an important politician, at least during this period of domestic political crisis. Lenin certainly valued Chicherin's abilities highly, describing his Foreign Commissar as 'an excellent worker. Full of initiative.'[31]

Chicherin also acted as the spokesman for Soviet foreign policy not only abroad, but in domestic political circles as well. He frequently authored articles in *Pravda* and *Izvestiia* which announced official policy or analyzed problems still under discussion.[32]

Chicherin's influence in the councils of state diminished, however, after Lenin's death, which deprived the Commissar of his most powerful supporter, and after the conclusion of the Locarno accords which, by effecting a *rapprochement* between Germany and the Western powers, seriously undermined Chicherin's policy of alliance with Berlin.[33] But even late in his tenure as NKID chief, Chicherin remained a redoubtable fighter for his Commissariat. For instance, when the Shakhty trial (which involved the prosecution of some German engineers on false charges of economic sabotage) threatened to damage relations between Moscow and Berlin, Chicherin, enlisting Rykov's assistance, managed to convince state prosecutor Krylenko that the trial should be managed so as not to discredit German industry in Russia as a whole.[34] Similarly, when ten thousand peasants of German Mennonite background sought immigration to Canada during the collectivization crisis in the fall of 1929, the Narkomindel insisted on granting them exit permits — again, to avoid difficulties with Berlin — in the face of stern resistance from the OGPU and the Commissariat of Internal Affairs.[35] In recent years Soviet scholars have also recognized Chicherin's influence in the decision-making process: 'Next to Lenin himself, there was no single individual who left such a deep imprint as he on foreign policy formulation during the early period of Soviet statehood.'[36]

The fact that the Politburo tended to be divided in its analysis of the world scene (e.g. on policy toward Poland in 1920, on the prospects of a German revolution in 1921 and 1923, on the Ghilan affair in Persia, or on policy toward the Chinese revolution) also strengthened the position of the Commissariat. Although at times the Narkomindel's freedom of maneuver was sharply restricted, on other occasions Soviet diplomats had the widest possible latitude. Thus, in 1920 Litvinov was authorized '. . .to carry on conversations in the name of the Government of the Russian Republic', and 'to conclude all kinds of agreements and treaties with the inclusion of all conditions and guarantees which he considers necessary and acceptable. . .', and also '. . .to negotiate and sign an agreement on the time, place, and preliminary conditions for the entry of Russia to peace negotiations with the governments of England, America,

Belgium, Italy, France, and Japan. . .'.[37]

The participation of the Soviet delegation at the Genoa conference in 1922 provides an excellent case study of the role of the Narkomindel in the formulation and execution of Bolshevik foreign policy. The Kremlin leadership regarded the conference as the potential source of both great opportunity and considerable danger for the USSR. Coming as it did on the heels of several important trade agreements with capitalist powers, which entailed at least de facto recognition of the Soviet regime, Moscow hoped that the diplomatic conclave at Genoa might lead to the granting of full de jure recognition of the Soviet state and to some much-needed economic and technological assistance from the advanced Western countries. Conversely, however, the Soviet leaders were well aware that capitalist circles in Europe sought by diplomatic means to recover the investments and the lucrative economic concessions in Russia which they had lost after the Bolshevik revolution.[38] Understandably, given the indisputable importance of the conference, preparations for Genoa occupied the top echelons of party and state leadership for several months before the diplomats actually convened. Several senior NKID officials, most notably Commissar Chicherin, participated extensively in the process of working out a set of objectives and a strategy for the Genoa meetings.

Work began on 5 January when the Politburo authorized the NKID to organize a preparatory commission with Chicherin in charge, to advise the party Central Committee on the elaboration of instructions for Soviet delegates to the conference. The preparatory commission supervised the drafting of background studies and position papers on a wide variety of subjects. It also advised the Central Committee on the press campaign to prepare the public for Genoa.[39] A few days later the Politburo appointed the Soviet delegation to the conference. The sixty-three-person group was led by Chicherin and included several other ranking Soviet diplomats (Litvinov, Krasin, Vorovskii, Ioffe) as well as representatives from each of the Union Republics and a host of experts on economic, geographical and military affairs. Chicherin subsequently sent Lenin detailed recommendations for the policies and strategies to be followed at Genoa which, after adding his own commentary, Lenin forwarded to the Politburo. The Central Committee and Politburo then deliberated at length over the position papers submitted by the Narkomindel and also considered additional suggestions and information from other state organs (the Commissariat of Foreign Trade, *Gosplan*, etc.). Finally, the Politburo approved a set of binding instructions, which had been drafted by Lenin, for its Genoa delegates.[40] The Politburo's detailed instructions notwithstanding, Chicherin enjoyed some freedom of tactical maneuver at the conference, at least in so far as he could subsequently defend the necessity of his actions.[41] In the event of unforeseen developments, however, the Commissar was required to submit the problem to a meeting of his delegation and transmit all opinions and suggestions to Moscow for final decision. On the whole it seems clear that Chicherin and his Commissariat exercised a significant, though far from exclusive, influence over the formulation of Soviet foreign policy in regard to the Genoa conference. The Narkomindel representatives also enjoyed a modicum of diplomatic flexibility in executing their directives. This flexibility enabled the Soviet diplomats to react sensitively to their political environment and, ultimately, to achieve a dramatic victory — the Rapallo Treaty.

Recent work in international relations theory has also begun to challenge the traditional picture of the Narkomindel which is based on the supposed separation of policy execution (i.e. diplomacy) and policy formulation. The systems analysts seek to demonstrate the integral connection and reciprocal nature of policy and implementation.[42] Not only are Politburo deliberations meaningless unless Soviet diplomats around the globe carry out Moscow's directives fully and effectively, but, in a very real sense, the way the diplomats implement their instructions strongly affects the character of Soviet foreign policy.[43] Furthermore, the diplomats at the missions abroad are still critically important in the policy-making process, even in this age of rapid communications, because they know the local situation at first hand and it is upon the information contained in their reports that policy must be based. Lenin is known to have valued and relied on the reports of his diplomats.[44] To cite another example, the question of tsarist debts became a major issue in the 1920 negotiations for an Anglo-Soviet accord, but while commercial interests in Britain demanded full restitution of tsarist obligations, some Labour Party and trade union spokesmen argued strongly against placing such demands on the Soviet Republic. When Chicherin heard of these developments, he eagerly pressed the head of the Soviet negotiating team, Leonid Krasin, for further information: 'Before we can come to a final decision with reference to British creditors,' the Commissar wrote, 'we must receive from you detailed data of the agitation which is being carried on in connection with this subject, details of the struggle, how wide it is and to what extent the masses are interested. . . . We are awaiting a detailed report from you. Write "very urgent" at the top of your ciphered message on this subject. This information is necessary in order to enable us to investigate the question of creditors here.'[45]

The status of several Narkomindel staff members as recognized 'experts' on particular geographic areas also added to the influence of the NKID in foreign policy-making. Thus, Khristian Rakovskii was regarded as the Eastern European expert both within the Commissariat and generally in Bolshevik circles. His opinions concerning this area often had a great affect on Soviet policy.[46] Similarly, Marchlewski and Radek were usually consulted on questions of Russo-Polish relations,[47] while the opinions of Rotshtein and Litvinov were widely respected on British affairs.[48]

The People's Commissariat of Foreign Affairs, in summary, was not the primary articulator of Soviet foreign policy. Its key officials were, however, part of a small foreign policy elite, drawn from various government bodies and party organs, which did determine the course of Soviet diplomacy. Its crucial role in interpreting the behavior of the outside world gave it added leverage. Finally, in the political environment of the succession struggle, the Narkomindel was able to achieve fairly great freedom of maneuver in carrying out the established policies.

THE NARKOMINDEL AND PARTY POLITICS

The relationship between the Commissariat of Foreign Affairs and the Communist Party of the Soviet Union was considerably more complex than merely the connections between the two in the policy-making process described above. The Narkomindel, as an institution, never had the same significance in Kremlin politics as the Politburo, the party Secretariat, the *Cheka* or even the *Gosplan*. Chicherin, its Commissar, did not even become a Central Committee member until 1925. The importance of the NKID, for matters of domestic politics, lay in the nature of its personnel.

The period from the October revolution to 1930 was a politically tumultuous epoch in the history of the Communist Party. Despite the facade of unity which party propaganda sought to erect, this era was characterized by fundamental disagreement on principle and prolonged factional squabbling. The question of whether or not to seize power in 1917 was only the first in a series of crucial debates which rocked the party. After their October victory, the Bolsheviks came close to schism over the terms of the Brest-Litovsk Treaty. United of necessity during the civil war, the party was attacked from within by the Workers' Opposition and the Democratic Centralists as soon as the Whites were defeated. The 1920s witnessed the greatest party crisis of all, the almost decade-long struggle for power among Lenin's lieutenants after his death. The Narkomindel was not always able to remain above this storm of controversy.

The precise role played by the Commissariat of Foreign Affairs in these intra-party struggles is difficult to determine. A number of scholars have maintained that the NKID served extensively as a 'dumping ground' or place of exile for the losers in this domestic political contest. This view implies that the Narkomindel was a particular haven for anti-Stalinist Old Bolsheviks, Trotskiites, former Mensheviks, Jews — in short, all those groups commonly identified with the opposition. By implication this interpretation also tends to denigrate the role of the NKID and of diplomacy in Soviet foreign policy.[49]

It cannot be denied that the employees of the Commissariat were, indeed, a rather cosmopolitan group, or that a number of prominent 'oppositionists' were to be found among their ranks. Commissar Chicherin, though he never personally engaged in the party's political wars, was far from universally popular with the communist elite. He had incurred Stalin's displeasure even before the revolution by his participation on an international socialist committee set up to investigate Bolshevik 'expropriations'.[50] Chicherin later fueled the General Secretary's hatred by criticizing his theses on the nationality question in Russia. Stalin became a frequent critic of the Narkomindel and the two men continued to harbor an ill-concealed detestation for each other.[51] Besides the Commissar, there were a few other members of the NKID whose relations with Stalin were less than cordial. The future dictator nurtured an intense dislike of Valerian Osinskii and of Krasin as well.[52] Stalin had also clashed with Sokol'nikov who, at the fourteenth party congress, had called for Stalin's dismissal from his post as General Secretary and had characterized his ideas on economics and foreign trade as 'entirely mistaken'.[53]

The first serious party crisis after the Bolsheviks had taken power, the debate over the Brest-Litovsk Treaty, found a number of present or future NKID members arrayed against Lenin. Krestinskii, Ioffe, Radek, Osinskii and Kollontai all attacked the proposed treaty as a betrayal of the revolution. Only a vigorous campaign by Lenin carried the issue for peace and narrowly averted a split in the party. The Russian Communist Party experienced another violent internal convulsion as the civil war drew to a close. The Group of Democratic Centralism emerged from the party's left wing in protest against the degeneration of democratic procedures within the Bolshevik camp, while trade union communists formed the Workers' Opposition to combat the current official labor policies. Two future Soviet diplomats were prominent among the leaders of these movements, Osinskii and Aleksandra Kollontai.

From the onset of Lenin's incapacitating strokes in 1922, the question of succession to the leader's mantle assumed central importance in Bolshevik politics. Trotskii was the obvious candidate and the Soviet political scene became polarized around the pro- and anti-Trotskii positions. The Commissariat of Foreign Affairs contained a number of what later came to be called 'Trotskiite deviationists'. Besides the first Commissar, himself, the list grew to include Ioffe, Rakovskii, Antonov-Ovseenko, Radek and Krestinskii. Later, after Trotskii had been defeated, Stalin turned on his fellow 'triumvirs' to remove yet another obstacle from his path to personal power. It was at this time that Kamenev and a few of his associates entered the foreign service.

Stalin, as General Secretary, was able on a number of occasions to use his organizational power physically to remove certain of his opponents from the conflict by means of diplomatic assignments to foreign countries. A few obvious examples stand out. Aleksandra Kollontai, who had a long record of ultra-left oppositional activity, received her first diplomatic post, at the Soviet embassy in Norway, in 1922. This served to remove the last prestigious defender of the Workers' Opposition from the political arena.[54] Rakovskii, who as Chairman of the Ukrainian Sovnarkom led the fight against Stalin's nationality policy, was quickly replaced by V.Ia. Chubar and dispatched to the embassy in London.[55] The Commissar for the Army, Antonov-Ovseenko, was relieved of his post by the triumvirs in 1923 on the grounds of 'incitement to insurrection' when he had asked his troops to declare themselves in favor of Trotskii.[56] The following year he was made *Polpred* for Czechoslovakia. The proposed ambassadorial assignment of Lev Kamenev to France in 1918 was probably not an instance of 'dumping', but rather an attempt to fill a critical position with a talented, high level Bolshevik.[57] Likewise, the appointment of Kamenev as the new head of the Soviet delegation at the Anglo-Russian trade negotiations in June of 1920 was confirmed with the support of Chicherin at Kamenev's own suggestion — over Lenin's objections.[58] However, after his participation in the mid-1920s in the ruling triumvirate, together with Zinoviev and Stalin, his subsequent appointment as the Soviet minister to Italy in 1927 was clearly a case of political exile. Krestinskii received similar treatment. He lost his powerful post as a Secretary of the Central Committee and was then dispatched to Berlin as Soviet representative because of his involvement with the Left Communists.

A number of 'oppositionists' saw service, at one time or another, in the Narkomindel and it seems that several prominent Soviet political figures received diplomatic posts abroad as a means of eliminating them from domestic struggles. That much is certain. That is not to suggest, however, that the Narkomindel was a hotbed of oppositional activity and intrigue, or that the principal domestic function of the Commissariat was to serve as a 'dumping ground' for political casualties.

Trotskii's connection with the Commissariat of Foreign Affairs was very brief and he left no lasting imprint upon the organization. Most notably, he failed to staff the Narkomindel with his supporters or to develop any significant following within the Commissariat. Chicherin was certainly no oppositionist even though he disliked Stalin. [59] Gustav Hilger claimed that the Commissar, in conversation with German Ambassador Count Brockdorff-Rantzau, declared that the supremacy of Trotskii and his faction would damage the Rapallo relationship and thus ruin Chicherin's foreign policy.[60] The Soviet foreign office, by its very nature as an organ of formal diplomacy, was predisposed to support Stalin's policy of Socialism in One Country which implied the (at least temporary) stabilization of relations with the Western powers and the diminution of Russian aid for foreign revolutionary activities, which had embarrassed and handicapped Soviet diplomacy. The implementation of the 'permanent revolution' doctrine, popularly attributed to Trotskii, or the continuation of Zinoviev's reckless adventurism in the Comintern, could not fail to undermine the efforts of the Foreign Commissariat to secure diplomatic recognition and economic assistance for the Soviet state.[61]

The composition, nature and tasks of the Foreign Commissariat precluded it from ever becoming a bastion of the Left-Communists during Lenin's lifetime or the subsequent Left-Opposition to Stalin. In the 1920s the leftist forces repeatedly indicted the majority leadership of the party with charges of bureaucractic degeneration and decay (*pererozhdenie*). In concrete terms these charges meant the estrangement of the various commissariats and party bureaus from the masses, the functionaries' supposed loss of 'true party spirit', and the diminution of revolutionary zeal among Soviet *chinovniki*. Although oppositionist diatribes seldom mentioned the Narkomindel, focusing instead on the domestic political and economic apparatus, the NKID evidenced all those characteristics so odious to the party's left wing. The upper levels of the Commissariat were dominated by men of bourgeois or even noble background, while its proletarian contingent was negligible. Worse yet, the revolutionary posturing so dear to much of the left was anathema to Chicherin and his colleagues. Both the nature and the mission of the Narkomindel were antithetical to all that the Left-Oppositionists represented.

Although diplomatic work met the approval of the so-called Right-Opposition, there is no evidence that the NKID, as an organization, was a tool of right-wing elements in Soviet politics. Chicherin, himself, sympathized with the rightist program,[62] but his Commissariat took no part in the struggle beyond defending its vested interest in a cautious foreign policy carried out by diplomatic means against the encroachments of the Comintern. Rather, Right-Oppositionist strength centered in the Supreme Economic Council, *Gosplan,* State Bank, and the Commissariats of Agriculture, Finance, Labor and Trade.[63]

The Narkomindel never became an active center of oppositional strength similar to the Leningrad party organization under Zinoviev or the *Gosplan* apparatus in the late 1920s. Opinion within the NKID on pressing political questions was usually divided among the various 'opposition' and the 'orthodox' positions. Thus, in 1918 on the question of one party dictatorship, the future diplomats Kamenev, Lunacharskii and Iurenev opposed the exclusion of other parties from the Soviets, while Trotskii, Ioffe and Sokol'nikov supported Lenin's program. Maksim Litvinov is an example of the orthodox Leninist-Stalinist influence in the Narkomindel.[64] It is also significant that a number of diplomats (e.g. Krestinskii, Antonov-Ovseenko and Kollontai) completely renounced 'factional' activity before the end of the decade.[65] The supposed oppositional nature of the Commissariat of Foreign Affairs has been too greatly stressed.

The 'dumping' thesis has been similarly overused. For example, Leonid Krasin spoke out against growing party centralism at the twelfth party congress in 1923, thus indirectly attacking Stalin. Professor Robert Daniels argues that 'in 1924, no doubt as an antidote to his critical frame of mind, [Krasin] was eased out and made Ambassador to France'.[66] This new position, however, need not necessarily imply a case of political exile since Krasin formerly had been the Commissar of Foreign Trade and also had completed a number of important diplomatic assignments previously. As a high ranking and experienced diplomat he was a logical choice for the embassy in Paris. This, moreover, was a difficult mission. France, the bulwark of European anti-communism and the sponsor of the *cordon sanitaire,* had finally recognized the Bolshevik regime. Moscow needed a diplomat with Krasin's skill and experience to assuage anti-Bolshevik sentiment in Paris and to negotiate the delicate problem of tsarist notes and bonds in the hands of French investors.[67]

The People's Commissariat of Foreign Affairs was not the only or even a principal place of exile for defeated political figures. When Stalin wanted to 'bury' a well-known oppositionist, the victim would be sent not to a prominent diplomatic post in one of the Western capitals, but to some bureaucratic backwater like the Scientific and Technical Department of the Supreme Economic Council. This actually happened to both Kamenev and Bukharin. To cite another example, when Nikolai Uglanov, Secretary of the Moscow party organization and, until then, a faithful Stalinist, began to experience doubts about the General Secretary's collectivization policy, Stalin saw to it that he was quickly replaced by Molotov and relegated to an honorific but relatively powerless post with the Commissariat of Labor. If the object of the leadership was merely to remove oppositionists from the levers of power in Moscow, then Siberia or Central Asia could serve as well or better than Paris or London. In 1918 the Ukrainian party and state apparatus actually became a stronghold of the Left Communists owing to the mass exile of leftist comrades from Moscow.

Diplomacy was too important a defensive weapon, given the encirclement of the weak socialist state by antagonistic capitalist powers, for Lenin or Stalin to undermine the efficiency of the Narkomindel by dumping quantities of oppositionists into its ranks.[68] Even those few vanquished rivals whose entry into the Commissariat clearly did involve political demotion and isolation were carefully selected for their suitability for diplomatic work. Lev Kamenev was known throughout the party for his tact, conciliatory nature and skill in negotiation, precisely the qualities required of a diplomat. Rakovskii, who replaced Krasin in Paris in 1925, was a similarly excellent choice for the post because of his mastery of foreign languages, extensive knowledge of Western politics, and his already established good working relationship with numerous French officials.[69]

The 'dumping' thesis can be applied legitimately to only a small minority of diplomatic appointments. A study of the long-term career patterns of Narkomindel appointees to responsible positions in the period from 1917 to 1930 shows that assignment to diplomatic work in many cases meant promotion or reward, rather than disgrace, and that the mere fact of appointment to the Commissariat had no political significance in itself[70] (see Tables 1-3). Persons receiving an assignment to the Narkomindel showed a generally upward trend in terms of career mobility in 36 percent of the cases studied, a downward trend in 22 percent of the cases, and no observable trend in 42 percent of the cases. Only 11 percent of all high and middle level diplomatic assignments gave evidence of involving obvious demotion or political isolation. The figures change only slightly when the data on the Narkomindel's top echelon (Commissars, Deputy Commissars, Collegium members, ambassadors, and heads of major departments) are studied separately. In this senior group 42 percent show an upward career pattern, 26 percent a downward trend, and 32 percent demonstrate no obvious trend. Only 12 percent of this group exhibit signs of having been diplomatic exiles.

These findings indicate that the Commissariat of Foreign Affairs cannot be characterized as a political purgatory for the losers in party struggles.[71] Diplomatic posts went to people with rising career patterns more often than to those with declining prospects. More important, assignment to the Narkomindel, as an independent factor, was unrelated to an individual's overall career pattern in an absolute ma-

Table 1
Career Mobility within the Narkomindel, 1917-1930
(i.e. diplomatic assignments only)[72]

Diplomatic Careers Showing:	All Responsible Officials		Top Echelon	
	N	%	N	%
An upward trend	140	32	60	43
A downward trend	73	17	24	17
No significant trend	225	51	56	40
Totals	438	100	140	100

Table 2
General Career Mobility of Diplomats, 1917-1930 (relating to
assignments previous and subsequent to an individual's first
diplomatic appointment — i.e. both diplomatic and non-diplomatic assignments)

Careers Showing:	All Responsible Officials		Top Echelon	
	N	%	N	%
An upward trend	155	36	59	42
A downward trend	95	22	36	26
No observable trend	178	42	44	32
Totals	428	100	139	100

jority of cases. The data shown in Table 2 suggest that the Commissariat in this period was neither a particularly advantageous base from which to launch a successful career in government service, nor a dumping ground for the politically beaten. The relative percentages expressed in Table 1 indicate that officials in the diplomatic corps were more likely to rise than to decline, if they showed any mobility at all. The Narkomindel was never a short cut to the top for the ambitious; diplomatic posts were never patronage plums for Stalin's Secretariat — largely because the educational and intellectual re-

Table 3
The 'Dumping' Thesis

	All Responsible Officials		Top Echelon	
	N	%	N	%
Diplomatic assignments involving obvious demotion or political isolation	48	11	17	12
Diplomatic assignments not involving obvious demotion or political isolation	383	89	125	88
Totals	431	100	142	100

quirements of diplomacy precluded filling the embassies in Paris or London with provincial party hacks. Many men, of course, made successful careers in the NKID. Aleksandr Troianovskii, for example, rose from his post as a humble Kremlin archivist to become ambassador to the United States. For some defeated oppositionists, such as Sokol'nikov or Piatakov, diplomatic assignments in the late 1920s marked their at least partial rehabilitation. The large number of Narkomindel officers whose careers seem to have been stalled (as represented by the 'No significant trend' column in Table1) resulted in part from the number of old revolutionaries who were recruited into the NKID in its early days, but who proved unsuited to diplomacy (e.g. I.A. Zalkind), and from the preference of the party leadership for filling important vacancies in the Commissariat from outside its ranks. The conclusion which emerges is that the Commissariat of Foreign Affairs had no specific political role during these years. It was, like most other governmental and party agencies, caught up in the general confusion of the early revolutionary period and ensuing succession struggle.

NOTES

1. Grzybowski, *Soviet Public International Law,* pp. 416-18.
2. *Sobranie uzakonenii,* 1923, vol. II, no. 107.
3. *Sobranie zakonov i rasporiazhenii,* 1925, no. 68.
4. Aspaturian, *Process and Power,* pp. 592-98. Also see N.V. Mironov, *Pravovoe regulirovanie vneshnikh snoshenii SSSR, 1917-1970gg.* (Moscow, 1971) for a recent Soviet treatment of this subject.
5. Lenin, *PSS,* vol. XLI, pp. 30-31. Also see Solov'ev, *Dvadtsat' piat' let,* p. 123; and Julian Towster, *Political Power in the U.S.S.R., 1917-1947* (New York, 1948), p. 162.
6. Lenin, *PSS,* vol. XLV, pp. 398-99.
7. *Der Zweite Kongress der Kommunistischen Internationale, Protokoll der Verhandlungen* (Hamburg, 1921), p. 94. Also see Liberman, *Building Lenin's Russia,* p.13.
8. Wheeler-Bennett, *Brest-Litovsk,* pp. 243-308. The treaty was also the subject of prolonged discussion at the seventh party congress in March of 1918. In general, foreign policy questions were seriously debated at party conferences and congresses during the first seven or eight years after the October revolution. With Stalin's rise to power, however, the congresses began to lose whatever informal powers of ratification of foreign policies they may previously have possessed.
9. For the Soviet view of the role of the party in foreign policy formulation see A.I. Stepanov, 'Leninskie printsipy partiinogo rukovodstva vneshnei politikoi i tvorcheskoe razvitie ikh KPSS na sovremennom etape', *Voprosy istorii KPSS,* 1976, no. 12, pp. 57-69; A.O. Chubar'ian, *V.I. Lenin i formirovanie sovetskoi vneshnei politiki* (Moscow, 1972); and V. Petrov, V. Belov and A. Karenin, *Leninskaia vneshniaia politika SSSR: razvitie i perspektivy* (Moscow, 1974), ch. I.
10. *Leninskii sbornik* (Moscow, 1975), vol. XXXVIII, pp. 367-68.
11. For example, *DVP,* vol. IX, p. 7.
12. Robert C. Tucker, 'Ruling Personalities in Russian Foreign Policy', in: Tucker, *The Soviet Political Mind* (New York, 1963), p. 157; Abdurakhman Avtorkhanov, *Stalin and the Soviet Communist Party: A Study in the Technology of Power* (New York, 1959), pp. 103-5; Boris I. Nicolaevsky, *Power and the Soviet Elite* (Ann Arbor, 1975 [1965]), pp. 93-97; Robert C. Tucker, *Stalin As Revolutionary, 1879-1929: A Study in History and Personality* (New York, 1973), p. 294; and Leonard Schapiro, *The Communist Party of the Soviet Union* (New York, 1971), p. 395. Actually, these intelligence-gathering systems were not just parallel, but interlocking. For speculation on Alexandra Kollontai's use of this 'personal secretariat' to make reports directly to Stalin, thus circumventing the Narkomindel apparatus, see Kaare Hague, 'Alexandra Mikhailovna Kollontai: The Scandinavian Period, 1922-1945', Ph.D. thesis, University of Minnesota, 1971, pp. 262-63.
13. *Leninskii sbornik,* vol. XXXVI, p. 205. Also see M.I. Trush, *Vneshnepoliticheskaia deiatel'nost' V.I. Lenina, 1917-1920: den' za dnem* (Moscow, 1963), p. 249.

14. For example, V.G. Trukhanovskii, et al., *Diplomaticheskaia deiatel'nost' V.I. Lenina* (Moscow, 1970), pp. 12ff; V.I. Popov, 'Lenin-osnovopolozhnik sovetskoi diplomatii', in: E.M. Zhukov, et al., eds., *Voprosy istorii vneshnei politiki SSSR i mezhdunarodnykh otnoshenii: sbornik statei pamiati akademika Vladimira Mikhailovicha Khvostova* (Moscow, 1976), pp. 62-85; and Chubar'ian, *V.I. Lenin i formirovanie sovetskoi vneshnei politiki,* pp. 283ff.

15. Fischer, *Soviets in World Affairs,* vol. I, p. 461. Warren Lerner, 'Poland in 1920: A Case Study in Foreign Policy Decision Making Under Lenin', *South Atlantic Quarterly,* 1973, LXXII, 3, pp. 407-8 also credits Lenin with, '. . .virtually dictatorial powers. . .'.

16. Georgii V. Chicherin, 'Lenin i vneshniaia politika', in: F.A. Rotshtein, ed., *Mirovaia politika v 1924g.: sbornik statei* (Moscow, 1925), p. 3.

17. *Izvestiia,* 30 January 1924.

18. Chicherin, *Stat'i i rechi,* p. 283.

19. For example, Lenin, even with the support of Trotskii and Krasin, suffered an at least temporary defeat in the Central Committee over the question of whether to maintain or loosen the monopoly of foreign commerce exercised by the Commissariat of Foreign Trade. See Richard B. Day, *Leon Trotsky and the Politics of Economic Isolation* (London, 1973), pp. 75-76.

20. Jon D. Glassman, 'Soviet Foreign Policy Decision Making', in: *Columbia Essays in International Affairs,* vol. III, Andrew W. Cordier, ed., *The Dean's Papers, 1967* (New York, 1968), p. 380. Also see William Perry Morse, Jr., 'Leonid Borisovich Krasin: Soviet Diplomat, 1918-1926', Ph.D. thesis, University of Wisconsin, 1971, for a sensitive description and analysis of the impact of a diplomat on policy formulation. Cf. Isaac Deutscher, *The Prophet Unarmed: Trotsky, 1921-1929* (New York, 1959), p. 56.

21. It is interesting to note that Stalin, who did not fit this description, participated infrequently in foreign policy debates at this time. Stalin had not spent much time abroad as had the other leading Bolsheviks and he did not have the foreign language skills necessary to follow the world press. Only in relations with some of the border states (especially Turkey), where the nationality question played a significant role in diplomacy, was Stalin considered something of an 'expert'. See Lenin, *Polnoe sobranie sochinenii,* vol. LIV, p. 58; Kapur, *Soviet Russia and Asia,* p. 95. Cf. Chubar'ian, *V.I. Lenin i formirovanie sovetskoi vneshnei politiki,* pp. 270 and 273; and Oleh S. Pidhainy, 'Stalin's Negotiations on Behalf of the Soviet Government with the Ukraine, November 30, 1917, and Conversation with Bakinskiy: The Suppressed Text', *New Review of East-European History,* 1963, III, 6, pp. 4-12.

22. For example, in September 1919 Russia and Estonia began peace negotiations. Then the White General Iudenich attacked Petrograd from Estonian territory. He was soon defeated and driven back by the Red Army. Trotskii wished to pursue him into his Estonian sanctuary and destroy his army. Chicherin, however, feared that such a violation of Estonian sovereignty would ruin the negotiations and perhaps even renew active hostilities with Estonia. He suspected that this possibility might have been Iudenich's original goal in invading Russia. Lenin supported the Foreign Commissar against the Red Army leadership. The pursuit was halted and subsequently the desired treaty was signed. Trotsky Archives, Harvard University, 22 October 1919, documents T-382, T-383 and T-384.

23. Liberman, *Building Lenin's Russia,* p. 13. However, Rykov once told Liber-

man that Lenin sometimes failed to support Rykov's initiatives at conferences, in spite of earlier pledges of assistance, if Lenin felt 'that the majority of the conferees [were] against [Rykov's] proposals. . .', ibid., pp. 68-69. It seems that Lenin's vaunted ability to decide all issues of policy may have been based, in part, on a keen sense of the distribution of opinion among party and government leaders even before their votes were formally polled. Also see Tucker, *Stalin As Revolutionary,* pp. 32-62 on Lenin's style of leadership.

24. Fischer, *The Soviets in World Affairs,* vol. I, pp. 463-64.

25. Barmine, *One Who Survived,* p. 213. Cf. Slusser, 'The Role of the Foreign Ministry', p. 227. Also see Glassman, 'Soviet Foreign Policy Decision Making', p. 380. Some of Stalin's excursions into diplomatic matters in the 1920s ended in defeats for him. Besedovskii claims that Stalin tried to circumvent the NKID and initiate negotiations for a *rapprochement* with Rumania through him. This initiative had to be abandoned under heavy pressure from the Narkomindel. Bessedovsky, *Revelations,* pp. 212-16.

26. Dean Acheson, 'Of Men I Have Known: Part Two, The Russians', *Saturday Evening Post,* 25 March 1961, CCXXXIV, 12, p. 31.

27. Hilger and Meyer, *The Incompatible Allies,* p. 115.

28. Bessedovsky, *Revelations,* p. 10.

29. Gordon Craig, *War, Politics, and Diplomacy* (New York and Washington, 1966), pp. 207-19. Also see Lord Vansittart, *The Mist Procession* (London, 1958), p. 269; Comte de Saint-Aulaire, *Je suis diplomate* (Paris, 1954), p. 106; and Ernst von Weizsäcker, *Erinnerungen* (Munich, 1950), p. 129. Cf. Harold Nicolson, *Diplomacy* (New York, 1964), p. 17.

30. For example, Von Laue, 'Soviet Diplomacy: G.V. Chicherin', pp. 234-5, 246-48, and 280; and Jan F. Triska and David D. Finley, *Soviet Foreign Policy* (New York, 1968), p. 37.

31. S. Aralov, 'On Lenin's Instructions', *International Affairs,* 1960, no. 4, p. 12.

32. Some of these articles were signed by Chicherin while others appeared over the pen names Mikhail Sharonov or *Osvedomlennyi* (the informed one). E.g. *Izvestiia,* 30 December 1924; 20 March, 30 June, 4, 28, 29 July, 1, 4, 11, 12, 18, 25, 30 August, 10 and 12 September 1925; and *Pravda,* 4 September 1924.

33. On the diminution of Chicherin's influence see Debo, 'George Chicherin', p. 353; Chossudovsky, *Chicherin,* p. 17; Andrei Gromyko, 'Diplomat leninskoi shkoly', *Izvestiia,* 5 December 1962; Gorokhov, Zamiatin and Zemskov, *G.V. Chicherin* (2nd edn.), pp. 208-10; Zarnitskii and Sergeev, *Chicherin,* pp. 238-39; memorandum by Louis Fischer of a conversation with Chicherin on 24 August 1929 in The Louis Fischer Papers, box 1, file 'Chicherin, George 1929', Princeton University Library.

34. Memorandum of conversation with Chicherin by Louis Fischer, 28 August 1929, in ibid. Despite this agreement, the NKID was still not entirely satisfied with Krylenko's handling of the trial.

35. See Harvey L. Dyck, *Weimar Germany and Soviet Russia, 1926-1933: A Study in Diplomatic Instability* (New York, 1966), pp. 162-80. Unfortunately, many of the Mennonites met a tragic fate when the Canadian government refused to accept them.

36. E.M. Chossudovsky, 'Lenin and Chicherin: The Beginnings of Soviet Foreign Policy and Diplomacy', *Millenium,* 1974, III, 1, p. 1. In another context the same author argued: 'Yet a study of the documentation pertaining to the Lenin-Chicherin

relationship shows that Georgy Vassilievich was not merely the executor and manager, but frequently also the originator of new approaches and concepts, many of which were subsequently endorsed by Lenin. And there were also situations where for want of centralized instructions Chicherin had to frame his own "directive" and get them approved *ex post*.' Chossudovsky, *Chicherin,* p. 11. In a 'forward' to another biography of Chicherin, Deputy Foreign Minister V.S. Semenov concluded that, '. . .in carrying out his tasks Chicherin was guided by the directives of the Party. But, at the same time, his personal contribution to the struggle against imperialism and intervention, for the break in the diplomatic blockade of the first state of workers and peasants is considerable.' Gorokhov, Zamiatin and Zemskov, *G.V. Chicherin* (1st edn.), p. 3.

37. *Leninskii sbornik,* vol. XXXIV, pp. 283-84. Cf. Girardet, 'Litvinov et ses énigmes', in: Duroselle, ed., *Les Relations Germano-Soviétiques,* pp. 124-31.

38. On Soviet policy at Genoa see Fischer, *The Soviets in World Affairs,* vol. I, pp. 318-54; Chubar'ian, *V.I. Lenin i formirovanie sovetskoi vneshnei politiki,* pp. 217-82; G.A. Trukan, ed., 'Doklad Ia. E. Rudzutaka o genuezskoi konferentsii', *Istoricheskii arkhiv,* 1962, no. 2, pp. 80-95; Liubimov and Erlikh, *Genuezskaia konferentsiia;* Akhtamzian, *Rapall'skaia politika,* pp. 49-80; and Freund, *Unholy Alliance,* pp. 84-140.

39. Evgeny Chossudovsky, 'Genoa Revisted: Russia and Coexistence', *Foreign Affairs,* 1972, L, 3, p. 562.

40. Lenin, *PSS,* vol. XLIV, pp. 371, 374-6, 388, and 581-82, and vol. XLV, pp. 34-35 and 171ff.; *Leninskii sbornik,* vol. XXXVI, pp. 409ff.; and Chicherin, *Stat'i i rechi,* pp. 284 ff. Also see L.A. Bezumenskii, 'Vladimir Il'ich Lenin-rukovoditel' sovetskoi delegatsii na genuezskoi konferentsii', in: Alfred Anderle, ed., *Rapallskii dogovor i problema mirnogo sosushchestvovaniia* (Moscow, 1963), pp. 58-84.

41. For example, although the Soviet delegation was instructed not even to consider the possibility of recognizing Russia's pre-revolutionary foreign debts, Chicherin hinted at just that possibility in a letter to Lloyd George in a gambit to prevent the premature rupture of negotiations. Some of his colleagues complained that the Commissar had violated his instructions but, after explaining the utility of this non-binding stratagem, Chicherin won the retrospective blessing of the Politburo. The latitude which Chicherin enjoyed, however limited, certainly paid dividends in this instance. By prolonging at least the appearance of substantive Anglo-Soviet negotiations Chicherin's maneuver contributed to the conclusion of the Rapallo Treaty with Germany. See Lenin, *PSS,* vol. XLV, pp. 163-64 and 539; and *DVP,* vol. V, pp. 259-60.

42. For example, see J.W. Burton, *Systems, States, Diplomacy and Rules* (London, 1968), pp. 198-99.

43. Nicolson, *Diplomacy,* pp. 39 and 143-44. In another context Stephen F. Cohen has argued that to understand the crucial role of administration it is only necessary to recall '. . .Stalin's great advantage over his opponents [in the late 1920s]; the Politburo made policy; but Stalin, through the Secretariat, implemented and thereby could transform it.' Cohen, *Bukharin and the Bolshevik Revolution,* p. 280.

44. Witness his annoyance with Ian Berzin, the Soviet representative in Bern, when Berzin failed to forward his reports to Moscow for several weeks in the summer of 1918. Lenin, *PSS,* vol. L, p. 102.

45. Telegram from Chicherin to Krasin on 25 June 1920. Quoted in Ullman, *Anglo-Soviet Accord,* p. 119.

46.   Fischer, *Men and Politics,* pp. 133-34.

47.   Lerner, 'Poland in 1920', pp. 412-13.

48.   Glenny, 'The Anglo-Soviet Trade Agreement', p. 78; Ullman, *Anglo-Soviet Accord,* p. 123; and Deutscher, *The Prophet Armed,* p. 463.

49.   Aspaturian, *Process and Power,* pp. 612 and 627. Also see Von Laue, 'Soviet Diplomacy: G.V. Chicherin', p. 257; Douglas Busk, *The Craft of Diplomacy: How to Run a Diplomatic Service* (New York, 1967), p. 4; Deutscher, *The Prophet Unarmed,* p. 338; and Adam Ulam, *Stalin: The Man and His Era* (New York, 1973), p. 272.

50.   Von Laue, 'Soviet Diplomacy: G.V. Chicherin', p. 247. Stalin and a number of other Bolsheviks had been implicated in a series of armed robberies, or 'expropriations', carried out to finance the party's activities. Also see Isaac Deutscher, *Stalin: A Political Biography* (New York, 1960), pp. 84ff. Paradoxically, Krasin had been even more deeply involved in the expropriations than Stalin, but he and Chicherin subsequently worked reasonably well together on diplomatic assignments. See Ulam, *Stalin,* pp. 61-69 and 90.

51.   Fischer-Chicherin Correspondence, Yale, box 1, folder no. 2, Chicherin to Fischer, 14 February 1930; and Von Laue, 'Soviet Diplomacy: G.V. Chicherin', p. 247.

52.   Liberman, *Building Lenin's Russia,* p. 166.

53.   *Chetyrnadtsatyi s''ezd vsesoiuznoi kommunisticheskoi partii (b): stenograficheskii otchet* (Moscow, 1926), p. 331.

54.   Margaret H. Pertzoff, 'Lady in Red: A Study of the Early Career of Alexandra Mikhailovna Kollontai', Ph.D. dissertation, University of Virginia, 1968, pp. 212ff.

55.   See Conte, 'Author de la polémique Rakovskij-Staline', pp. 111-17; and Robert V. Daniels, *The Conscience of the Revolution* (New York, 1969), p. 187.

56.   Roland Gaucher, *Opposition in the U.S.S.R., 1917-1967* (New York, 1969), p. 92.

57.   Cf. Debo, 'Litvinov and Kamenev', pp. 472-73.

58.   Lenin, *PSS,* vol. LI, pp. 236 and 438.

59.   It is significant that Chicherin was never disgraced or even publicly criticized by the Stalinists. As late as the tenth anniversary of Chicherin's entry into the NKID (30 May 1928) both *Pravda* and *Izvestiia* carried laudatory articles on the Foreign Commissar.

60.   Hilger and Meyer, *Incompatible Allies,* p. 213.

61.   Throughout the 1920s Commissar Chicherin waged a long, and only partially successful, campaign to disassociate the Narkomindel and the government which it represented from the activities of the Comintern. See G.V. Chicherin, 'Za piat' let', *Mezhdunarodnaia zhizn',* 1922, no. 15; and Hilger and Meyer, *Incompatible Allies,* pp. 108-10. On the battle of slogans, socialism in one country vs. permanent revolution, see Day, *Leon Trotsky,* pp. 126-27. Even though, as Day demonstrates, 'permanent revolution' was not Trotskii's policy in the mid-1920s, Trotskii and that slogan were widely identified in the public mind.

62.   L. Fischer to W.W. Ewer, 11 June 1930, box 1, Fischer Papers, Princeton.

63.   Cohen, *Bukharin and the Bolshevik Revolution,* p. 233; and Michael Kitaeff, *Communist Party Officials: A Group of Portraits* (New York, 1954), p. 49.

64.   Litvinov was reticent in expressing his opinion of Stalin, though once he complained in private that Stalin, 'doesn't know the West. If our opponents were a bunch

of shahs or sheikhs he would outwit them.' Ilya Ehrenburg, *Post-War Years, 1945-1954* (London, 1966), p. 278.

65. Kollontai, for example, publicly attacked the anti-Stalinist opposition in an article entitled, 'Oppozitsiia i partiinaia massa', *Pravda,* 30 October 1927. Also see Beatrice Brodsky Farnsworth, 'Bolshevism, the Woman Question, and Aleksandra Kollontai,' *The American Historical Review,* 1976, LXXXI, 2, pp. 292-316.

66. Daniels, *Conscience of the Revolution,* p. 195.

67. Fischer, *The Soviets in World Affairs,* vol. II, pp. 570-79; and Morse, 'Leonid Borisovich Krasin', pp. 206-35.

68. The presence of even a few prominent oppositionists in the Narkomindel created problems for both the Soviet regime and the governments to which the diplomatic exiles were accredited. When Rakovskii was the Soviet *Polpred* in England between 1923 and 1925, the British Foreign Office feared that, as a Trotskiite, he might not adequately represent Moscow. See Foreign Office document no. 371-11017-N712/114/38, William Peters to Austin Chamberlain, 30 January 1925. In another instance, when Dutch diplomats sought to contact Krestinskii, then *Polpred* in Berlin, about opening negotiations for a Dutch-Soviet treaty, his Chargé, V.K. Aussem, intimated that the Dutch should approach Moscow through Rotshtein, rather than through Krestinskii who was in such disfavor at the Kremlin that his effectiveness was impaired. See Richard K. Debo, 'Dutch-Soviet Relations, 1917-1924: The Role of Finance and Commerce in the Foreign Policy of Soviet Russia and the Netherlands', *Canadian Slavic Studies/Revue canadienne d'Etudes slaves,* 1970, IV, 2, p. 214.

69. Anatole de Monzie, *Destins hors série* (Paris, 1927), pp. 23-39; Stuart Schram, 'Christian Rakovskij et le premier rapprochement franco-soviétique', *Cahiers du monde russe et soviétique,* 1960, I, 2, pp. 218-20; and Gabriel Gorodetsky, *The Precarious Truce: Anglo-Soviet Relations, 1924-27* (Cambridge, 1977), pp. 5-6, n. 10. Professor Alfred E. Senn has suggested, in a reversal of the usual 'dumping' interpretation of Rakovskii's diplomatic career, that 'once Stalin's victory at home over the Trotskyites was assured, Rakovsky's days in the diplomatic service had to be numbered'. Senn, 'The Rakovsky Affair: A Crisis in Franco-Soviet Relations, 1927', *Études slaves et est-européennes/Slavic and East European Studies,* 1965-66, III-IV, p. 115.

70. This conclusion is reinforced by the recent, but as yet unpublished, findings of Professor Jan Triska of Stanford University who conducted roughly similar tests covering a larger time span with a much larger sample. Triska found no significant correlation between assignment to the diplomatic corps and political exile.

71. The dumping thesis can, however, legitimately be applied to the Narkomindel in later periods, especially in the years immediately following the death of Stalin. See Aspaturian, *Process and Power,* pp. 615-22 and 628-31.

72. The figures in Tables 1-3 are based on an examination of all appointments to diplomatic or central administrative work at a 'responsible' level (i.e. Commissar through third secretary or attaché) in the NKID, where sufficient biographical data are available to determine the career pattern of each individual. Technical and other minor personnel are excluded. The category 'Top Echelon' refers to Commissars, their Deputies, Collegium members, *Polpredy* and heads of major departments. The determination of rising or falling career patterns within the Narkomindel (Table 1) is relatively easy to do since all positions are listed in the same hierarchy of ranks. Assessing the direction of long-term career patterns (Table 2), especially in cases where an in-

dividual worked either previously or subsequently for an agency other than the Narkomindel, is more difficult. In such cases determinations of the trajectory of career patterns were made by common sense rather than any bureaucratic table of ranks. Thus, a former Red Army general who was assigned as a second secretary in Bulgaria would be considered demoted, while an ambassador who later became Commissar of Agriculture would obviously have been promoted. Special weight was given to positions in the party apparatus. Thus, a person who was a Secretary of the Central Committee and who was later made ambassador to Berlin is regarded as having suffered a substantial demotion, despite the importance and prestige of his diplomatic mission.

6

IDEOLOGY AND DIPLOMACY

Evaluating the role of ideology in Soviet diplomacy is a difficult task. The problem involves not only attempting to assess how beliefs affected actions, but also trying to discover exactly what elements constituted the world view or ideology of Soviet diplomats during the period from 1917 to 1930. Soviet scholars have not seen these questions as especially challenging. For them ideology is synonymous with Marxism-Leninism, a genuinely scientific world view which, they believe, gives Soviet diplomats a substantial advantage over their benighted, non-Marxist rivals.[1] Many Western observers, while denying the alleged scientific infallibity of the dogma, nonetheless agree about the importance of Marxism-Leninism in Soviet diplomacy. They contend that the ideology serves as a medium of communication, a guide to the analysis of objective phenomena, a blueprint for action, and a mechanism for the conferring of 'legitimacy' on Soviet actions.[2]

None of these opinions provides a satisfactory answer to the question of the role of ideology in Soviet diplomacy. Part of the problem is that Marxism-Leninism is not an unambiguous and rigidly codified body of doctrine concerning international relations. The writings of Marx and Engels, and even of Lenin, do not constitute a useful manual for the day-to-day operations of socialist diplomacy. At best the 'sacred texts' provide a rough frame of reference for categorizing experiences. The tenets of Marxism-Leninism are obviously not the only elements forming the *Weltanschauung* of the Soviet diplomat, either. Many other influences (nationalism, idiosyncratic prejudices, non-Marxist conceptions of foreign affairs, etc.) contribute to the particular intellectual framework with which each Soviet diplomat approaches his tasks.

MARXISM AND SOVIET DIPLOMACY

Although the ideas of Marx and Lenin were not the only influences affecting the Soviet diplomat's perspective on international affairs, they probably were the most important ingredient in his world view.

The overwhelming majority of the Soviet diplomatic corps considered themselves to be disciples of Marx. Their perceptions of reality were fundamentally conditioned by the Marxist framework. The foreign nations with which they were to maintain relations were above all *capitalist* states. It was the bourgeoisie who made all of the political decisions and the state was seen as merely the instrumentality of this dominant class. As Khristian Rakovskii explained, 'foreign policy. . . is only a projection of domestic policy and, clearly, has a close relationship to the form of political and social organization of the nation and to its institutions generally'.[3] This identification of foreign states (and by extension, of their representatives) with the hated oppressors of the masses logically led the Narkomindel staff to view both 'capitalist' governments and diplomats with a certain hostility. From this starkly Manichean perspective, the USSR represented all the forces of right and justice while the capitalist powers embodied the essence of evil. The Constitution of 1924 bluntly summarized the dichotomy: on one side the Soviet camp, bastion of peace, freedom and equality — on the other, the camp of capitalism, seething with hatred, slavery and war.[4] The 'two-camp' doctrine constituted a bias and an emotional attitude which at times hindered the ability of the Soviet diplomat to assess contemporary international developments realistically. As a recent commentator humorously put it, 'one gets the impression that the two-camp thesis is akin to the White Rabbit's watch, which, because it did not run, was exactly right twice a day: the accuracy of the two-camp thesis depends on a reality that will conveniently adapt to the model'.[5]

Theoretical considerations also led the Soviets to expect a particular pattern of behavior from the bourgeois states. It was taken as axiomatic that the capitalist powers would use any means and every opportunity to destroy the young socialist state. In 1917 all of the Bolsheviks felt that only the imminent pan-European proletarian revolution would save the Soviet experiment from annihilation at the hands of the Russian and international bourgeoisie. The Leninists were hopeful, however, because they firmly expected that their own uprising would serve as the detonator for the greater revolution. These beliefs explain why the first Foreign Commissar, Trotskii, felt that he would have little diplomatic work to do and why some Soviet diplomats were willing to engage in compromising revolutionary activities in the countries to which they were accredited during the first few years after the October revolution. Even after the hoped-for world revolution failed to materialize and the 'international bourgeoisie' proved unable to crush the RSFSR, Soviet diplomats continued to expect the worst from their opponents:

> Capitalism has transformed into the field of international relations the same methods applied by it in 'regulating' the internal economic life of the nations. The path of competition is the path of systematically annihilating the small and medium-sized enterprises and of achieving the supremacy of big capital. World competition of the capitalist forces means the systematic subjection of the small, medium-sized and backward nations by the great and greatest capitalist powers.[6]

Bolshevik fears were well founded to the extent that there was considerable anti-communist sentiment among ruling circles in the West.[7] The readiness with which the British Conservatives pounced on the so-called 'Zinoviev' letter in 1924 in order to undermine the Anglo-Soviet *rapprochement* and the same party's staging of the Arcos raid and subsequent rupture of diplomatic relations with the USSR are cases in point.[8] Even so, the pervasive climate of hostility and distrust bred by this combination of doctrine and events lessened the Soviet diplomat's ability to perceive the true motivations behind the diplomatic activities of the capitalist states and to predict the reaction of the Western powers to Soviet initiatives. Foreign statesmen simply did not always behave like the pawns of capital that they were alleged to be. The diplomatic initiative paralleling the introduction of the NEP in 1921 is an example. The Kremlin leadership assumed that the capitalist states would be unable to resist lucrative opportunities to exploit Russian economic concessions. In reality such offers did not overcome the anti-Bolshevik policies of the more conservative Western governments. The international position of the Soviet Republic did improve after 1921, but not as a result of satisfying the capitalists' acquisitive desires. In Britain it was the electoral victory of the Labour Party, rather than any change of heart by the pro-capitalist Conservatives, which made possible better relations with the RSFSR.[9]

The preoccupation of Soviet diplomats with matters of socio-economic class also led them to attach great significance to working class movements abroad. For example, in the summer of 1925 when anti-communist Members of Parliament pressed the new Conservative British government as to whether it was considering a breach of relations with the Soviet Union, Foreign Secretary Austin Chamberlain replied in the negative. Soviet diplomats, who had feared that the Conservatives would use the 'Zinoviev' letter affair as an excuse for a rupture, were greatly relieved. In a report to Chicherin, Ian Berzin, the Soviet Chargé in London, expressed his belief that pressure from the trade unions had played a large part in preventing Chamberlain and Baldwin from severing relations with Moscow. Berzin was in error, however, since the representations of the Trades Union Council on the subjects of the Bolsheviks and the Chinese situation had reached Prime Minister Baldwin only after the Cabinet had already held its deliberations on these matters.[10]

To supplement their study of Marx and Engels, Soviet diplomats could also turn to Lenin's major treatise on the international system, *Imperialism*. Marx had noted that, 'the need of a constantly expanding market for its products chases the bourgeoisie over the whole surface of the globe. It must nestle everywhere, settle everywhere, establish connections everywhere'.[11] Lenin developed an elaborate theory about the nature of this capitalist expansion. The capitalist world, he argued, was highly unstable by its very nature. The economic development of each capitalist state was 'uneven' and 'disproportionate'. Thus, the rate of development of currently powerful states like England, which had begun the process of modernization relatively early, had slowed, while countries whose industrialization had begun later, like Germany or Japan, were now experiencing rapid rates of development. Just as the latter were overtaking the former economically, so too these newly emerging powers were challenging the formerly dominant great powers for political supremacy. Lenin went on to contend that the bourgeoisie of each rival power were organizing and centralizing their respective economies and governments to a greater degree than before. But, as each became better organized and more fully developed, their rates of productivity (and, therefore, the returns on their investments) diminished. To deal with this problem each of the powers established a vast colonial empire. These colonies served as markets for the surplus goods of the mother country and could also absorb capital investment more profitably. In addition, super-profits from the exploited colonies allowed the capitalists to ameliorate the lot of their own proletariat at least partially, and thus, temporarily, to lessen class conflict.

The number of exploitable colonial areas was limited, however, while the appetite of the imperialists was insatiable. As more and more recently developed powers entered the imperialist competition, a vicious scramble ensued among them for the redivision of the colonial world. To make matters worse, the colonial peoples were beginning to chafe under the harsh oppression of the imperialists. Lenin, therefore, predicted that a long series of inter-imperialist wars would dominate world politics. Periods of peace would be the exception, amounting to no more than temporary truces between the inevitable conflicts. Furthermore, emergent national liberation movements in the colonies would begin to challenge imperialist domination in bloody uprisings. The advent of socialism in one or more countries would add a third element of conflict to the situation. The new socialist state, or states, would face enormous danger from the hostile imperialist camp but, given the faltering nature of world capitalism and the awakening of the colonial world, the forces of socialism would enjoy equally great opportunities in their struggle with the enemy.[12]

These ideas, developed by Lenin in 1916, provided Soviet diplomats with a framework for interpreting the confused international scene. It is obvious though that the formulation and execution of Soviet foreign policy involved more than the mechanical application of doctrinal prescriptions. The Bolsheviks had always been realists in a Machiavellian sense of the word. The ability and the willingness to do what was necessary to gain and then to retain power had characterized Bolshevik policy since Lenin's return to Russia in April of 1917. The ideas developed in *Imperialism* supplied the theoretical justification for making necessary accommodations with the capitalist states, in addition to suggesting where the most advantageous compromises might be made.

The expected European-wide revolution failed to materialize and consequently the Soviet state was thrown back on its own resources. The preservation of Soviet power by any means possible became the overriding task. The pressure of events forced doctrinal revision. Karl Radek argued that the world revolution might not come in the form of a cataclysmic global explosion but might take the less dramatic but equally effective form of a slower corrosive process. The RSFSR would thus be obliged, in the meantime, to seek a modus vivendi with the bourgeois governments while the revolution was developing.[13] Under these conditions, even alliances with imperialist powers were permissible.[14] The task of the Bolshevik diplomat was to purchase a 'breathing space' in which the Soviet state could develop its resources and await the revolution.[15] Chicherin and his colleagues at the Narkomindel began to stress the possibility of (at least temporary) peaceful coexistence with the capitalist states.[16] The Russian communists had not abandoned their hostility toward, or fear of, the great powers, but the outcome of the civil war and foreign intervention had modified their expectations concerning capitalist behavior.

Lenin's *Imperialism* suggested two possible strategies which Soviet diplomats could use in the defense of the socialist fatherland, the exploitation of divisions among the powers and the enlistment of the oppressed colonial peoples in the struggle against the imperialists. In the Leninist view, capitalism was not a monolithic entity but rather the bourgeoisie was divided against itself by its own greed. The Bolshevik leader explained the diplomatic implications of this situation to the eighth Congress of Soviets in 1920:

> As long as we are alone and the capitalist world is strong, our foreign policy must consist in part in the exploitation of contradictions. (Of course, to defeat all the imperialist powers would be the nicest thing of all, but we shall not be in a position to accomplish this for a long time yet.) Our survival depends on the existence of fundamental disagreements among the imperialist powers on the one hand, and, on the other, on the fact that the victory of the Entente and the Treaty of Versailles have plunged the vast majority of Germans into conditions in which they cannot live.[17]

Commissar Chicherin became the chief executor of this policy and the Rapallo Treaty with Germany was his greatest triumph. His whole career was devoted to fighting the League of Nations, an organization which, to him, was the embodiment of Anglo-French capitalist domination. The tactic of allying with one great power against another, although it found sanction for the Bolsheviks in Lenin's writing, was scarcely a Marxist concept. It was the same balance of power strategy employed by the most able diplomats of the Old Regime. With Chicherin and a surprising number of his colleagues in the Narkomindel, the Marxist-Leninist world view was integrally blended with elements of more traditional diplomatic wisdom. The responsibilities of power and the prolonged experience of actual negotiation with representatives of the capitalist states forced Soviet diplomats to moderate some of their doctrinaire attitudes and opinions. Compare, for instance, the heated debates over the question of accepting the Brest-Litovsk Treaty in 1918 with the widespread popularity of the Rapallo Treaty in Bolshevik circles. The latter was more favorable to Russia, but it still involved a political alliance, and military collaboration, with a regime which suppressed its native communists.

The Bolsheviks also laid special stress on cooperation with underdeveloped nations in the struggle against the European great powers.[18] Soviet diplomats strove to encourage the anti-colonialist movements because such activities weakened the power of the imperialist states and at the same time identified the Soviet Republic with a progressive cause. For once Lenin had a good word for the bourgeoisie:

> This [here Lenin was specifically referring to the Chinese revolution] means that the east has finally taken the road to the west, that fresh hundreds and hundreds of millions of human beings will henceforth take part in the struggle for the ideals to which the west has attained by its labors. The western bourgeoisie is rotten, and is already confronted by its gravediggers — the proletariat. But in Asia there is still a bourgeoisie capable of standing for a sincere, energetic, consistent democracy, a worthy comrade of the great teachers and revolutionaries of the end of the eighteenth century in France.[19]

The forces of 'national liberation' were seen as valuable allies of the USSR because they were to play the progressive role of bringing the benighted colonial populations out of darkness and smashing the strangle hold of imperialism on the world. Chicherin instructed his diplomats assigned to Asian countries that 'our policy in the east is never aggressive, it is always exclusively a policy of the national liberation of nations'.[20]

The means whereby the contradictions among capitalist powers could be exploited and alliances with the national bourgeoisie of the third world could be consumated was, of course, diplomacy. 'Bourgeois diplomacy' had traditionally been held in ill repute among Marxists. Stalin's opinion, enunciated in 1913, was probably typical. 'A diplomat's words have no relation to action — otherwise what kind of diplomacy is it? Words are one thing, actions another . . . .Sincere diplomacy is no more possible than dry water or iron wood.'[21] Nevertheless, diplomacy became a necessity. The Foreign Commissar, himself, was the archetype of the flaming revolutionary turned professional diplomat. Many of the Narkomindel's chief diplomats experienced a similar metamorphosis. Diplomatic activity may have seemed strange at first, but Chicherin, Litvinov, Krasin and their colleagues were soon very much at home in striped pants. The substance of capitalist diplomacy remained suspect, but doctrinal scruples about the method were soon overcome.

The receding of any possibility of world revolution in the near future not only modified the Marxist-Leninist view of the world, it also provided the opportunity for other influences, antithetical to socialist ideas, to manifest themselves in Soviet diplomacy. The men responsible for the formulation and execution of Soviet foreign policy were increasingly concerned with the interests of the Soviet state at the expense of 'proletarian internationalism'. This evolution of perspective proceeded gradually. In the early days of Soviet power Lenin had forcefully asserted that: 'We defend neither great-power. . .nor national interests, we hold that the interests of socialism, the interests of world socialism, are more important than national interests, more important than the interests of the state. . .'.[22] The behavior of the Soviet delegation at the Brest-Litovsk discussions made it clear that the Bolsheviks were not seriously worried about territorial issues. It was the social struggle within each territory that concerned them. The settling of the social issue (i.e. the victory of the world proletariat) would automatically take care of questions of secondary importance including problems of sovereignty and territorial rights.

The great social dislocations which accompanied the World War gave promise of widespread revolutionary successes, but the promises remained largely unfulfilled. The Soviet Republic stood out as the one tangible gain of the revolutionary movement. As hopes for further upheavals in Europe and America dimmed, more and more Bolsheviks came to feel that the defense of the one existing socialist state was a legitimate cause. By 1927 Stalin could claim that 'an internationalist is one who unreservedly, without hesitation, without conditions, is ready to defend the Soviet Union because it is the base of the world revolutionary movement'.[23]

From the defense of Bolshevik Russia as the center of the world communist movement to the defense of the USSR as a national state was only a short step. Although in theory the two positions were widely separated, in practice the former, given the political situation in Europe, logically led to the latter. This identification of the international proletarian cause with the interests of the Soviet state was especially pronounced in the Narkomindel, an organization whose chief purpose was the protection of that state. Moreover, Soviet diplomats began increasingly to analyze the international position of the Soviet Union in terms of the *historic* interests of the Russian state. Commissar Chicherin personified this tendency. England had been the principal rival of Imperial Russia in the nineteenth century and the Commissar saw in the current difficulties between the USSR and Great Britain a continuation of that rivalry. Chicherin's writings on Asia were full of allusions to earlier British imperialism and to the policies of Tsar Alexander II and his Foreign Minister, Gorchakov.[24] He even advised his diplomats in the Asian countries to study the history of nineteenth-century tsarist diplomacy for a better understanding of their problems.[25] Chicherin's analysis of European affairs was similarly grounded in his broad knowledge of diplomatic history.[26] In a letter to a friend he described himself lecturing the Politburo in 1927 on the Metternichian alliance system (which he called the Monarchintern), and the role of Tsar Nicholas I in it, as an object lesson concerning German foreign policy.[27]

Despite Lenin's denial of any interest in petty territorial issues, the Narkomindel took a strongly nationalist position on the matter of Russian sovereignty. The 'Bessarabian question' is a case in point. Imperial Russia had annexed that Rumanian principality in the nineteenth century, but the Rumanians had reoccupied the area immediately after World War I. Khristian Rakovskii, then the Soviet ambassador in London, and Chicherin (supported by Stalin) championed the Soviet claim.[28] Similarly, the Soviet government often asserted its rights under the terms of old tsarist treaties. In 1923, for example, when representatives of Britain, France and Spain met in Paris to draw up a new statute regulating the international position of Tangier, the USSR was excluded from the deliberations even though Imperial Russia had been a signatory of the Algeciras agreement in 1906. Therefore, Moscow informed the three Western participants that it reserved the right not to recognize any changes in the old Act of Algeciras.[29]

RED DIPLOMACY

Soviet commentators have often claimed that Soviet diplomacy, inspired by the ideas of Marx and Lenin and grounded in the interests of the working class, is of a new type, qualitatively superior to 'bourgeois diplomacy'.[30] Its uniqueness is said to lie in its openness, honesty, and genuinely peaceful and humanitarian character. Western diplomats, while agreeing that Soviet diplomacy is indeed different from their own practice, have vigorously denied any claims

of superiority for the Narkomindel's techniques. Sir Harold
Nicolson's opinion is typical of this point of view.

> Mr. W.P. Potjomkin [V.P. Potemkin], in his *History of Diplomacy,*
> assured us that the Russians possess one powerful weapon denied to their op-
> ponents — namely 'the scientific dialectic of the Marx-Lenin formula.' I have
> not observed as yet that this dialectic has improved international relationships,
> or that the Soviet diplomatists and commissars have evolved any system of
> negotiation that might be called a diplomatic system. Their activity in foreign
> countries or at international conferences is formidable, disturbing, compulsive.
> I do not for one moment underestimate either its potency or its danger. But it is
> not diplomacy: it is something else.[31]

None of these descriptions accurately characterizes Soviet diplomacy
as it was practised during the first fourteen years after the October
revolution. If the diplomacy of Metternich, Castlereagh and Alexander I is taken as the norm, then perhaps the Narkomindel's techniques were novel, but then so was the diplomacy of Woodrow
Wilson.

Soviet diplomacy was remarkable for the emphasis it placed on the
public relations value of diplomatic activity. In the early days after
the revolution, propaganda and diplomacy were almost synonymous
at the Commissariat of Foreign Affairs. It could scarcely have been
otherwise. The Bolshevik regime, militarily weak and desperately in
need of peace, was faced by hostility on all sides. At Brest-Litovsk
words were the only weapons at its command. The Brest-Litovsk
talks were the prototype of Soviet diplomacy from 1917 to 1921.
Trotskii openly explained the Soviets' strategy:

> Sitting at one table with them [the representatives of Imperial Germany,
> Austria-Hungary, Bulgaria, and Turkey] we shall ask them explicit questions
> which do not allow any evasion, and the entire course of the negotiations, every
> word they or we utter, will be taken down and reported by radiotelegraph to all
> peoples, who will be the judges of our discussions. Under the influence of the
> masses, the German and Austrian Governments have already agreed to put
> themselves on the dock. You may be sure, comrades, that the prosecutor, in the
> person of the Russian revolutionary delegation, will be in its place and will in
> due time make a thundering speech for the prosecution about the diplomacy of
> all imperialists.[32]

At Brest-Litovsk, in Lenin's Decree on Peace and on many subsequent occasions, the Bolsheviks sought to appeal to the peoples of
the world, over the heads of the bourgeois diplomats, in an effort to
foster revolution or, failing that, at least to force the Western

governments to modify their anti-Soviet policies under the pressure of public opinion.[33] The Soviet diplomats who negotiated with the Germans in 1917 and 1918 claimed that 'the Russian delegation represents the interests of the entire democratic world. . .'.[34] Throughout the period of Russia's isolation during the civil war and intervention, 'diplomacy' by public proclamation over the radio was almost the only means the NKID had for communicating with the outside world. Even after formal relations had been re-established with most European countries, Moscow never forgot the propaganda value inherent in diplomatic exchanges. When Franco-Russian negotiations over debts and credits reached an impasse in May of 1927, Rakovskii, the Soviet representative in Paris, gave an interview to *Paris Soir* which was a transparent attempt to appeal to the French holders of old Russian bonds and thus to bring the pressure of public opinion to bear on the recalcitrant Poincaré government.[35] Besides mobilizing world opinion, public diplomacy could also be used to expose the mendacity of imperialist foreign policy. Commissar Chicherin delighted in publicly unmasking the hypocrisy of his rivals. In 1922 at the Genoa conference he boldly proposed general disarmament and also demanded that representatives of the colonial peoples be admitted to the sessions on an equal basis with the diplomats of the great powers. Neither suggestion was at all realistic, but Chicherin's tactics had great propaganda value and such 'demands' could always be dropped as a concession during negotiations.

These techniques employed by Soviet diplomats, although they brought forth cries of outrage from their opponents, were in reality not so novel. The general principle of open diplomacy found its most eloquent defender not in Lenin, but in Woodrow Wilson. An official of the American Department of State, in reference to Wilson, recently claimed that: 'The "American" method [of diplomacy] was characterized by the extension of democratic ideals from the national to the international arena, egalitarianism, public negotiations, summitry, and attempts to influence and use public opinion.'[36] For that matter, the eighteenth-century *philosophes* had decried the evils of traditional diplomacy, while their disciples, the American and French revolutionaries, had talked of the need for a new diplomacy.[37] By the early twentieth century 'old diplomacy' was widely criticized by Western political leaders.[38] Entente diplomats also engaged in the practice of appealing to peoples over the heads of their governments. The Allied representatives in Russia in 1917 and 1918 never recognized the Soviet regime. After the fall of the Provisional Government these diplomats claimed to be accredited directly to the Russian people and they issued anti-Soviet statements to the general public.[39] In terms of the relationship between foreign policy and public opinion, Soviet diplomacy was only quantitatively different from its predecessors and rivals. The Bolsheviks were merely quicker to perceive the new styles in diplomacy demanded by the age of mass communications and mass politics.

The Narkomindel, moreover, soon began to balance its propaganda offensives with more traditional diplomatic initiatives wherever possible. Diplomatic notes, formal negotiation, even secret treaties, increasingly replaced the earlier style of diplomacy by proclamation and denunciation. Soviet proclamations about open diplomacy did not prevent Kopp and Stomoniakov from entering into a series of top secret military negotiations with Weimar Germany between 1920 and 1922.[40] These talks resulted in *sub rosa* military cooperation between Moscow and Berlin to circumvent the disarmament clauses of the Versailles treaty. Nor did it take the Narkomindel representatives long to master the arts of diplomatic dissimulation. The negotiations for the Rapallo treaty provide an excellent example. Knowing that the German delegation was greatly concerned about the possibility of an Anglo-Soviet *rapprochement* which would further deepen Germany's isolation, Ioffe told Baron Ago von Maltzan that talks with the British at the Villa d'Albertis were proceeding satisfactorily. In fact, those negotiations had foundered on the problem of tsarist debts, but Ioffe's clever fabrication helped stampede the panicky Germans into signing the treaty of Rapallo.[41] To cite another example, during the Anglo-Soviet negotiations of August 1920 Kamenev deliberately misrepresented to the British the armistice terms the Bolsheviks hoped to impose on the Poles. He did so in order to gain time and to prevent Great Britain from becoming directly involved in the Russo-Polish conflict.[42]

The Commissariat of Foreign Affairs gradually was able to command the services of a corps of skilled and able diplomats. A few of the party comrades assigned to the NKID in its first years, notably Zalkind and A.M. Makar, proved temperamentally unsuited to diplomatic work,[43] but most of the new diplomats adapted to their duties very well. At its best, Soviet diplomacy could be superb. Chicherin's rebuttals at Genoa to the arguments of Lloyd George on the question of tsarist debts were examples of the highest diplomatic skill.[44] The British Prime Minister later told Ivan Maiskii: 'It wasn't easy for Chicherin at Genoa: one against us all! But he maneuvered superbly and at the same time firmly defended the positions of his government. Though no agreement was reached Chicherin personally proved himself a splendid diplomat.'[45] The great economist, J.M. Keynes, who also attended the Genoa conference, similarly praised the Soviet Foreign Commissar as one of the most accomplished diplomats in Europe.[46] Beyond Chicherin, in Litvinov, Krasin, Rotshtein, Maiskii and Dovgalevskii, the Narkomindel possessed diplomats of the first rank.

No unique Soviet style can be identified in either the realm of Bolshevik diplomatic practice or in the personal manner of Soviet diplomats. To a great extent, the necessities of protecting the USSR, and therefore of maintaining peaceful relations with the capitalist countries, imposed the usages of bourgeois diplomacy on the representatives of the socialist state.

THE NARKOMINDEL AND REVOLUTION

The role played by the Narkomindel and its diplomats in the world revolutionary movement has been a hotly disputed issue. The anticommunist opponents of the Soviet state have pictured Soviet embassies as centers of subversion, intrigue and espionage. Spokesmen for the NKID have vigorously denied these charges. The problem is compounded by the extreme scarcity of reliable evidence concerning this question. It seems safe to say, however, that neither side in the argument has presented the whole truth.

The Bolsheviks at first believed that only the occurrence of further socialist revolutions, especially in the industrialized countries of Europe, could prevent the reactionary powers from crushing the Soviet regime. Under these circumstances the promotion of revolutions abroad became a cardinal policy of the state. The first Narkomindel representatives thought of themselves not merely as diplomatic agents of the Soviet government accredited to one of the bourgeois states, but as representatives of the revolutionary Russian working class to the proletariat of the country to which they were sent. In the face of what appeared to be a united front of capitalist hostility to the socialist experiment, the Russian communists had scarcely another choice. In the period from 1917 to 1921, when the RSFSR had neither great military power nor any significant diplomatic leverage and when it was threatened on all sides by civil war, foreign intervention and émigré intrigue, a revolutionary appeal to the world proletariat was one of the few options open to the desperate Bolsheviks.

After 1921, with the consolidation of its political, economic, and military power and the consequent rise of its diplomatic stock, the Soviet regime became more willing not only to sign but, to a great extent, to fulfill pledges prohibiting propaganda and other activities hostile to its treaty partners. Increased diplomatic opportunities coupled with the failure of the revolutionary movements in Western Europe meant that there was now more to be gained through normal channels. In this drastically changed environment, any connections with radical agitation proved to be liabilities for the Soviet diplomats. The Narkomindel rapidly divested itself of such activities. Dedicated communists serving in the Comintern came to feel that the Bolsheviks were sacrificing the hallowed principles of proletarian internationalism in order to secure the interests of their state.[47] This shift from revolutionary agitation to more traditional diplomacy occurred gradually and not without some ambiguity.

The Bolsheviks expected that an insurrection would break out soon in Imperial Germany. Consequently their embassy in Berlin, directed by Adolf Ioffe, expended more time and effort on revolutionary activities than on diplomacy. In an interview with the American journalist Louis Fischer, Ioffe candidly admitted that:

> His embassy in Berlin served as a staff headquarters for a German revolution. He bought secret information from German officials and passed it on to radical leaders for use in public speeches and articles against the government. He bought arms for the revolutionaries and paid out 100,000 marks for them. Tons of anti-Kaiser literature were printed and distributed at the Soviet Embassy's expense. 'We wanted to pull down the monarchist state and end the war,' Joffe said to me [Fischer]. 'President Wilson tried to do the same in his own way.' Almost every evening after dark, Left-wing independent socialist leaders slipped into the embassy building in Unter den Linden to consult Joffe on questions of tactics. He was an experienced conspirator. They wanted his advice, guidance and money. 'In the end, however,' Joffe commented ruefully, 'they, we, accomplished little or nothing of permanent value. We were too weak to provoke a revolution.'[48]

The German authorities soon found a pretext to expel Ioffe and the whole Soviet mission. The next Soviet representative in Berlin, Viktor Kopp, who arrived in 1920 as the head of a trade delegation, carefully limited his contacts with the local communists.

Other Narkomindel diplomats emulated Ioffe's tactics. Especially in Asia, Soviet representatives attempted to foment revolutions.[49] The NKID Department of the East was charged with preparing reports on revolutionary activities and movements in Asia.[50] The Narkomindel also issued the announcement of the first congress of the Communist International and both Chicherin and Reinshtein attended its opening session, sitting on the platform.[51] The Comintern seems to have occasionally used the diplomatic courier service as part of its communications system.[52] The Narkomindel apparently also provided cover for Comintern field agents by employing them in its embassies. It has been claimed, for example, that I.D. Ianson, who served in various diplomatic capacities in Tokyo during the 1920s was really a representative for the Comintern and Profintern in Japan, while a certain Mirov-Abramov, a member of the Press Department of the Berlin embassy, was the Comintern representative from 1921 to 1930.[53] There was, in addition, considerable exchange of personnel between the Third International and the Commissariat of Foreign Affairs. Soviet diplomats who also spent some time working in the Comintern include Berzin, Holzman, Kamenev, Karakhan, Kobetskii, Kurskii, Litvinov, Lorents, Manuilskii, Marchlewski, Narimanov, Radek, Raskol'nikov, Shumiatskii, Sokol'nikov, Stuchka, Trotskii and Vorovskii. F.F. Raskol'nikov, for instance, who had formerly been the Soviet representative in Afghanistan and who would subsequently be the Russian ambassador in Estonia, interrupted his diplomatic career for several years in the mid-1920s to serve as head of the Eastern Department at Comintern headquarters. Bolsheviks who were familiar with conditions abroad and knew foreign languages were scarce and therefore were often shuttled to whatever agency needed them at the moment.

These revolutionary activities soon became a liability to Soviet diplomats. By 1921 the Kremlin was beginning to learn that revolutions could not be provoked by the intrigues of diplomats and that such attempts undermined the relationship between the Soviet diplomat and the government to which he was accredited. Since the world revolution was obviously not imminent, the emphasis of Bolshevik policy shifted to the protection of the Soviet state by diplomatic means. In this situation the Narkomindel was forced to do everything possible to disassociate itself from its former revolutionary activities and connections. The very existence of the Communist International, openly dedicated to the overthrow of the capitalist order, was a source of great embarrassment for the Soviet diplomats (see figure 1).

Figure 1. The famous *Pravda* cartoon of Zinoviev and Chicherin titled 'Friendly Jests' and captioned 'Comrade Zinoviev delivers a speech. . .'[54]

Chicherin labored long and hard to deny any connection between his Commissariat and the Third International:

> The Communist Party stands at the head of a great government. As a government it enters into relations with all other governments and establishes close friendly relations, guarding the vital political and economic interests of its republic. It conducts a state policy determined by the interests of the laborers. State policy and party policy are strictly separated. Speaking in the name of the government organs we leave the second [i.e. party policy] on the side. The fate of the communist movement, the success and experience of communist parties belongs in the realm of other organs. Our attention is given to the fate of the Soviet government.[55]

Chicherin's only contribution to *Kommunisticheskii internatsional,* the Comintern journal, was an article in which he attempted to draw a clear distinction of both organization and function between the

Soviet state and the Third International.[56] Following this line of argument, Litvinov told Lord Curzon that the Comintern in Moscow had no more connection to the Soviet government than the Second International in Brussels had to the Belgian government. He claimed that officials of the RSFSR might be members of the Comintern as private individuals in the same way that some Belgian or British ministers were members of the Second International.[57] Such arguments did not convince many Western diplomats. Chicherin even went so far as to ask Lenin and Trotskii to resign from the Executive Committee of the Comintern in order to improve the image of the Soviet government in the European capitals.[58] The Foreign Commissar and his Deputy, Litvinov, also strongly opposed any sort of open aid on the part of the RSFSR to foreign revolutionary movements.[59]

The Soviets began to employ the device of anti-propaganda clauses inserted in their treaties to reassure foreign governments of the legitimacy of their intentions. The Brest-Litovsk Treaty had contained such a provision which the Bolsheviks had frequently and openly violated. To achieve recognition from the European powers, however, the Narkomindel had to ensure the faithful execution of such pledges, at least to the extent of barring openly revolutionary agitation by its diplomats. Anti-propaganda clauses became a regular feature of Soviet treaties. In an exchange of notes with the British in 1923 the USSR promised not to support financially, 'or by another means persons, agencies, organizations or institutions which have the aim of spreading disaffection, or supporting rebellion in any part of the British Empire. . .'.[60] The Soviet authorities did actually close a school for propagandists in Tashkent, curtail the activities of the Council of Action in Baku, and instruct their diplomats in Afghanistan and Persia that they must observe the anti-propaganda provisions of the Anglo-Soviet treaties and refrain from 'artificial attempts to introduce communism'.[61]

The Soviet embassy in Berlin had been involved in minor, but highly embarrassing, ways in the abortive 1923 uprising of German communists. A Comintern agent code-named Petrov, using the cover of embassy employment, had managed the transmission of funds with which to buy arms for the insurgents.[62] The pathetic failure of the uprising together with the strain that Soviet involvement put on Russo-German relations apparently taught the Bolshevik leaders two hard lessons. First, the anticipated European revolution — even in the homeland of Marx — was not an imminent probability. Secondly, the futile efforts of Soviet diplomatic agents to promote foreign revolutions under such conditions could only undercut the effectiveness of the Narkomindel without producing any commensurate gains for the revolutionary movement. The Commissariat of Foreign Affairs, therefore, informed its diplomats in 1924 that they were to avoid all compromising activities. 'It goes without saying that diplomatic missions are appointed by each of the parties establishing diplomatic relations for purposes which exclude propaganda in the country to which they are accredited.'[63]

The security and the prospect of profitable economic exchanges which came with recognition by the great powers could not be gambled away for the petty gains which Soviet diplomats might achieve by dabbling in local politics. Although there were a few exceptions, on the whole the Narkomindel carefully avoided involvement in overtly revolutionary affairs. In 1927 the British used the pretext of supposed irregular activities by Soviet trade representatives possessing diplomatic immunity to break relations with the USSR. The documents published by the British government did not prove its case, and even the authenticity of those papers is suspect.[64] The French used a similar pretext in the same year to demand the recall of Khristian Rakovskii from Paris. Rakovskii had been in Moscow at the sessions of the Communist Party Central Control Commission when he signed an oppositionist statement which declared that 'every honest proletarian in the capitalist countries must work effectively towards the defeat of his government. . .', and that 'all soldiers of foreign countries who do not desire to help their slavemasters. . .' should desert to the Red Army. This was actually not a serious attempt to arouse the French workers and soldiers. It created a scandal in Paris only because elements within the French government, deeply hostile to the communist state, were already looking for an excuse to break relations with Soviet Russia.[65] It was only in China, already racked by revolution and civil war, that Soviet diplomats openly participated in revolutionary movements.[66]

In the first years after the October seizure of power, the emphasis of Soviet foreign policy was clearly on spreading the revolution to Europe and Asia, and the Narkomindel worked toward that goal. It was even hoped that the new association of working class parties, the Comintern, would soon replace the imperialist state system and, with it, bourgeois diplomacy. Given these expectations, the early subservience of the NKID to the Third International is easily explicable. With the decline in revolutionary prospects, however, the relationship between the two organizations was reversed. Having failed to carry out its revolutionary mission, the Comintern sank to the status of a tool manipulated by the Kremlin to ensure the predominance of the CPSU in the world communist movement and to mobilize that movement in support of Soviet foreign policy objectives.[67] The International thus became, at least in some instances, the servant of the Narkomindel. Article fourteen of the twenty-one conditions for admission to the Comintern demanded from all communists, 'unconditional support for every Soviet republic in its struggle against counter-revolutionary forces'.[68] Successive Comintern congresses throughout the decade never failed to voice their support of the Soviet Union and its current foreign policy.[69] Individual communist parties were pressed into service, too. In 1927 when Voikov, the Soviet representative to Warsaw, was assassinated and Moscow was gripped by a war scare, the fourth congress of the Polish Communist Party resolved that its chief duty at the moment was to defend the USSR.[70] The foreign communist parties were frequently used in this manner to mobilize public support whenever the Narkomindel was engaged in important negotiations with a Western government.

Neither sentiment nor Marxist scruple was allowed to overshadow *raison d'etat*. The NKID established good relations with Kemal Pasha's Turkey and Mussolini's Italy, despite the savage repression meted out to communists in those countries. Foreign communists sometimes criticized Soviet diplomacy, but with Moscow dominating the International, they were powerless to alter the situation.[71] Within Bolshevik ranks as well, the Foreign Commissariat was held in low esteem by the militant left-wing of the party.[72] The revolutionary credentials of Chicherin, Litvinov, Krasin and their comrades could not be doubted, but they labored in a field where radical phrasemongering and insurrectionary intrigue could only be counterproductive. According to Louis Fischer, Litvinov, 'repeatedly said in private that he never saw the sense of antagonizing a great power like England for the sake of Persia or Afghanistan or even China'.[73]

Although Soviet diplomatic missions soon severed most of their ties with overtly revolutionary groups, they did attempt to maintain contact with the workers' movements in the countries to which they were accredited. Ivan Maiskii served as the liaison between the Soviet embassy in London and the more militant sections of the British trade unions.[74] He kept Moscow informed about current tendencies among the English workers. Upon occasion the Soviets tried to use these links with the labor movement for diplomatic purposes. When the Conservatives ousted the MacDonald government in 1924 and evidenced their intent to reverse the developing Anglo-Soviet *detente,* the Russians hoped that pressure from the British Trades Union Council would reorient British foreign policy.[75]

After 1924 the Narkomindel's embassies continued to harbor a few Comintern and Profintern agents, but their activities were more carefully circumscribed and most of them apparently found more congenial niches in the less sensitive posts of the Soviet foreign trade missions. The Comintern also remained a source of embarrassment for Soviet diplomacy, though more because of its rhetoric than its actions. There was no more talk of 'closing up shop' at the Foreign Commissariat. Ironically, it was the Third International which was eventually 'cast into the dustbin of history'.

THE NARKOMINDEL AND ESPIONAGE

The role of Soviet diplomatic missions in espionage operations has also been greatly exaggerated. The small amount of reliable evidence available on this subject suggests that the Narkomindel's embassies occasionally provided cover for members of the Soviet intelligence network, but that this practice was soon restricted. Chicherin and Litvinov vigorously argued against any ties between the NKID and spy rings.[76] By 1927 the diplomatic and intelligence services had been decisively separated from each other.[77] Most embassies included a sizable contingent of *Cheka* (later GPU) officers, but their principal duties involved monitoring the political loyalty of the mission staff and combating anti-Soviet intrigues among Russian émigré circles.[78] Their functions of intelligence gathering and analysis were usually carried out by the traditional methods of combing the foreign press and sifting the diplomats' reports of conversations with their foreign colleagues.[79]

The foreign missions of the NKID were often denounced as centers of revolutionary agitation and spying.[80] There was a large and eager market for such stories not only among hostile Western governments, but also within the conservative scholarly community.[81] Most of these indictments were pure fabrication. After the initial burst of revolutionary enthusiasm had subsided, certainly by 1921, Soviet diplomats engaged in very few compromising revolutionary or espionage activities.[82] The diplomatic pouch might still occasionally be used to send messages or funds to foreign radicals, but even that practice was declining. Alexander Barmine's memoirs reveal that Soviet embassies were much duller places than the émigré spy novels depicted them.

> . . .I shall have to disappoint readers who expect me as a former Soviet diplomat to make sensational revelations about secret activities involving the GPU and the Comintern. The legation [in Athens] as such had nothing to do with the work of the GPU and neither Kobetsky [Soviet minister in Greece] nor I knew anything about it — except that its agents, naturally, were in the staff watching us.
>
> Of the Comintern's activities, also, I have little to say. We had no connection with its work at all. The Foreign Office still kept aloof in those days, strictly adhering to the principle that the Soviet Government and the Communist International were distinct entities. In obedience to this principle, we even abstained from contact with Communist members of the Greek Parliament, though often meeting other members. . . .
>
> . . .At the time when the Soviets were poor and revolutionary, the intervention of their diplomatic and trade representatives in labor movements was much exaggerated and a great fuss made about it. As a matter of fact, the Communist International had its own channels of communication with Moscow, and the GPU ran its own secret service. We diplomatic and commercial agents confined ourselves as stricly as possible to our legitimate tasks.[83]

The tasks facing the Narkomindel — protecting the Soviet state from renewed intervention and securing the profitable trade and loans necessary under the NEP — were too important to permit Soviet diplomats to risk compromising their missions by engaging in petty revolutionary intrigues.

NOTES

1. For example, V.P. Potemkin, ed., *Istoriia diplomatii* (Moscow, 1945), vol. III, pp. 763-64.

2. William Zimmerman, *Soviet Perspectives on International Relations, 1956-1967* (Princeton, 1969), pp. 282-83; and Aspaturian, *Process and Power*, p. 337.

3. Christian Rakovsky, 'The Foreign Policy of Soviet Russia', *Foreign Affairs*, 1926, IV, 4, p. 574.

4. *Annuaire diplomatique*, 1927, p. 129.

5. Zimmerman, *Soviet Perspectives*, p. 84.

6. Leon Trotsky, *What is a Revolutionary Programme?* (Colombo, 1956), p. 4.

7. See William Appleman Williams, 'American Intervention in Russia: 1917-1920', in: David Horowitz, ed., *Containment and Revolution* (Boston, 1967), pp. 26-75; and two works by Mayer, *Wilson vs. Lenin,* and *Politics and Diplomacy of Peacemaking.*

8. On the 'Zinoviev' letter affair see Gorodetsky, *Precarious Truce,* pp. 35-52; Gabriel Gorodetsky, *The Other 'Zinoviev' Letters: New Light on the Management of the Affair* (Tel-Aviv, 1976); *Anti-sovetskie podlogi: istoriia fal'shivok, faksimile i kommentarii* (Moscow, 1926), ch. III; Robert D. Warth, 'The Mystery of the Zinoviev Letter', *South Atlantic Quarterly,* 1950, XLIX, 4, pp. 441-53; and Lewis Chester, Stephen Fay and Hugo Young, *The Zinoviev Letter* (Philadelphia, 1967). Cf. Natalie Grant, 'The "Zinoviev Letter" Case', *Soviet Studies,* 1967, XIX, 2, pp. 264-77; Sibyl Crowe, 'The Zinoviev Letter: A Reappraisal', *The Journal of Contemporary History,* 1975, X, 3, pp. 407-32; and Paul Blackstock, *Agents of Deceit: Frauds, Forgeries and Political Intrigue among Nations* (Chicago, 1966), pp. 103-28. On the rupture of relations between Great Britain and the USSR see Robert D. Warth, 'The Arcos Raid and the Anglo-Soviet "Cold War" of the 1920's', *World Affairs Quarterly,* 1958, XXIX, 2, pp. 115-51; M. Tanin, 'Anglo-sovetskii razryv i problema edinogo imperialisticheskogo fronta', *Bol'shevik,* 1927, no. 11-12, pp. 59-68; and L.M. Khinchuk, *Kistorii anglo-sovetskikh otnoshenii* (Moscow and Leningrad, 1928), ch. XII.

9. Gorodetsky, *Precarious Truce,* pp. 7-35; and Daniel F. Calhoun, *The United Front: The TUC and the Russians, 1923-1928* (Cambridge, 1976), ch. I and II. Similarly, when Mussolini's Italy granted de jure diplomatic recognition to the USSR in 1924, Vorovskii, the Soviet representative in Rome attributed it to '. . .the profit seeking of the business community which overcame the instinctive anti-Communism of the Fascists in determining Italian foreign policy toward the USSR'. Vorovskii to NKID, Arkhiv Vneshnei Politiki SSSR, quoted in V. Sokolov, 'Break Through the Diplomatic Blockade (Fiftieth Anniversary of the Period of Recognition of the USSR)', *International Affairs,* 1974, no. 6, p. 86.

10. *DVP,* vol. VIII, p. 419; British Foreign Office document no. 370-11016-N3904/102/38; and Gorodetsky, *Precarious Truce,* p. 71.

11. Karl Marx and Friedrich Engels, 'Manifest der Kommunistischen Partei', *Werke* (Berlin, 1964), vol. IV, p. 465.

12. On Lenin's ideas about imperialism see Alfred G. Meyer, *Leninism* (New York, 1962), ch. XI; and Saul Norman Silverman, 'A World to Win: A Study of the Roots of Pre-Revolutionary Development of the Bolshevik Approach to World Affairs', Ph.D. dissertation, Yale University, 1963, pp. 563-66; and James W. Roberts, 'Lenin's Theory of Imperialism in Soviet Usage', *Soviet Studies,* 1977, XXIX, 3, pp. 353-72.

13. Karl Radek, *Die auswärtige Politik Sowjet-Russlands* (Hamburg, 1921), pp. 37-38.

14. 'Ein neues Dokument W.I. Lenins', *Beiträge zur Geschichte der Arbeiterbewegung,* 1963, V, 4, pp. 79-86.

15. Outsider, 'Vneshniaia politika SSSR bez lenina', *Izvestiia,* 22 January 1922, p. 2. Also see Lenin, *PSS,* vol. XLII, p. 22 and vol. XLIV, pp. 304-5; and *Leninskii sbornik,* vol. XXXVIII, p. 293.

16. Chicherin, *Stat'i i rechi,* pp. 172-78.

17. Lenin, *PSS,* vol. XLII, p. 105. Lenin's tactics also included the exploitation of differences within each capitalist state as well as those between the imperialist powers. For an analysis of disagreements within imperialist foreign policy-making elites and Soviet attempts to exploit those differences see Boris Shtein, *'Russkii vopros' v 1920-1922gg.* (Moscow, 1958).

18. G.V. Chicherin, 'Rossiia i aziatskie narody', *Vestnik NKID,* 1919, no. 2.

19. Lenin, *PSS,* vol. XXI, p. 402.

20. Quoted from the Central Political Archive of the Institute of Marxism-Leninism by M. Trush, 'A Diplomat of the Leninist School: For the 100th Anniversary of the Birth of G.V. Chicherin', *International Affairs,* 1972, no. 12, p. 70.

21. I.V. Stalin, *Sochineniia* (Moscow, 1946), vol. II, p. 277. Also see Potemkin, ed., *Istoriia diplomatii,* vol. III, p. 702.

22. Lenin, *PSS,* vol. XXXVI, pp. 341-2

23. Stalin, *Sochineniia,* vol. X, p. 61.

24. See, for instance, Chicherin, 'Rossiia i aziatskie narody'.

25. Aralov, *Vospominaniia sovetskogo diplomata,* p. 15.

26. For example, Chicherin, *Stat'i i rechi,* pp. 67-86. In this article Chicherin elaborately paralleled the post-1815 Congress System with Europe after the Versailles Treaty.

27. Chicherin to Fischer, 14 February, 1930, Fischer-Chicherin Correspondence, Yale, box 1, folder 2.

28. Fischer, *Men and Politics,* p. 135. Iurenev, the *Polpred* in Rome, was also an advocate of Bessarabia's annexation. See his interview in *Giornale d'Italia,* 21 February 1925.

29. USDS, Research and Analysis Report no. OCL-3489.1, 'The USSR and the Colonial Problem, Part I: Africa'; and *Izvestiia,* 4 July 1945.

30. For example, V.A. Zorin, *Osnovy diplomaticheskoi sluzhby* (Moscow, 1964), pp. 27ff. and 51ff.

31. Harold Nicolson, *The Evolution of Diplomacy* (New York, 1962), pp. 120-21.

32. Trotskii, *Sochineniia,* vol. III, part II, p. 178.

33. Soviet diplomats later tried to bypass the Auswärtiges Amt entirely by opening direct negotiations with the *Rat der Volksbeauftrachten.* See Moritz Schlesinger, *Erinnerungen eines Aussenseites im diplomatischen Dienst* (Köln, 1977), pp. 31-5.

34. *Izvestiia,* 23 November 1917.

35. *Paris Soir,* 4 May 1927; and Senn, 'The Rakovsky Affair', pp. 108-9 and 115-16.

36.   John Ensor Harr, *The Professional Diplomat* (Princeton, 1969), p. 17.

37.   Felix Gilbert, 'The "New Diplomacy" of the Eighteenth Century', *World Politics,* 1951, IV, 1, pp. 1-39.

38.   See Aubrey L. Kennedy, *Old Diplomacy and New* (London, 1922), pp. 364-65; Gordon Craig, *War, Politics, and Diplomacy,* pp. 207-19; and Paul Gordon Lauren, *Diplomats and Bureaucrats: The First Institutional Responses to Twentieth-Century Diplomacy in France and Germany* (Stanford, 1976), passim.

39.   For example, *K russkomu narodu* (Archangel, [1918]). Of course, even under the 'old diplomacy' the most astute diplomats, men such as Canning, Palmerston and Bismarck, were well aware of the importance of public opinion and its manipulation. See Nicolson, *Diplomacy,* pp. 37-38.

40.   See Freund, *Unholy Alliance,* ch. III-IV.

41.   See Fischer, *The Soviets in World Affairs,* vol. I, pp. 337-42. Cf. Liubimov and Erlikh, *Genuezskaia konferentsiia,* pp. 65-73.

42.   See Ullman, *Anglo-Soviet Accord,* ch. V-VI.

43.   USDS, 701.6157/11, report from US Embassy in Oslo, 31 October 1927. Also see Richard Debo's comments on Krestinskii's shortcomings as a diplomat. Debo, 'Dutch-Soviet Relations', pp. 216-17.

44.   Liubimov and Erlikh, *Genuezskaia konferentsiia,* pp. 50-64.

45.   I.M. Maisky, 'Diplomats of the Lenin School: Georgi Chicherin', *New Times,* 1967, no. 44, p. 12.

46.   The *Manchester Guardian,* 19 April, 1922; and Liubimov and Erlikh, *Genuezskaia konferentsiia,* pp. 142-51.

47.   Ypsilon (pseudonym for Karl Volk), *Pattern for World Revolution* (Chicago and New York, 1947), p. 77.

48.   Fischer, *Men and Politics,* p. 26. Also see A.A. Ioffe, 'Germanskaia revoliutsiia i rossiiskoe posol'stvo', *Vestnik zhizni,* 1919, no. 5, pp. 35-46; and Baumgart, *Deutsche Ostpolitik,* pp. 334-63.

49.   G.V. Chicherin, *The Foreign Policy of Soviet Russia* (London, 1919), p. 31; and Barmine, *One Who Survived,* p. 97.

50.   *Spravochnik tsentral'nykh i mestnykh uchrezhdenii RSFSR,* p. 157.

51.   *Der I. Kongress der Kommunistischen Internationale: Protokoll der Verhandlungen in Moskau vom 2. bis zum 19. März 1919* (Hamburg, 1921), pp. 6 and 54-6.

52.   Ypsilon, *Pattern for World Revolution,* p. 109.

53.   G.Z. Bessedovsky, *Den Klauen der Tscheka Entronnen: Erinnerungen* (Leipzig, 1930), p. 26; and Elisabeth K. Poretsky, *Our Own People: A Memoir History of 'Ignace Reiss' and His Friends* (Ann Arbor, 1969), p. 53.

54.   *Pravda,* 19 July 1924.

55.   G.V. Chicherin, 'Za piat' let', *Mezhdunarodnaia zhizn',* 1922, no. 15. Also see Hilger and Meyer, *The Incompatible Allies,* pp. 108-10.

56.   G.V. Chicherin, 'Mezhdunarodnaia politika dvukh internatsionalov', *Kommunisticheskii internatsional,* 1919, no. 6, pp. 817-28.

57.   *DVP,* vol. IV, pp. 374-80.

58.   *Leninskii sbornik,* vol. XXXVI, pp. 338-39.

59.   Arthur U. Pope, *Maxim Litvinoff* (New York, 1943), p. 168, and Avtorkhanov, *Stalin and the Soviet Communist Party,* p. 180.

60.   *DVP,* vol. VII, pp. 330 and 334.

61. Ibid., vol. IV, pp. 165-68; Stephen White, 'Communism and the East: The Baku Conference, 1920', *Slavic Review*, 1974, XXXIII, 3, pp. 504-6; and White, 'Colonial Revolution and the Communist International', *Science and Society*, 1976, XL, 2, pp. 177-78.

62. Germany, Auswärtiges Amt, Handakten Wallroth, bd. 10, no. 5265/318063-6, Wallroth to Brockdorff-Rantzau. Also see Boris Bajanov [Bazhanov], *Avec Staline dans le Kremlin* (Paris, 1930), pp. 190-98; Herbert Helbig, *Die Träger der Rapallo-Politik* (Göttingen, 1958), pp. 160-61; Werner T. Angress, *Stillborn Revolution: The Communist Bid for Power in Germany, 1921-1923* (Princeton, 1963), pp. 395, and 419, n. 104; R.P. Morgan, 'The Political Significance of the German-Soviet Trade Negotiations, 1922-5', *The Historical Journal*, 1963, VI, 2, pp. 253-71; and Freund, *Unholy Alliance*, p. 187.

63. *Sobranie zakonov*, 1924, vol. I, no. 26, pp. 402-3.

64. Fischer, *The Soviets in World Affairs*, vol. II, pp. 686-89. Also see note 8.

65. Ibid., vol. II, pp. 707-16; and Senn, 'The Rakovsky Affair', pp. 102-17.

66. M.S. Kapitsa, 'Lev Karakhan', and R.A. Mirovitskii, 'Mikhail Borodin', in: *Vidnye sovetskie kommunisty — uchastniki kitaiskoi revoliutsii* (Moscow, 1970), pp. 5-40; and Fischer, *The Soviets in World Affairs*, vol. II, ch. XXIII.

67. On the evolution of the Comintern see Moore, *Soviet Politics*, p. 215; and Bernard S. Morris, *International Communism and American Policy* (New York, 1966), pp. 3-43.

68. Bela Kun, ed., *Kommunisticheskii internatsional v dokumentakh* (Moscow, 1933), p. 103.

69. For example, Jane Degras, ed., *The Communist International, 1919-1943: Documents* (London, 1960), vol. II, pp. 111-12 and 145.

70. Ponomaryov, *History of Soviet Foreign Policy*, p. 264.

71. British communists, for example, frequently criticized the bourgeois 'commercialism' which they believed dominated Krasin's mission in London. See Liberman, *Building Lenin's Russia*, p. 165.

72. This attitude even found its way into Soviet literature. In Isaak Babel's *Red Cavalry*, Sidorov, an ultra-revolutionary red cavalryman who wants a diplomatic assignment in Italy so he can shoot the King and spark an insurrection, tells a friend, 'Don't mention Kings or shooting to the Tzeka [Central Committee, i.e. the Collegium] in the Narkomindel. They will only pat you on the head and mumble: "A romantic".' Babel, *Red Cavalry* (London, 1929), pp. 39-40.

73. Louis Fischer, *The Life and Death of Stalin* (New York, 1952), p. 114.

74. I.M. Maiskii, 'Iz londonskikh vospominanii', *Novyi mir*, 1968, no. 4, pp. 212-16.

75. G. Gorodetsky, 'The Soviet Union and Britain's general strike of May 1926', *Cahiers du Monde Russe et Soviétique*, 1976, XVII, 2-3, p. 289.

76. Bessedovsky, *Revelations*, p. 162; G.S. Agabekov, *G.P.U. zapiski chekista* (Berlin, 1930), p. 22; and Reswick, *I Dreamt Revolution*, p. 195. The GPU did provide some useful services for the Narkomindel, however, such as the training of experts in code work — including the decipherment of codes used by rival diplomatic services. See Besedovskii's article in *La Matin*, 16 May 1930.

77. David J. Dallin, *Soviet Espionage* (New Haven, 1955), pp. 40-41.

78. On the subterranean war between the GPU and anti-Soviet émigré political and terrorist groups see Gerson, *The Secret Police in Lenin's Russia*, pp. 231-32; and Paul W. Blackstock, *The Secret Road to World War Two: Soviet versus Western In-*

telligence, 1921-1939 (Chicago, 1969), passim. Unfortunately, none of the studies on Soviet intelligence activities meet the usual scholarly standards because of the highly unreliable nature of the available source material.

79.   Bessedovsky, *Revelations,* pp. 243-49.

80.   For example, ibid., pp. 10-12 and 30; K.V. Ozols, *Memuary poslannika* (Paris, [1938]), ch. XVI; and J.R.D. Bourcart, *L'Espionnage Soviétique* (Paris, 1962), pp. 16-17 and passim.

81.   A US State Department official admitted that the American government sustained an on-going effort to collect anti-Soviet stories of all kinds. See John Campbell White, The Reminiscences of John Campbell White, Oral History Project, Columbia University, 1953, p. 69. Also see Pavel Milioukov, *La Politique Extérieure des Soviets* (Paris, 1936), pp. 254-5; and Barmine, *One Who Survived,* pp. 193-94.

82.   After Litvinov lost control of the NKID in 1937 the situation changed and NKVD agents were once again given license to expand their covert operations, using diplomatic posts as cover. See *Report of the Royal Commission Appointed under Order in Council P.C. 411 of February 4, 1946. . .* (Ottawa, 1946); Aleksandr Kaznacheev, *Inside A Soviet Embassy: Experiences of a Russian Diplomat in Burma* (Philadelphia and New York, 1962), passim; Vladimir and Evdokia Petrov, *Empire of Fear* (New York, 1956), ch. XXII and passim; and Dallin, *Soviet Espionage,* ch. VIII-IX.

83.   Barmine, *One Who Survived,* pp. 278 and 195.

7

THE DESTRUCTION
OF THE NARKOMINDEL

The structure of the Narkomindel was modified in detail during the 1930s, but the overall functioning of the NKID remained much the same. Chicherin formally retired as Foreign Commissar on 21 July 1930, to be succeeded by his Deputy, Litvinov. In actuality, Litvinov had already replaced his ailing chief during the two preceding years. In May of 1934 the NKID lost its Collegium in a government-wide reorganization which involved the abolition of collegia in all the People's Commissariats.[1] Litvinov retained the services of two principal assistants, Krestinskii as First Deputy Commissar and Boris Stomoniakov as Second Deputy Commissar. The motives of the government in abolishing the collegia in all the commissariats probably had nothing to do with the NKID, but the foreign office was included in the directive for the sake of uniformity. Just four years later collegia were reintroduced into all commissariats.[2] The political-geographic departments of the Narkomindel were also reorganized along the following lines in the early 1930s:

The First Western Department — for relations with Scandinavia, the Baltic and Finland,

The Second Western Department — for the Balkans, Czechoslovakia, Austria, Germany, Switzerland, Luxembourg and the low countries,

The Third Western Department — dealing with France, Italy, Great Britain, the British Commonwealth and the Americas,

The First Eastern Department — for relations with countries of the Near and Middle East,

The Second Eastern Department — for Mongolia, Tannu-Tuva and the Far East.[3]

In addition, a Department of International Problems was created in the early 1930s to deal with international diplomatic conferences. It was apparently replaced in 1935 by a new subdivision of the NKID

Secretariat — the Service for League of Nations Affairs.[4] The Economic and Legal Department was divided into two separate components as it had been in the early days of the Commissariat.

The only other significant structural modification of the Narkomindel involved the abolition of Soviet consulates abroad and the reciprocal closing of foreign consulates in the USSR. The middle and late 1930s, the period of the Great Purges, was a time of spy-scares, xenophobia and general insecurity within Soviet society. The Stalinist regime wanted to limit contacts between its citizens and foreigners to a minimum and it also wished to prevent inquisitive foreign consular officials from uncovering embarrassing examples of the horrors of collectivization, rapid industrialization and the purges. By the end of 1938 the foreign diplomatic colony was strictly limited to the environs of Moscow. The NKVD did its best to isolate the foreign diplomats from any but the most superficial contact with the Soviet people.[5]

While the consular service shrunk to nothing, the number of Soviet diplomatic missions continued to expand. Litvinov's greatest victory in this regard was the establishment of diplomatic relations with the United States in 1933.[6] The USSR also exchanged diplomats with Spain and Uruguay in that same year. Then, in 1934, Hungary, Rumania, Bulgaria, Albania and Czechoslovakia accorded de jure recognition to the Soviet Union, and in 1935 Colombia, Belgium and Luxembourg followed suit. The Narkomindel's representatives also began to attend the major international conferences between 1927 and 1934, and in the latter year the USSR finally joined the League of Nations.

The decade also witnessed a substantial reorientation in Soviet foreign policy. The Kremlin leadership at first followed a cautious and conciliatory approach toward the new Hitler regime in Germany, even to the extent of passively watching the massacre of the KPD without protest. The anti-Soviet character of the Führer's policy, however, forced the USSR to abandon the Rapallo line and seek an accommodation with the Western democracies. Japanese aggression in the Far East also began to stir fears in Moscow of the harrowing possibility of a two front war. After the Soviet entry into the League, Litvinov became the most eloquent tribune at Geneva for collective action against the fascist menace. The Narkomindel launched a parallel campaign to secure bilateral treaties of mutual defense. The 1935 mutual assistance pacts with France and

Czechoslovakia were the notable successes of this approach, while the failure to reach a similar agreement with Great Britain was its signal defeat.[7]

THE END OF A GENERATION OF SOVIET DIPLOMATS

Georgii Chicherin and his assistants had constructed a well-functioning foreign ministry and recruited a capable group of diplomats during the first thirteen years after the October revolution. Commissar Chicherin's work and the continuing efforts of his successor, Maksim Litvinov, were completely undone, however, by the Great Purges of 1937-38 which decimated the Soviet diplomatic corps and completely smashed the Narkomindel organization in Moscow. The diplomatic world was shocked when, one by one, the most able representatives of the USSR began to disappear into the maw of the *Ezhovshchina*. Between 1925 and 1936 the foreign office had issued an annual personnel register, the *Ezhegodnik NKID/Annuaire diplomatique*. Its publication was discontinued in 1936, obviously to prevent embarrassment, since the list of Stalin's victims read like a who's who of Soviet diplomats.

The victims included Deputy Foreign Commissars Krestinskii and Sokol'nikov; as well as former Deputy Commissar and then ambassador to Turkey Karakhan, ambassador to Finland E.A. Asmus, ambassador to Hungary Aleksandr Bekzadian, ambassador to Latvia Stefan Brodovskii, ambassador to Poland Ia. Kh. Davtian, ambassador to Norway I.S. Iakubovich, ambassador to Germany K.K. Iurenev, ambassador to Turkey Mikhail Karskii, ambassador to Rumania M.S. Ostrovskii, ambassador to Spain Marsel' Rozenberg, ambassador to Afghanistan B.E. Skvirskii, ambassador to Mongolia V.K. Tairov and ambassador to Denmark Nikolai Tikhmenev; and Narkomindel department heads V.N. Barkov (Chief of Protocol), E.A. Gnedin (Press Chief), D.G. Shtern (of the Second Western Division) and V.M. Tsukerman (of the Central Asian Division), to name only a few of the more prominent officials. Some legations, most notably the Soviet mission in republican Spain, were completely decimated, while at the Commissariat in Moscow certain departments (e.g. the Third Western Division) experienced three or four changes in command within twenty months. Diplomats serving abroad were recalled without warning while those working in the Commissariat's Moscow offices often simply vanished.[8] They were arrested and either executed or imprisoned in the infamous camps.

Most of them disappeared into the anonymity which shrouded the whole purge operation, although a few (e.g. Krestinskii and Sokol'nikov) were put on display at the show trials. It was even rumored in 1938 that a special trial of diplomats was in preparation which would feature Antonov-Ovseenko, the Soviet Consul-General in Barcelona and a great hero of 1917, though such a spectacle never materialized.[9]

Despite the grim rumors which circulated about the fate of their colleagues, most Soviet diplomats abroad seem to have obeyed their recall orders willingly enough, although a few may well have been kidnapped from their own embassies by the NKVD.[10] Their acquiescence was undoubtedly caused by a variety of motives — for many, their sense of duty; for others, disbelief that such horrors could occur in the homeland of socialism; or alternatively, that the purges would affect them; and, in some cases, the simple lack of viable alternatives. To avoid difficulties the government cunningly lured many of its representatives home. M.S. Ostrovskii, Soviet ambassador to Rumania, refused his summons until he received assurances of his future safety from Marshal Voroshilov. The Marshal's promises notwithstanding, Ostrovskii was arrested at the border.[11] Fedor Raskol'nikov, Soviet ambassador in Bulgaria, refused to return to Russia, fleeing instead to France, only to die within a few months under suspicious circumstances.[12] The Soviet Chargé d'Affaires in Athens, Aleksandr Barmin, was more fortunate than many of his associates. He made good his escape, became an American citizen, and wrote a popular volume of memoirs about his grizzly experiences.[13]

The years of the 'great terror' were filled with grim ironies for the diplomats. Not only were Litvinov and his colleagues powerless in the face of the onslaught, the Foreign Commissariat was even forced to justify the slaughter and to aid in its execution. Soviet representatives who lived in fear of their own recall were obliged to assure foreigners as to the justice of the trials and of the guilt of their condemned comrades.[14] Similarly, in 1937 the Consular Division of the NKID issued a certificate to the effect that Kjeller Airdrome near Oslo could and did receive civilian flights even during the winter. This certificate was used by the state in the trial of Piatakov in support of his confession that he had flown to Norway in December of 1935 for a secret meeting with Trotskii. Critics of the trial had pointed out that the airfield in question was not serviceable in the winter.[15]

The extreme secrecy which surrounded most of the purges — the fact that many victims became 'unpersons' — makes it difficult to assess their impact on the Soviet diplomatic service with a great degree of precision. A few tentative judgments will be advanced, however. Considering all responsible officials who comprised the Commissariat's staff throughout the 1920s, there is reliable evidence that at least 20 percent of this group was purged. (In this context the term 'purge' implies arrest followed by execution, imprisonment or exile, but not the transfers and minor demotions that are common to the organizational politics of any large bureaucratic entity.) For an additional 14 percent of these employees it is possible to obtain detailed career information from some point in the 1920s but abruptly terminating in 1937 or 1938. It seems reasonably safe to assume that they, too, were purge victims. Adding these two categories together, it appears that at least 34 percent of the Narkomindel's entire staff was purged. The available data further indicate that 7 percent of the total group under consideration were definitely not purged (i.e. they are known to have survived, escaped arrest, and maintained positions in government or party service). Also 14 percent of the group either died or defected to the West before the Great Purges began. Unfortunately this analysis leaves fully 45 percent of the group unaccounted for. In the main, these were lower grade diplomats and departmental staff employees within the Commissariat who were visible in the relatively open 1920s, but for whom adequate career data are lacking for the 1930s. Some of this group undoubtedly suffered in the purges, but it is impossible to determine what proportion.

The picture becomes much clearer, however, if the sample taken for analysis includes only the elite of the foreign service (i.e. Commissars, Deputy Commissars, Collegium members and ambassadors — well over one hundred people for the 1920s). Within this group 44 percent definitely are known to have been purged, while another 18 percent are likely victims since they disappeared at the height of the terror. Thus, on one hand, a minimum of 62 percent of these top level diplomats and Commissariat officials fell in the *Ezhovshchina*. On the other hand, only 16 percent of this sample remained at their posts unscathed (though not necessarily without some loss in influence or rank), and another 14 percent avoided destruction either by defecting or by dying before the purges occurred. This leaves only 8 percent in the 'insufficient information' category.

The general impression among contemporary foreign observers of the Great Terror was that the Narkomindel, together with the Soviet military officer corps, was hit harder by this political holocaust than any other branch of the government or the party apparatus. Severyn Bialer speculates that '. . .in the prevailing paranoiac atmosphere of spy-hunting. . .', diplomats were inevitable targets because of their constant contact with foreigners, many of whom were presumed to have been foreign intelligence agents.[16] However, Roy Medvedev's recent study of the purge era demonstrates that the damage was extensive in every commissariat.[17] The foreign service and the Red Army may only have appeared especially ill-favored to the outside world because of the high visibility of diplomats and generals.

In order to effect a thorough purging, the Narkomindel was infiltrated at the highest levels by the NKVD. Actually, Stalin and the secret police had long maintained a network of informers in the diplomatic ranks. For example, Konstantin Umanskii, of the NKID Press Department, was surreptitiously referred to as *'Chekistik'* (the little Chekist) by his colleagues because he was widely suspected to have been not only an informer, but a *provocateur* as well.[18] Yet when the terror began in earnest, mere spies were no longer sufficient. In 1937 Vasilii Korzhenko, a political police official, was placed in charge of the Commissariat's Personnel Department. Korzhenko's daughter relates that he 'was not concerned with diplomacy but had absolute power over Foreign Office employees from cipher clerks to ambassadors. . .not only in Moscow but throughout the world. . . . Father's job was to see that everyone kept the party line. If they made one slip, he put through an order for their immediate recall and banishment.'[19] Subsequently Korzhenko, himself, was purged and replaced by an even more powerful veteran Chekist, Vladimir Dekanozov, who became Deputy Commissar of Foreign Affairs in 1939.[20] Most Soviet diplomats in the field were purged during the *Ezhovshchina,* from mid-1936 through 1938, while the Narkomindel's central staff was effectively destroyed by Dekanozov in 1939. In that year the American Embassy in Moscow reported to Washington that 'with only few exceptions, almost the entire staff of the Commissariat has changed since Molotov assumed the functions of the Commissariat for Foreign Affairs. . . . Among the minor officials of the Foreign Office at least 90 percent have been replaced since the appointment of Molotov.'[21]

This radical displacement of personnel combined with the atmosphere of terror must have brought the normal functioning of Soviet diplomacy almost to a complete halt. Reflecting on the period just before his own defection in 1937, Barmin comments:

> I was uneasy, for I was conscious of a mysterious process developing in my own country. The Commissariat of Foreign Affairs seemed to be suffering from a strange torpor. For some months I had been left without instructions or information. Krestinskii, deputy to Foreign Commissar Litvinov, had just been relieved of his post. The signature of Stern, director of the German and Balkan Department, had suddenly ceased to appear to official documents. My dispatches remained unanswered.[22]

American diplomats reported that the *Ezhovshchina* had so paralyzed the Narkomindel that Russia's representatives could no longer be relied upon either to explain Soviet policies adequately or to convey foreign views to the Kremlin with any precision. Loy Henderson, the American Chargé in Moscow, commented that, 'Some of the officials of the People's Commissariat for Foreign Affairs are so patently in abject terror that one must pity them. They fear to talk on almost any subject and apparently dread meeting foreign visitors, particularly those from the local diplomatic corps.'[23] Pierrepont Moffat of the State Department's Division of European Affairs was equally critical in his assessment of Dmitrii S. Chuvakhin, the First Secretary who then headed the Soviet Embassy in Washington: 'I have talked with Henderson about the Soviet Chargé. His name is Chuvakhin. Henderson confirms my impression that he is thoroughly scared and not the sort of man who would either trust his own judgment or assume any responsibility. I asked Henderson if he could get a message straight; Henderson replied definitely in the negative.'[24]

The Nazi-Soviet Pact of August 1939, an extremely delicate affair handled with great skill by the Russians, constitutes the one major exception to this general picture of disorganization and immobilizing fear. It should be noted, however, that at the crucial stages these negotiations were handled directly by Stalin and his protégé, Molotov. The only experienced Soviet diplomat to play a significant role in these *pourparlers* was G.A. Astakhov, the Embassy Counsellor in Berlin, and he was involved principally in the preliminaries.[25] In the main, the devastated Commissariat of Foreign Affairs was hard pressed to carry out even the most elementary diplomatic tasks.

Amidst this general chaos and carnage, only a few prominent Soviet diplomats managed, inexplicably, to survive: Commissar Litvinov and his Deputy, Vladimir Potemkin, as well as Soviet ambassador to Sweden Aleksandra Kollontai, ambassador to Great Britain Ivan Maiskii, ambassador to France Iakov Surits, ambassador to Italy Boris Shtein, ambassador to the United States Aleksandr Troianovskii and Counsellor at the Embassy in Washington Konstantin Umanskii. Certainly this tiny nucleus did provide a bare minimum of continuity between the pre- and post-purge diplomatic corps, and they also served to train the new generation of Soviet diplomats. It is impossible, though, to tell why these particular individuals escaped the Great Purges. There seems to have been little correlation between a diplomat's chances for survival and his past political associations. While one surviving diplomat, Sergei Kavtaradze, was widely known as a crony of Stalin, Maiskii and Potemkin were former Mensheviks and Troianovskii had maintained connections with Bukharin. Even Ilia Ehrenburg, a close friend of Litvinov, was baffled as to why the Foreign Commissar was spared while his whole organization was destroyed. 'Why, having put to death almost all of Litvinov's assistants, did he [Stalin] not have the obstreperous Maxim himself shot? It is extremely puzzling, certainly Litvinov expected a different ending. From 1937 until his last illness he kept a revolver on his bedside table because, if there were to be a ring at the door in the night, he was not going to wait for what came after.'[26]

Even those diplomats who managed to avoid the ravages of the *Ezhovshchina* now found their role and influence in Soviet diplomacy totally eclipsed by new men. Litvinov lost all touch with the foreign policy-making process after his forced retirement as Commissar in 1939. Although he continued to serve as the nominal chief of the party Central Committee's Foreign Affairs Information Bureau and as a deputy on the Supreme Soviet, he was rarely seen in public and was clearly out of favor at the Kremlin.[27] Litvinov was also dropped from the Central Committee in February of 1941 for 'inability to discharge obligations'. The former Commissar was rescued from anonymity and given the crucial Washington embassy later that same year, however, when the fortunes of war brought Russia into alliance with the Western powers. Nonetheless, Litvinov's influence remained quite limited. He complained to the American Under Secretary of State, Sumner Welles, '. . .that he was unable to communicate with Stalin, whose isolation bred a distorted view of the West. . .'.[28] He was recalled in 1943 and replaced by the young Andrei Gromyko. Litvinov continued to hold the title of Deputy Foreign Minister, but according to Ehrenburg, he was left to languish in bureaucratic backwaters and soon pensioned off.[29] At about the same time Ivan Maiskii lost his post in London to another novice diplomat, F.T. Gusev. Maiskii was 'promoted' to Deputy Commissar and assigned to relatively minor tasks in connection with the reparations problem — much to his surprise and against his will.[30] Other Narkomindel veterans (e.g. Shtein, Surits, Troianovskii) who had held prestigious ambassadorial appointments, now found themselves relegated to minor functions deep within the bowels of the Commissariat. Thus, by the end of 1943 the Chicherin-Litvinov generation of Soviet diplomats had almost entirely passed from the scene.[31]

This mass exodus of the older generation opened the Narkomindel to the entrance of a new one. Between 1937 and 1944 a new, Stalinist Narkomindel was created. In these years the Commissariat, soon to be renamed the Ministry of Foreign Affairs, was flooded with inexperienced but eager recruits who quickly assumed responsible positions and, even today, still dominate the Soviet *corps diplomatique*. From among this group Andrei Gromyko has become the Soviet Foreign Minister, while Valerian Zorin, Nikolai Fedorenko, Iakov Malik, Arkadii Sobolev and Fedor Gusev have headed Russian embassies in major capitals around the globe. This batch of inexperienced young men was leavened with a sprinkling of high ranking Stalinists and seasoned journalists in order to provide a crucial minimum of leadership and knowledge of the outside world. For example, the prosecutor in the great purge trials, Andrei Vyshinskii, and the General Secretary of the Profintern, Solomon Lozovskii, both became Deputy Commissars under Molotov, while a veteran foreign correspondent, N.G. Pal'gunov, took over the NKID Press Department.

The profile of this second generation of Soviet diplomats differs markedly in several important respects from that of the old diplomatic corps of the Chicherin and Litvinov years. First of all, these recent recruits constituted a new generation in the most literal sense. The average age in 1938 of high ranking NKID officials who were purge victims was 55 years, while their replacements had an average age upon entering the foreign service of 33 years and a modal age of 31 years. In its early days the Narkomindel had drawn most of its personnel from the middle classes (about 70 percent), but with a significant admixture of nobles (17 percent). Workers and peasants made up only a tiny fraction (9 and 5 percent, respectively) of the corps at that time. Because of the insufficiency and unreliability of data on social class in the Stalinist period it is impossible to give exact percentages on the social origins of those diplomats recruited during or soon after the purges. However, it can be said with reasonable assurance that the sons of peasants and workers far outnumbered all others combined in this group. The two generations also differ in educational background. In the 1920s the NKID could boast that its diplomats were alumni of leading Russian, European and American universities. In contrast, many members of the new generation had no post-secondary education and those who did have advanced training typically attended various kinds of technical institutes.[32] Few of them had studied the liberal arts and almost none had attended foreign universities. The two generations of diplomats differ greatly in nationality terms as well. Only a minority (42 percent) of the veteran foreign service officers had been of Great Russian extraction, and the Commissariat had included representatives from all the important ethnic groups of the old tsarist empire. In contrast, Great Russians comprised fully 80 percent of the new recruits in the NKID.

Perhaps a more important contrast, though, was the radically different formative experiences that each group had undergone. During the Chicherin and Litvinov era most of the important diplomatic posts had gone to men of the revolutionary intelligentsia from tsarist days. Their common experiences included the underground struggle against the autocracy, long periods of exile (often abroad), the thrilling victories of the February and October revolutions in 1917 and the grim years of the Russian civil war. These men were genuine intellectuals and cosmopolitans. Almost half of them came from the ranks of the Old Bolsheviks. The 'Gromyko cohort' presents a sharp contrast. The typical member of this second generation was only twelve years old when the Bolsheviks seized power in Petrograd. These men spent the formative years of their adolescence in the NEP period of Soviet history when Stalin was besting his rivals for Lenin's mantle. Few of them were proficient in foreign languages and even fewer had traveled outside of Russia.[33] Their diverse former careers included work in industry, education, the military, other branches of government bureaucracy and the party apparatus. Gromyko had been a Senior Research Associate in agricultural economics at the Institute of Economics of the Academy of Science; N.I. Sharonov, the new Ambassador to Greece and Albania, had directed the chartering of foreign steamers for Soviet use; Vladimir Derevianskii, the new Ambassador to Finland, had been the manager of an electrode factory in Moscow. Significantly, a large proportion of them had joined the party quite recently, some as late as 1938. This is, no doubt, the reason why this group survived the Great Purges which had destroyed much of the party elite. In all these respects the second generation diplomats shared the same social, political and educational profile as other members of the post-purge generation who were flooding into the sorely depleted ranks of the government and the party.[34]

Numerous historians have hypothesized that Stalin could find widespread support for the purges and could replace his victims readily, precisely because the first generation to mature under Soviet rule was now ready and anxious to displace their elders.[35] The transition from the Chicherin-Litvinov generation to the Gromyko generation in the Soviet diplomatic service provides a good example of this phenomenon. Actually, this development had begun even before the Great Terror. A trickle of men who fit the second generation profile had entered the Narkomindel between 1931 and 1936 (e.g. Nikolai Generalov, Evgenii Rubinin, and Ivan Samylovskii). From 1937 onwards the trickle became a deluge. Apparently the Stalinist party Secretariat, which was ultimately responsible for allocating party talent, had already decided to refashion the Foreign Commissariat more to its liking. Although the *Ezhovshchina* did not initiate the process, it radically accelerated the infusion of new cadres into the Narkomindel and, thereby, drastically heightened their impact on the diplomatic service. Certainly this new 'Soviet' generation would have eventually dominated the NKID even without the purge, but it would have done so only gradually (as was the case before 1937), and it would have remained a minority within the Commissariat for several more years. Most importantly, the new men would have begun in lesser positions and received valuable in-service training under the tutelage of veteran diplomats.[36]

These changes in personnel inevitably led to an alteration in the style of the Narkomindel's operation as well. Pressed into responsible positions with no experience and little training, the novice diplomats foundered on occasion and they adopted a hyper-cautious approach to diplomacy that often led their foreign colleagues to exasperation. A drastic restriction in freedom of maneuver is one of the hallmarks of the new NKID. Even in the Stalinist 1930s, Commissar Litvinov seems to have enjoyed a reasonable degree of autonomy as the spokesman for Soviet foreign policy at Geneva. As one knowledgeable observer noted:

> Litvinov was never a member of the all-powerful Politburo in Moscow. It was often asserted by well-informed persons that he had no real influence and was merely a mouthpiece of the inner cabinet. No one who witnessed his activities in Geneva could readily believe this. It is not hard to see when a delegate is merely acting on instructions. Litvinov rarely asked for time to consult his government; he seemed always ready to decide on the spot when to press his argument, to propose a compromise, or to resign himself to accepting the majority view. It was clear that he had at least as free a hand as was generally given to the Foreign Ministers of the democratic powers.[37]

Soviet diplomats never again exercised this kind of latitude.[38] This applied even to Commissar Molotov, who at that time appears to have been one of Stalin's most trusted lieutenants. In the judgment of Gustav Hilger, a veteran German diplomat who participated along with the Soviet Foreign Commissar in the negotiation of the Nazi-Soviet Pact of 1939,

> Molotov is a highly efficient administrator, a capable executive of policies that are handed down to him, and an experienced bureaucrat. In contrast to his predecessor in the Foreign Commissariat, however, he has no creative mind. In negotiations which I witnessed or in which I took part, he never showed any personal initiative, but seemed to keep strictly to the rules laid down by Stalin. When problems came up, he would regularly say that he had to consult his 'government'.[39]

Yet another important change related to the Great Purges saw the NKID drawn deeply into espionage work. Between 1924 and approximately 1937 Soviet career diplomats remained relatively free of compromising entanglements with either revolutionary movements or covert intelligence operations.[40] With the onset of the purges, however, the NKVD moved into the Foreign Commissariat in force (Korzhenko, Dekanozov, et al.), and apparently began to involve foreign service personnel directly in their clandestine activities.[41]

The new breed of Soviet diplomats differed from their predecessors in two other important ways. They were farther removed from the decision-making process in foreign affairs, and Stalin may have perceived them to have been more reliable instruments for the execution of his policy. The Foreign Commissariat had played a significant role in policy formulation under Chicherin and Litvinov, but the purges changed all that. After 1939 the only politically influential officials in the Narkomindel were Stalin's personal representatives, Molotov and Vyshinskii. In addition, the new generation of diplomats would carry out Stalin's instructions fully and precisely (within the limits set by their abilities and lack of experience) without question or challenge. Certainly the NKID had always been efficient and reliable in the execution of official policy. Nevertheless, the pathologically suspicious dictator undoubtedly preferred totally dependent servitors to knowledgeable men capable of independent judgment.

The Great Terror accomplished the near total destruction of that talented and urbane corps of diplomats organized under Commissars Chicherin and Litvinov. The new Ministry of Foreign Affairs which emerged from the purges differed radically from its predecessor in the nature of its personnel, in the style of its diplomacy and in its relationship to the political leadership of the state.

THE GREAT PURGES AND FOREIGN POLICY

Some scholars have suggested that the purge of the Soviet foreign office must have been part of Stalin's on-going campaign to crush his opponents. They have emphasized the supposedly oppositionist stance of the Narkomindel as the primary motive for its destruction.[42] This view must be rejected on two grounds. First, it fails to harmonize with the general nature of the purges. Several recent studies have shown that the destruction of genuinely oppositionist factions was a minor theme of the purges (even though most victims were *accused* of left or right deviationism), since these groups had already been destroyed or paralyzed much earlier. The main thrust of the Great Terror of 1937-38 was directed against the Stalinists themselves and against those who generally accepted Stalin's leadership.[43] Secondly, this characterization of the NKID is simply inaccurate. A detailed analysis of politics and political opinion within Chicherin's Commissariat reveals a group in which almost all elements of the Soviet political spectrum are represented, and which can in no way be labeled anti-Stalinist in the aggregate.

A more widely accepted theory identifies foreign policy considerations as a primary motive behind the Great Purges. According to this interpretation, collective security, the policy of attempting to strengthen the resolve of the League of Nations and to secure bilateral pacts (especially with Britain and France) against the menace of Nazi aggression, was never Stalin's policy. Rather, Stalin is alleged to have contemplated the Nazi-Soviet Pact in 1934 or even earlier. Such a pact, it is argued, would have been no merely defensive agreement, but an active partnership of the two 'totalitarian' powers for massive territorial aggrandizement.[44] But Stalin's path to Hitler was blocked, in this view, by a moderate faction in the Politburo which apparently enforced the collective security campaign against his will. Hence, the Great Terror. By destroying the veteran Bolshevik cadres whose ideological scruples are said to have blocked an agreement with Nazi Germany, Stalin is supposed to have freed himself for a sinister deal with Hitler in 1939. The show trials then served as a signal to Hitler that Stalin was ready for an alliance.[45]

The nature of the purges, far from demonstrating the validity of this thesis, points in the opposite direction. First of all, the fact that the *Ezhovshchina* significantly diminished the national power and prestige of the USSR seems to indicate that it was not motivated by foreign policy considerations. The destruction of the officer corps and much of the technical intelligentsia substantially weakened the bargaining position of the Russians in seeking an alliance with either the Western powers or Hitler. Secondly, if the Great Terror is construed as a prerequisite to the Nazi-Soviet Pact, then its impact on the Narkomindel is inexplicable. Certainly Litvinov and some of his associates were closely identified with a strongly anti-German interpretation of collective security.[46] They were, in a sense, pro-British. But, there was also the pro-German, Chicherin faction of the NKID which, although its dean had retired from the diplomatic service, could have been restored to its former leading role in the Commissariat. The purge of the diplomatic corps, however, did just the opposite. The pro-Rapallo wing of the Narkomindel (Krestinskii,[47] Karakhan, et al.) was completely destroyed, while Anglophiles like Litvinov and Maiskii and Germanophobes like Kollontai survived! The arrest of Karl Radek is significant in this context as well. Radek, though not formally a diplomat, had been instrumental previously in bringing Moscow and Berlin together and he had even participated in an earlier, ill-starred campaign for fascist-communist cooperation.[48]

Finally, the contention that a purge of the Bolshevik elite was necessary before any agreement with Hitler could be negotiated is insupportable.[49] The Peace of Brest-Litovsk had created considerable controversy in party circles but, as a necessity for the physical security of the regime, it had been signed nonetheless. In Marxist terms the Nazi dictatorship of the 1930s was neither more nor less suitable as a treaty partner for a 'workers' state' than imperial Germany had been in 1918. Bukharin and his faction would certainly have noisily opposed any deal with Nazism, but would they have been any more effective then than they had been in decrying the collectivization of agriculture (which had led to a full-scale civil war in the countryside and which both the left and right oppositions had attacked)? The purges, either in general or in the diplomatic corps specifically, simply make no sense in terms of *any* foreign policy objectives.

There is an alternative explanation of the Great Purges which does seem to fit what is known of their impact on the Commissariat of Foreign Affairs. In an apparent departure from his earlier emphasis on foreign policy motives, Robert Tucker has laid the groundwork in his admirable, recent biography of Stalin's early years for an interpretation of the purges as primarily a psychological phenomenon — a bloody trauma necessary to bring Russia's external view of Stalin and his own internal image of himself into alignment. In Tucker's words, 'In the terror of the thirties, untold thousands of loyal party members and other Soviet citizens would have to be condemned as covert enemies of the people so that Djugashvili could prove to himself and Russia that he was really Stalin.'[50] The purges may well have been a bloody exercise in biographical revision — an attempt to eliminate from public life those who knew (and could not repress the knowledge) how small had been Stalin's role in 1917, or how badly he had bungled some of his responsibilities during the civil war, or how little weight his opinions on foreign affairs had carried in the early 1920s. Fortunately for Stalin, his decision to deal with that generation of Old Bolsheviks (who had often wounded his ego and who could never accept his self-image as reality) coincided with the emergence of the first generation to mature under Soviet rule.[51] These latter young men absorbed the 'cult of personality' with their school assignments. After graduation they learned quickly that the Stalinist course was also the route to their own advancement. In that the Narkomindel of Chicherin and Litvinov was dominated by the old revolutionary intelligentsia, a cosmopolitan and cultured assemblage, its destruction helped Stalin to remodel the party in his own image.

NOTES

1. *Sbornik zakonov,* series I, 1934, no. 15, article 103.
2. Towster, *Political Power in the USSR,* pp. 290-92.
3. *Ezhegodnik NKID/Annuaire diplomatique,* 1935, pp. 116-18.
4. Ibid., p. 115; and Andrei A. Gromyko et al., eds., *Diplomaticheskii slovar'* (Moscow, 1964), vol. III, p. 483.
5. Nora Murray, *I Spied for Stalin* (New York, 1951), p. 65.
6. On the establishment of Soviet-American diplomatic relations see Joan Hoff Wilson, *Ideology and Economics: U.S. Relations with the Soviet Union, 1918-1933* (Columbia, 1974), passim; and E.I. Krutitskaia and L.S. Mitrofanova, *Polpred Aleksandr Troianovskii* (Moscow, 1975), pp. 140-61.
7. On Soviet diplomacy in the 1930s see Henry L. Roberts, 'Maxim Litvinov', in: Craig and Gilbert, eds., *The Diplomats,* pp. 344-77; Duroselle, ed., *Les Relations Germano — Soviétiques;* and William Evans Scott, *Alliance Against Hitler: The Franco-Soviet Pact* (Durham, 1962).
8. Purged diplomats disappeared not only from their embassies, but from the pages of history as well. None of them was mentioned in the first edition of the *Diplomaticheskii slovar'* (Moscow, 1948), but the names of a few (e.g. Iurenev, Skvirskii) reappeared in the second edition (Moscow, 1960-64), and a few more (e.g. Davtian) were named in the third edition (Moscow, 1971). The names of such prominent purge victims as Kamenev, Rakovskii and Sokol'nikov have also been deleted from their dispatches published in *Dokumenty vneshnei politiki.*
9. Robert Conquest, *The Great Terror: Stalin's Purge of the Thirties* (New York, 1973), p. 609.
10. For an account of a foiled kidnap attempt see Barmine, *One Who Survived,* pp. 12-16.
11. Ibid., p. 21.
12. Ibid.; and R.A. Medvedev, *K sudu istorii* (New York, 1974), p. 795, n. 87. Ilia Ehrenburg claims that Raskol'nikov 'had a nervous breakdown and died'. Ilya Ehrenburg, *Memoirs: 1921-1941* (Cleveland and New York, 1963), p. 469. Also see V.S. Zaitsev, 'Geroi oktiabria i grazhdanskoi voiny', *Voprosy istorii KPSS,* 1963, no. 12, pp. 90-94.
13. See note 10 above.
14. Ivan Maiskii has noted that the purges made it difficult for him to deal with even those sections of Western public opinion usually sympathetic to the USSR. See B.

Shou i drugie: vospominaniia (Moscow, 1967), pp. 82-83.

15. See *Report of the Court Proceedings in the Case of the Anti-Soviet Trotskyite Center* (Moscow, 1937), p. 443.

16. Severyn Bialer, 'Andrei Andreevich Gromyko', in: George Simmonds, ed., *Soviet Leaders* (New York, 1967), p. 166.

17. Medvedev, *Let History Judge,* ch. VI.

18. Reswick, *I Dreamt Revolution,* pp. 153-54.

19. Murray, *I Spied for Stalin,* p. 83.

20. See M. Loginov, 'Kul't lichnost chuzhd nashemu stroiu', *Molodoi kommunist,* 1962, no. 1, pp. 53-54.

21. *Foreign Relations of the United States: The Soviet Union, 1933-1939* (Washington, 1952), p. 772.

22. Barmine, *One Who Survived,* p. 3.

23. Henderson to Secretary of State, 10 June 1937, USDS 861.00/11705.

24. Moffat to Sumner Welles, 3 August 1939, USDS 701.6111/954.

25. For a thorough discussion of these negotiations see Gerhard L. Weinberg, *Germany and the Soviet Union, 1939-1941* (Leiden, 1954), pp. 4-52.

26. Ilya Ehrenburg, *The Post-War Years, 1945-1954* (London, 1966), p. 277. N.S. Khrushchev alleges that the NKVD actually planned to murder Litvinov, disguising the crime as a traffic accident. Khrushchev does not explain why these plans were never carried out. *Khrushchev Remembers* (Boston, 1970), p. 278.

27. Louis Fischer notes that 'Litvinov retired to a bungalow in the woods outside Moscow. He played much bridge, learned to type, read poetry and fiction, and took long walks. He was completely isolated from Soviet politics.' See Fischer, *The Life and Death of Stalin,* p. 56. This picture is confirmed by Ehrenburg, *Post-War Years,* pp. 276-78.

28. Vojtech Mastny, 'The Cassandra in the Foreign Commissariat: Maxim Litvinov and the Cold War', *Foreign Affairs,* 54, 2, p. 368; and *Foreign Relations of the United States, 1943,* vol. III, pp. 522-24.

29. Ehrenburg, *Post-War Years,* p. 279.

30. Ivan Maisky, *Memoirs of A Soviet Ambassador, The War: 1939-1943* (New York, 1967), pp. 365-81. Maiskii left the Ministry of Foreign Affairs in 1946 when he was elected a member of the prestigious Academy of Sciences. He was subsequently arrested in February of 1953 in what may have been the advent of a new Great Purge. Stalin died just two weeks later, but Maiskii remained in custody until his trial in the summer of 1955. Although charged with treason and espionage, he was found guilty only of certain 'errors' in the performance of his former diplomatic duties, and sentenced to six years in prison. Maiskii was immediately pardoned by the Presidium of the Supreme Soviet, reinstated in the party, and permitted to resume his academic work. See Alexander Nekrich, 'The Arrest and Trial of I.M. Maisky', *Survey,* 1976, XXII, 3-4, pp. 313-20.

31. Historians differ in their estimates as to why Stalin chose to remove the last remnant of Narkomindel veterans from major responsibilities in 1943. Adam Ulam argues that Stalin's post-Teheran confidence in his ability to deal with the Western leaders made him feel less dependent on the old-line, professional diplomats. See Ulam, *Stalin ,* p. 292. Ehrenburg believes that the withdrawal of such pro-Western ambassadors as Litvinov and Maiskii was intended as a sign of Stalin's displeasure over the continued postponement of a second front in France. Ehrenburg, *The War:*

1941-1945 (Cleveland and New York, 1964), p. 119. Vojtech Mastny has gone so far as to suggest that the dismissal of these two living symbols of inter-Allied cooperation may have been intended by Stalin as a signal to Hitler of Russia's willingness to consider a separate peace. Mastny, 'The Cassandra in the Foreign Commissariat', p. 368.

32. For example, Anatoly Dobrynin graduated with a degree in engineering from the Aviation Institute. His subsequent assignment to the Narkomindel came as a complete and apparently not altogether pleasing surprise. Iakov Malik graduated from the Kharkov Institute of National Economy, while Arkadii Sobolev received his diploma from the Leningrad Electrical Engineering Institute.

33. Charles E. Bohlen, who served in the American Embassy in Moscow during the purges, comments: 'Most of the new officials seem to have been selected because of their non-experience or non-connection with foreign affairs. Among the new officials mentioned in an Embassy dispatch was Andrei Gromyko. This was the first time, I think, that anyone had ever heard the name Gromyko in the foreign service of the Soviet Union. During this period, he came to lunch at Spaso House, and I think it was the first time he had ever had a meal with foreigners. It was quite apparent that Gromyko, a professor of Economics, had virtually no knowledge of foreign affairs. He was ill at ease and obviously fearful of making some social blunder during the luncheon.' Bohlen, *Witness to History, 1929-1969* (New York, 1973), p. 65. Also see David Kelly, *The Ruling Few: Or the Human Background to Diplomacy* (London, 1952), p. 374.

34. For example, new recruits into the party apparatus showed many of these same career characteristics. Cf. Schapiro, *The Communist Party of the Soviet Union*, pp. 440-44; and A.L. Unger, 'Stalin's Renewal of the Leading Stratum: A Note on the Great Purge', *Soviet Studies*, 1969, XX, 3, pp. 321-30.

35. There is no evidence, however, that the purge of the Narkomindel was either caused or greatly expanded by ruthless careerism. For the most part the new generation of diplomats was brought into the Commissariat from outside in order to replace veterans who had already been purged or were foredoomed if still in place.

36. A statistical profile of the Narkomindel staff in 1933, published by the government, showed that the personnel characteristics of the Commissariat were changing only gradually since Chicherin's retirement. The foreign office was still a bourgeois stronghold, although the percentage of responsible officials from working class backgrounds had risen from 9 to 19 percent. The educational level of the NKID remained high, too, with nearly 60 percent of its officials having graduated from one or another sort of higher educational institution. See *Sostav rukovodiashchikh rabotnikov i spetsialistov soiuza SSR*, pp. 296-303.

37. F.P. Walters, *A History of the League of Nations* (London, 1952), vol. I, pp. 358-59.

38. Philip E. Mosely, who served with many of these new generation Soviet diplomats on various inter-Allied commissions at the close of World War II, described them as men with no initiative or latitude in negotiations who were hamstrung by their instructions from Moscow. He noted, too, that they lacked knowledge or understanding of foreign nations and that they were uncomfortable — even 'wooden' — in negotiating. They also seemed nearly paralyzed by the fear of failure. See Mosely, *The Kremlin and World Politics* (New York, 1960), pp. 3-41. Also see Stephen D. Kertesz, 'Reflections on Soviet and American Negotiating Behavior', *The Review of Politics*, 1957, XIX, 1, pp. 3-36. Not surprisingly, Litvinov was also highly critical of the men who had replaced him at the top of the Narkomindel apparatus. He told an American

journalist that the Foreign 'Commissariat is run by three men [i.e. Molotov, Vyshinskii and Dekanozov] and none of them understand America or Britain'. Quoted in Mastny, 'Cassandra', p. 371.

39. Hilger and Meyer, *Incompatible Allies,* p. 290.

40. See Chapter 6 in this volume, and Alexandre Barmine, 'A Russian View of the Moscow Trials', *International Conciliation: Documents for the Year 1938,* no. 337, pp. 48-49.

41. Iakov Malik is a good example of the new generation of Soviet diplomats who were willing to carry out, and even to supervise, covert espionage operations. See Jack Anderson and Les Whitten, 'Soviet U.N. Envoy Linked to Spying', *The Washington Post,* 11 February 1975.

42. Aspaturian, *Process and Power,* pp. 628-30. This view of the Narkomindel is shared by David J. Dallin, *From Purge to Coexistence* (Chicago, 1964), p. 212.

43. Cohen, *Bukharin and the Bolshevik Revolution,* p. 346; and Ulam, *Stalin,* p. 393.

44. Robert C. Tucker, 'Stalin, Bukharin and History as Conspiracy', in: *The Great Purge Trial* (New York, 1956), p. xxxvi. Also see Slusser, 'Role of the Foreign Ministry', pp. 214-30; and George F. Kennan, *Russia and the West under Lenin and Stalin* (New York, 1961), pp. 288-91 and 296. For earlier expressions of this interpretation of the purges see Boris Nikolaevskii, 'Stalin i ubiistvo kirova', *Sotsialisticheskii vestnik,* 1956, no. 10, p. 186 and no. 12, pp. 239-40; Franz Borkenau, *European Communism* (New York, 1953), pp. 117, 132-35 and 234-35; W.G. Krivitsky, *I Was Stalin's Agent* (London, 1939), pp. 18-34 and 37-40; and Erich Wollenberg, *The Red Army: A Study of the Growth of Soviet Imperialism* (London, 1940), p. 237. Cf. Daniels, *The Conscience of the Revolution,* p. 382. Daniels moots the opposite possibility, namely that '. . .fear of criticism of his [Stalin's] impending alliance with democratic forces abroad, contributed to his decision to liquidate the oppositionists'.

45. Tucker, 'Stalin, Bukharin and History as Conspiracy', pp. xxxvi-xxxix; and Slusser, 'Role of the Foreign Ministry', p. 231.

46. For discussions of Litvinov's political orientation and his role in Soviet diplomacy see Girardet, 'Litvinov et ses énigmes', pp. 103-35; and Roberts, 'Maxim Litvinov', pp. 344-77.

47. Krestinskii is an especially good example of a pro-German diplomat who fell victim to the purges. The staff of the German embassy in Moscow considered him an important advocate of Russo-German cooperation. See Herbert von Dirksen, *Moscow, Tokyo, London: Twenty Years of German Foreign Policy* (London, 1957), p. 91. For instance, it was Krestinskii who, as Deputy Commissar of Foreign Affairs, had tried to prevent the rapid deterioration of relations between the USSR and Hitler's Germany in October of 1933. The Führer, however, had no interest in a rapprochement with the Soviet Union. Krestinskii's aborted mission to Berlin is discussed in Gerhard L. Weinberg, *The Foreign Policy of Hitler's Germany: Diplomatic Revolution in Europe, 1933-36* (Chicago, 1970), p. 81. At his trial Krestinskii was, of course, accused of striving '. . .to hamper, hinder and prevent the normalization of relations between the Soviet Union and Germany along normal diplomatic lines. . .'. Tucker and Cohen, eds., *The Great Purge Trial,* p. 51. This seems to have been precisely the reverse of the truth.

48. Radek's role in Russo-German relations and his dealings with various right-wing circles in Germany are described in Lerner, *Karl Radek.*

49. Even Litvinov, that undisputed champion of collective security, had hinted at the possibility of a rapprochement with Germany when he said 'We certainly have our own opinion about the German regime. We certainly are sympathetic toward the suffering of our comrades [i.e. the KPD]; but you can reproach us Marxists least of all for permitting our sympathies to rule our policy. All the world knows that we can and do maintain good relations with capitalist governments of any regime including Fascist. We do not interfere in the internal affairs of Germany or of any other countries, and our relations with her are determined not by her domestic but by her foreign policy.' M.M. Litvinov, *Vneshniaia politika SSSR* (Moscow, 1935), p. 70.

50. Tucker, *Stalin as Revolutionary,* p. 493.

51. Stalin's letter of 1925 to Arkadi Maslow, a leader of the German Communist Party, gives early evidence both of his low regard for the intelligentsia and of his plans for remolding Soviet elites. 'We in Russia have also had a dying away of a number of old leaders from among the *littérateurs* and the old "chiefs". . . . This is a necessary process for a renewal of the leading cadres of a living and developing party.' I.V. Stalin, *Sochineniia,* vol. VII, p. 43. Also see Stalin, *Sochineniia* (Stanford, 1967), vol. I (XIV), p. 245.

8

CONCLUSION

At its inception in October of 1917 the People's Commissariat of Foreign Affairs was intended to be little more than an agency for the dissemination of propaganda and the publication of the secret treaties of the Entente. Contrary to expectations, by 1930 the Narkomindel had become a typical European diplomatic establishment, closely paralleling in form and function the British Foreign Office or the Quai d'Orsay. In 1917 the Bolsheviks had confidently expected that the rest of Europe's exploited proletariat would soon follow their example in throwing off the oppressive yoke of the aristocrats and capitalists. The Russian communists had misinterpreted the situation in the advanced industrial nations, however. Although serious disturbances flared up throughout Europe at the close of World War I, the rebellions were either crushed or, where successful, channeled along nationalist or liberal democratic lines. The Soviet Union was destined to remain an isolated outpost of communism for decades. As the prospects of world revolution receded ever further into the future, Lenin and his followers were forced to adopt a policy of defending the lone socialist state by any means available, including the arts of traditional, bourgeois diplomacy. The Narkomindel developed in response to this need to protect the RSFSR while the revolutionary movement in the West was given more time to mature.

Trotskii, Chicherin, Zalkind and their comrades, who were responsible for organizing the Commissariat of Foreign Affairs, created the new institution in an ad hoc fashion, responding to the needs of the moment. There was little in the pre-revolutionary writings on Marxism-Leninism to guide their work since the revolutionaries had planned to overthrow the bourgeois international state system rather than to participate in it. Lenin's *Imperialism* provided a general interpretation of world politics in the era of advanced capitalism but it had nothing to say about the practice or institutions of 'socialist diplomacy'. In the absence of guidance, the organizational structure of the Commissariat was patterned, for the most part, on that of its tsarist predecessor. The Functional divisions were set up to handle the administrative problems common to any bureaucracy, while geographic units were established to supervise relations with various combinations of foreign countries (the border states, the Central Powers, the Western Allies, the neutrals, etc.). The only novel aspect of this structure was the institution of revolutionary propaganda agencies as part of the diplomatic service. Even in this respect, Narkomindel propagandistic activities were not entirely without precedent. Both the Auswärtiges Amt and the Quai d'Orsay had already developed their own propaganda apparatus in response to the advent of the mass circulation press and the intrusion of the general populace into international politics.[1]

Creating a foreign office in Petrograd (later in Moscow) proved to be a much easier task than establishing a network of missions abroad. The majority of diplomats in the Imperial service, as well as the appointees of the Provisional Government, were unwilling to serve the Soviet regime or even to turn over to it the funds, documents, and buildings of the Russian embassies, nor were many of the capitalist powers anxious to receive Bolshevik emissaries. It was not until the general normalization of relations with the outside world in the period from 1921 to 1924 that the Soviet government was able to establish its official representatives in the great capitals of the West.

Since only a handful of members of the tsarist diplomatic service volunteered to serve under Trotskii and Chicherin, a whole new corps of diplomats had to be recruited. The Commissariat of Foreign Affairs was fortunate to have at its disposal a body of new employees who were familiar with social and political conditions throughout Europe and who had mastered numerous foreign languages — the men of the Russian pre-revolutionary, radical emigration. These men had been forced to flee Imperial Russia because of their political beliefs and had settled in the great cities of Europe and America. They were a cosmopolitan group comprised of Great Russians, Ukrainians, White Russians, Jews, Germans and many other nationalities. They also represented the whole spectrum of pre-revolutionary Russian radical politics: Bolsheviks, Mensheviks, Socialist-Revolutionaries, even Liberals and Anarchists. These men, who filled almost all of the important posts in the Narkomindel, were overwhelmingly of middle class origin and most of them had been college educated. Their ranks were augmented by a number of foreign radicals who came to Russia to examine and to participate in the socialist experiment, and by cadres of state and party bureaucrats. The NKID was open to middle and even lower class elements, as well as women and ethnic minorities (especially Jews) to a much greater degree than were other European foreign services.[2]

Comparison of the Russian and German foreign offices in the 1920s and 1930s presents some interesting contrasts. Both the Narkomindel and the Auswärtiges Amt experienced revolutionary changes of regime, during 1917 in Petrograd and during both 1918 and 1933 in Berlin. Unlike the NKID which was thoroughly Bolshevized in the wake of the October revolution, the Wilhelmstrasse was not radically transformed after the Kaiser's fall. The so-called Schüler reforms, which were intended to open the German diplomatic service to the non-privileged strata of society and to subordinate it to republican control, never succeeded in democratizing the Auswärtiges Amt. Diplomats of pre-war vintage, especially such aristocrats as Ago von Maltzan and Karl von Schubert, continued to dominate the upper echelons of the Wilhelmstrasse. For such men Weimar was an object of toleration rather than loyalty. The National Socialist seizure of power produced no great upheaval in the German foreign office, either. The career diplomats, with notably few exceptions, proved willing to execute the new dictator's foreign policies, though none of them were Hitler's disciples. It was only after 1937 that the Nazis purged the Wilhelmstrasse and Ribbentrop achieved full control of Germany's diplomatic establishment.[3] The Narkomindel was from its inception a thoroughly integrated component of the Soviet system, whereas the Auswärtiges Amt sought to maintain a degree of independence from the Weimar and Nazi regimes.

Some scholars have suggested that the NKID was used principally by the Soviet leaders to exile their domestic opponents. Thus, a dissident Central Committee member might be appointed *Polpred* to Afghanistan and in so doing be removed from his sources of power and influence. This practice does not seem to have been very common, however. Almost all of the political currents and party factions which dominated Soviet politics in the 1920s were represented among the personnel of the NKID. Although some prominent 'oppositionist' leaders were given foreign diplomatic assignments as a means of isolating them from the struggles racking the Russian Communist

Party, the Narkomindel was not generally a place of exile or a stronghold of the opposition as some writers have claimed. The Foreign Commissariat did not play any identifiable role in Soviet politics during this period.

The Narkomindel did have an important part in the process of foreign policy formulation. The NKID was responsible for providing information on the international scene upon which the foreign policy of the USSR was based. According to the constitution, questions concerning foreign relations were to be decided by the Congress of Soviets and by the Council of People's Commissars. In actual practice Soviet foreign policy was formulated in the higher councils of the Communist Party. This does not mean, however, that the Commissariat of Foreign Affairs was merely the mechanical executor of policies handed down from above. A number of the Commissariat's higher ranking members were also part of that interlocking directorate of prominent party and government officials who formed the Soviet foreign policy elite and actually determined the course of the state in world affairs. The Narkomindel had as much or more freedom of action and influence on policy than did other European diplomatic chancelleries.[4] At the same time, the diplomatic irresponsibility which had characterized the Imperial Foreign Ministry did not recur in the NKID.

Both partisans and opponents of the Soviet Union have claimed that 'socialist diplomacy' is something qualitatively different from 'bourgeois diplomacy'. The former see the uniqueness of 'socialist diplomacy' in its openness, honesty and genuinely peaceful and humanitarian character, while the latter attack it as treacherous, deceptive or 'Byzantine'. Such polemics shed little light on the subject. The teachings of Marx and Lenin provided the Narkomindel representatives with certain attitudes (mainly hostile) toward the capitalist state system and also with some categories of analysis (monopoly capitalism, national bourgeoisie, etc.), but they presented no coherent system of diplomatic practice or theory. Soviet diplomacy in the 1920s was different from the classical diplomacy of the eighteenth and nineteenth centuries in that it was adapting itself to the 'new diplomacy' of the era of mass communications and mass participation in politics. Some early Bolshevik diplomats were deeply involved in promoting workers' insurrections in the capitals of the great powers, but as the interests of the Soviet state came to predominate over those of proletarian internationalism, the techniques and the style of the Narkomindel's diplomats became less and less distinguishable from those of their bourgeois colleagues.

In the 1920s the Commissariat of Foreign Affairs became one of the more important organs of the Soviet government. All of this would change with the advent of Stalin's domination, but while the heirs of Lenin were contesting the succession, the Narkomindel enjoyed a substantial degree of influence and independence in diplomatic matters. The fledgling Foreign Commissariat served the Soviet state well during its first decade. It secured treaties of peace and friendship with the Asian and East European neighbors of the USSR, and it won the diplomatic recognition of all the great powers except the United States. Narkomindel representatives labored tirelessly to prevent the formation of anti-Soviet coalitions and to expose the moralistic pretensions of the imperialist states. Given the initial isolation and weakness of the RSFSR, these were no mean accomplishments. Soviet diplomacy failed, however, to secure the foreign credits and technical assistance which Russia's damaged economy required. It also failed to achieve genuine security for the Soviet Union as the war scare of 1927 demonstrated. But the hopes for massive capitalist assistance in building communism and for absolute security in an age of anxiety were never realistic goals. The successes of the Narkomindel, though limited, stand as tributes to the diplomatic skill of Chicherin, Litvinov and their colleagues — the first generation of Soviet diplomacy.

NOTES

1. Lauren, *Diplomats and Bureaucrats,* pp. 91, 130-31 and 179-207. Cf. Zara Steiner, *The Foreign Office and Foreign Policy, 1898-1914* (London, 1969), pp. 211-12.

2. See Lamar Cecil, *The German Diplomatic Service, 1871-1914* (Princeton, 1976), pp. 58-68, 97-103 and 173-76; Steiner, *The Foreign Office and Foreign Policy,* pp. 16-19 and 174-75; Zara Steiner and M.L. Dockrill, 'The Foreign Office Reforms,

1919-1921', *The Journal of History*, 1974, XVII, 1, pp. 131-56; and Paul Seabury, *The Wilhelmstrasse: A Study of German Diplomats Under the Nazi Regime* (Berkeley and Los Angeles, 1954), pp. 152-53. Even in the American foreign service, blacks and women were largely excluded. Robert D. Schulzinger, *The Making of the Diplomatic Mind: The Training, Outlook, and Style of United States Foreign Service Officers, 1908-1931* (Middletown, 1975), pp. 108-10.

3. Seabury, *The Wilhelmstrasse*, pp. 9-71; Hans-Adolf Jacobsen, *Nationalsozialistische Aussenpolitik, 1933-1938* (Frankfurt a.M., 1968), pp. 252-318; Weinberg, *The Foreign Policy of Hitler's Germany*, pp. 35-36; and Craig, *War, Politics, and Diplomacy*, pp. 421 ff.

4. Alan J. Sharp, 'The Foreign Office in Eclipse, 1919-1922', *History*, 1976, LXI, 202, pp. 198-218; Steiner, *The Foreign Office and Foreign Policy*, pp. 173-76; and Cecil, *The German Diplomatic Service*, ch. VI and VII and pp. 320-22.

BIBLIOGRAPHICAL ESSAY

The official publications of the Commissariat of Foreign Affairs, supplemented by archival reports on the NKID prepared by the diplomatic and intelligence services of other countries, provide basic information about the structure of the Soviet diplomatic corps. Unfortunately three important sources — the archives of the Ministry of Foreign Affairs, the personnel files of the party Secretariat and the minutes of Central Committee and Politburo meetings — remain closed to Western investigators. Thus, it is difficult to give more than tentative answers to some questions, such as why the Narkomindel was founded in 1917 when the Bolsheviks did not foresee the establishment of normal diplomatic relations with the capitalist powers, or why certain individuals were transferred into or out of the foreign office. This lack of Soviet archival materials is compensated for, in part, by the published *Dokumenty vneshnei politiki SSSR* series and by the accounts of Soviet diplomatic activity contained in foreign archives. The American, West German and British diplomatic archives were especially useful in this regard. The intercepts of secret Narkomindel wireless messages which have been quoted and analyzed by Richard Ullman in *The Anglo-Soviet Accord* also give a picture of Soviet diplomacy rare in its candor. Finally, some archival material is contained in the more recent works of Soviet historians. Such sources are fragmentary, however, and it seems that Soviet scholars do not have free access to the full range of relevant documents in the archives of the USSR. Apparently only high officials are able to consult freely such important collections as the voluminous correspondence between Commissar Chicherin and the Central Committee.

Insights concerning the negotiating style and world view of Narkomindel members have been gleaned from the published and archival records of actual negotiations as well as from the memoirs of Soviet diplomats and their foreign colleagues. Every effort has been made to evaluate critically statements of opinion by and about Soviet diplomats. The memoir literature relating to the NKID is extensive but extremely uneven in quality. Obvious forgeries — for example, 'M. Litvinov', *Notes for a Journal* — have been discounted, while works whose internal inconsistencies and blatant rumor-mongering make them highly suspect (e.g. Bessedovsky's *Revelations of a Soviet Diplomat*) have been used with great caution. In general it has been the author's policy to accept memoir evidence on important matters only where it could be corroborated by other sources. The memoirs of two Soviet defectors, Barmin and Liberman, have proven quite valuable as have the reflections of the veteran German diplomat Gustav Hilger. Diplomatic memoirs published in the USSR (e.g. those by Aralov and Maiskii), though useful, are generally disappointing in that they tend to be eliptical, if not thoroughly tendentious, on the most crucial problems of foreign and domestic politics.

The sections dealing with the personnel composition of the Commissariat of Foreign Affairs are based on the author's compilation of biographical data on Soviet diplomats and Narkomindel officials. Sources of biographical information include autobiographies, biographies, memoirs, documents, press clippings, reference tools and works of scholarship as listed in the bibliography. The richest collections of relevant personnel data are found in the special biographical files compiled by the library of the Hoover Institution on War, Revolution and Peace at Stanford University and similar files prepared by the former Institute for the Study of the USSR in Munich. These sources are supplemented by the records of the Auswärtiges Amt in Bonn, the State Department's Decimal File housed in the United States National Archives and the British Foreign Office 'Russia Correspondence' which has been published recently on microfilm. The press clippings files of the Institut für Auswärtige Politik in Hamburg, the Institut für Weltwirtschaft an der Universität, Kiel, and the Institut für Wirtschaftsforschung in Hamburg also proved valuable.

It has been possible to compile the biographies of about 650 high and middle level foreign service officials for the years from 1917 through 1930. This 'sample' includes approximately 95 percent of all high level Commissariat officials (i.e. Commissars, Deputy Commissars, ambassadors and heads of major departments) for these years, and about 70 percent of the remaining middle level officials (i.e. secretaries and attachés, responsible officials of major departments and heads of minor departments). Although no official figures have been published, the central Narkomindel headquarters, its republican and regional offices, and the diplomatic and consular missions abroad employed around 3,000 people during the period under discussion, but the great majority of them were engaged at minor or technical posts (i.e. in Soviet terminology they were not 'responsible' officials), so they are not considered in this study. The 'sample' of diplomats included in this collective biography is obviously biased in favor of several groups (i.e. the highest ranking diplomats; diplomats having served in America, Britain or Germany where the archives are open; prominent opponents of Stalin and purge victims; and well known radicals — in short, those groups receiving the most publicity). It is not likely, however, that this bias in the sample has seriously distorted the study. The data available on diplomats who are not included in the groups mentioned above fail to highlight any marked tendencies not evidenced by the group as a whole.

The author must acknowledge his intellectual debt to those scholars who previously have written about the Narkomindel (especially Von Laue, Aspaturian, Slusser, Magerovsky, Iroshnikov, Bakhov and Chossudovskii). Although in many ways the conclusions reached in the present study vary substantially from those arrived at in these earlier treatments of the NKID, the path-breaking work of these men has materially assisted the author in his labors.

SELECTED BIBLIOGRAPHY

Archival Sources

British Foreign Office. Russia Correspondence, 1781-1945.
  Wilmington, Del.: Scholarly Resources, 1975.
Columbia University, The Oral History Collection.
  Davis, Malcolm W. 'The Reminiscences of Malcolm W. Davis.' 1950.
  Poole, DeWitt Clinton. 'The Reminiscences of DeWitt Clinton Poole.' n.d.
  White, John Campbell. 'The Reminiscences of John Campbell White.' 1953.
Germany, Auswärtiges Amt. Bonn.
  Akten betreffend: Die diplomatische Vertretung Russlands im Auslande. Bd. 19-20
    (1 Jan. 1915-Feb. 1920). Russland No. 87.
  Akten betreffend: Die diplomatischen und konsularischen Vertretungen Russlands
    in Deutschland. Bd. 1-8 (March 1920-Oct. 1931). Politik 9, Russland.
Harvard University, The Trotsky Archive.
The Hoover Institution on War, Revolution and Peace.
  Hoover Institution Library.
    Biographical files on persons connected with the Russian revolution and with
      early Soviet history.
    Perso-Russian Treaties and Notes of 1828-1931. [typescript] J. Rives Childs,
      ed. and trans.
  Hoover Institution Archives.
    The Lastours Papers.
    The V.A. Maklakov Collection.
    The Nikolaevskii Collections.
    The Okhrana Files.
    Otdel pechati narodnogo komissariata po inostrannym delam: skhemy i proekty.
      (n. p., 1927)
    The Papers of the Russian Imperial Delegation in Berlin, 1918-1930.
    Selected Items from the David R. Francis Collection at the Missouri Historical
      Society, pertaining to the Russian Revolution of 1917.
Institut für Auswärtige Politik, Hamburg, Clippings archive, file 'R-d'.
Institut für Weltwirtschaft an der Universität, Kiel.
  Russland: Politik — Äussere Politik (1/VIII/1920-31/XII/1933).
  Sowjetunion: Politik — Diplomaten und Handelsvertreter des Inlands im Ausland.
  Sowjetunion: Politik, Recht, Verwaltung — Diplomaten und Handelsvertreter d.
    Auslands im Inland.
Hamburgisches Weltwirtschaftsarchiv, Institut für Wirtschaftsforschung, Press
  clippings files and Personenarchiv.
Institute for the Study of the USSR, Munich,
  Biographical files.
Princeton University, Firestone Library. The Louis Fischer Papers.
United States National Archives
  State Department, Decimal File.

Office of Strategic Services [and subsequently Department of State], Research and Analysis reports.
Yale University Library, Fischer (Louis) Collection.

Published Documents and Documentary Collections

Akten zur Deutschen Auswärtigen Politik, 1918-1945. Serie B. Göttingen, 1966-.
Biulleten. Moscow, 1920-1922.
'Bolshevik Propaganda.' Hearings before a Subcommittee of the Committee on the Judiciary, United States Senate, 65th Congress, 3rd Session and thereafter, pursuant to S. Res. 439 and 469. February 11, 1919, to March 10, 1919. Washington, 1919.
Bunyan, James and H.H. Fisher, eds. *The Bolshevik Revolution, 1917-1918: Documents and Materials.* Stanford, 1934.
Bunyan, James T., ed. *Intervention, Civil War and Communism in Russia, April-December 1918: Documents and Materials.* Baltimore, 1936.
Chetyrnadtsatyi s"ezd vsesoiuznoi kommunisticheskoi partii (b): stenograficheskii otchet. Moscow, 1926.
Clissold, Stephen, ed. *Soviet Relations with Latin America, 1918-1968: A Documentary Survey.* London, 1970.
Cumming, C.K. and Walter W. Pettit, eds. *Russian-American Relations, March, 1917-March, 1920: Documents and Papers.* New York, 1920.
Degras, Jane, ed. *Calendar of Soviet Documents on Foreign Policy, 1917-1941.* London, 1948.
_____ *The Communist International.* 3 vols. London, 1956-1965.
_____ ed. *Soviet Documents on Foreign Policy.* 3 vols. London, 1951-1953.
Dekrety sovetskoi vlasti. Moscow, 1957-.
Desiat' let sovetskoi diplomatii: akty i dokumenty. Moscow, 1927.
'Diplomatic and Consular Law of the USSR', *Soviet Statutes and Decisions: A Journal of Translations,* III, 2-3 (Winter-Spring 1967), pp. 7-148.
Documents on British Foreign Policy, 1919-1939. Series I. 3 vols. London, 1947-1949.
'Documents on the Comintern and the Chinese Revolution', *China Quarterly,* no. 45 (1971), pp. 100-15.
Dokumenty i materialy po istorii sovetsko-chekhoslovatskikh otnoshenii. Moscow, 1963.
Dokumenty velikoi proletarskoi revoliutsii. Moscow, 1938.
Dokumenty vneshnei politiki SSSR. Moscow, 1957-.
Der I. Kongress der kommunistischen Internationale: Protokoll der Verhandlungen in Moskau vom 2. bis zum 19. März 1919. Hamburg, 1921.
Eudin, Xenia Joukoff, and Robert M. Slusser, eds. *Soviet Foreign Policy, 1928-1934: Documents and Materials.* 2 vols. University Park, 1966-1967.
Eudin, X.J., and Harold H. Fisher, eds. *Soviet Russia and the West, 1920-1927: A Documentary Survey.* Stanford, 1957.
Eudin, X.J., and Robert C. North, eds. *Soviet Russia and the East, 1920-1927: A Documentary Survey.* Stanford, 1957.
Ezhegodnik narodnogo komissariata po inostrannym delam/Annuaire diplomatique du Commissariat du peuple pour les Affaires Etrangères. Moscow, 1925-1935.

Foreign Relations of the United States, 1933-1939. Washington, 1952.

Gankin, Olga Hess and H. H. Fisher, eds. *The Bolsheviks and the World War: The Origin of the Third International.* Stanford, 1940.

Godovoi otchet za 19-- god k s"ezdu sovetov SSSR. Moscow, 1919-1924.

Gregor, Richard, ed. *Resolutions and Decisions of the Communist Party of the Soviet Union.* Vol. II. *The Early Soviet Period: 1917-1929.* Toronto and Buffalo, 1974.

Hardwick, Thomas W. *The Status and Activities of L. C. Martens, Representative of the Russian Socialist Federal Soviet Republic, as shown in the evidence before the subcommittee of the Committee on Foreign Relations of the United States Senate.* N.p., [1920].

House of Representatives. *Investigations of Communist Propaganda: Report no. 2290 from the Special Committee to investigate Communist Activities in the United States* (17 January 1931). Washington, 1931.

K russkomu narodu. Archangel, (1918).

Kliuchnikov, Iu. V. and A. Sabanin, eds. *Mezhdunarodnaia politika noveishego vremeni v dogovorakh, notakh, i deklaratsiiakh.* 3 vols. Moscow, 1925-1926.

Kommunisticheskaia partiia sovetskogo soiuza: v rezoliutsiiakh i resheniiakh s"ezdov, konferentsii i plenumov TsK. 4 vols. Moscow, 1953-1960.

Kommunisty v sostave apparata gos. uchrezhdenii i obshchestvennykh organizatsii (Itogi vsesoiuznoi partiinoi perepisi 1927 goda). Moscow, 1929.

Konsulskii ustav soiuza SSR. Moscow, 1926.

Konsulskii ustav soiuza SSR s postateinymi primechaniiami (material sobran po ianvar'ia 1931 goda) sostavlen pravovym i konsulskim otdelami narodnogo komissariata po inostrannym delam. Moscow, 1931.

'*Krasnaia kniga*', *sbornik diplomaticheskikh dokumentov o russko-pol'skikh otnosheniiakh 1918-1920g.* Moscow, 1920.

Kun, Bela, ed. *Kommunisticheskii internatsional v dokumentakh.* Moscow, 1937.

Kurdiukov, I., *et al.*, eds. *Sovetsko-kitaiskie otnosheniia 1917-1957: sbornik dokumentov.* Moscow, 1959.

McNeal, Robert H., ed. *Resolutions and Decisions of the Communist Party of the Soviet Union.* Vol. III. *The Stalin Years: 1929-1953.* Toronto and Buffalo, 1974.

Mezhdunarodnaia politika RSFSR v 1922g. Moscow, 1923.

Mezhdunarodnaia zhizn'. Moscow, 1922-1930.

Modzhorian, L. A. and V. K. Sobakin, eds. *Mezhdunarodnoe pravo v izbrannykh dokumentakh.* Moscow, 1957. 3 vols.

Papers Relating to the Foreign Relations of the United States, 1918, Russia. Washington, 1931.

Papers Relating to the Foreign Relations of the United States, 1919, Russia. Washington, 1937.

Papers Relating to the Foreign Relations of the United States, 1920-1933. Washington, 1935-1948.

Piatyi sozyv vserossiiskogo tsentral'nogo ispolnitel'nogo komiteta, 1919. Moscow, 1919.

Polnyi svod zakonov rossiiskoi imperii. A. A. Dobrovol'skii, ed. Petersburg, 1911.

Proceedings of the Brest-Litovsk Peace Conference. The Negotiations between Russia and the Central Powers, 21 November 1917-3 March 1918. Washington, 1918.

Protokoly tsentral'nogo komiteta RSDRP (avgust 1917-fevral'1918). Moscow, 1929.

Report of Court Proceedings in the Case of the Anti-Soviet Trotskyite Centre. Moscow, 1937.

Report of Court Proceedings: The Case of the Trotskyite-Zinovievite Terrorist Centre. Moscow, 1936.

The Report of the Royal Commission appointed under order in Council P.C. 411 of February 5, 1946, to investigate the facts surrounding the communication, by public officials and other persons in positions of trust, of secret and confidential information to agents of foreign power. June 27, 1946. Ottawa, 1946.

Russian Information and Review [title varies]. London, 1921-1925.

Sbornik deistvuiushchikh dogovorov, soglashenii i konventsii zakliuchennykh RSFSR s inostrannymi gosudarstvami. Moscow, 1924-.

Sbornik polozhenii, instruktsii i rasporiazhenii po upravleniiu delami N.K.I.D. Moscow, 1925.

Sbornik sekretnykh dokumentov iz arkhiva byvshego ministerstva. Moscow, 1917-1918.

Sbornik zakonov i rasporiazhenii rabochego i krest'ianskogo pravitel'stva s 1-go ianvaria 1918 goda — po 1-oe aprelia 1918 goda. Moscow, 1918.

Sed'moi ekstrennym s"ezd RKP (b), mart 1918 goda. Moscow, 1962.

S"ezdy sovetov vserossiiskie i soiuza SSR v postanovleniiakh i rezoliutsiiakh. Moscow, 1925.

XVI s"ezd vsesoiuznoi kommunisticheskoi partii (bol'shevikov): stenograficheskii otchet. Moscow, 1931.

Sobranie uzakonenii i rasporiazhenii rabochego i krest'ianskogo pravitel'stva. Petrograd (then Moscow), 1917-1938.

Sobranie zakonov i rasporiazhenii rabochekrest'ianskogo pravitel'stva SSSR. Moscow, 1924-1938.

Soglasheniia sovetskogo soiuza s inostrannymi gosudarstvami po konsul'skim voprosam (sbornik). G. E. Bilkov and I. P. Blishchenko, eds. Moscow, 1962.

Sostav rukovodiashchik rabotnikov i spetsialistov SSR. Moscow, 1936.

Sovetsko-afganiskie otnosheniia 1919-1969gg.: dokumenty i materialy. Moscow, 1971.

Sovetsko-germanskie otnosheniia ot peregovorov v Brest-Litovske do podpisaniia Rapall'skogo dogovora. 2 vols. Moscow, 1968-1971.

Sovetsko-mongolskie otnosheniia, 1921-1974: sbornik dokumentov. Moscow, 1975.

United States, Congress, 91st. *The Soviet Approach to Negotiation.* Washington, 1969.

'Soviet International Law: Legal Status of Foreigners in the USSR', *Soviet Statutes and Decisions: A Journal of Translations,* III, 1 (Fall 1966), pp. 7-120.

'Soviet Public International Law', *Soviet Statutes and Decisions: A Journal of Translations,* III, 4 (Summer 1967), pp. 7-95.

Soviet Union Review. Washington, 1923-1934.

Spravochnik tsentral'nykh i mestnykh uchrezhdenii R.S.F.S.R. partiinykh organizatsii i professional'nykh soiuzov. 2nd edn. Moscow, 1920.

Tarify konsul'skikh sborov i instruktsiia po primeneniiu. Moscow, 1923.

Trotskii, Lev D. *The Trotsky Papers, 1917-1922.* 3 vols. Jan M. Meijer, ed. The Hague, 1964.

Vestnik narodnogo komissariata inostrannykh del. Moscow, 1919-1922.

Vestnik tsentral'nogo ispolnitel'nogo komiteta, soveta narodnykh komissarov i soveta truda i oborony SSSR. Moscow, 1923.

Vos'maia konferentsiia RKP (b) dekabr' 1919 goda. Moscow, 1961.

Vos'moi s"ezd RKP (b), mart 1919 goda. Moscow, 1959.

Vtoroi vserossiiskii s"ezd sovetov. Moscow, 1928.

Der Zweite Kongress der Kommunistischen Internationale, Protokoll der Verhandlungen. Hamburg, 1921.

Reference Works

Bol'shaia sovetskaia entsiklopediia. 1st edn. Moscow, 1926-1931. 65 vols. 2nd edn. Moscow, 1949-1958. 51 vols. 3rd edn. Moscow, 1970-.

Bratskaia mogila: biograficheskii slovar' umershikh i pogibshikh chlenov moskovskoi organizatsii RKP. 2 vols. Moscow, 1922-1923.

Crowley, Edward L., Andrew I. Lebed and Dr Heinrich E. Schulz, eds. *Party and Goverment Officials of the Soviet Union, 1917-1967.* Metuchen, 1969.

—— *Prominent Personalities in the USSR: A Biographic Directory Containing 6,051 Biographies of Prominent Personalities in the Soviet Union.* Metuchen, 1968.

—— *The Soviet Diplomatic Corps, 1917-1967.* Metuchen, 1970.

'Deiateli soiuza sovetskikh sotsialisticheskikh respublik i oktiab'rskoi revoliutsii: avtobiografii i biografii', *Entsiklopedicheskii slovar' russkogo bibliograficheskogo institut granat.* Moscow, 1929. Vol. XLI, parts I-III.

Ezhegodnik bol'shoi sovetskoi entsiklopedii. Moscow, 1958-.

Gromyko, Andrei A., et al., eds. *Diplomaticheskii slovar'.* 2nd edn. Moscow, 1960-1964. 3 vols.

—— *Diplomaticheskii slovar'.* 3rd edn. Moscow, 1971-1973. 3 vols.

Haupt, Georges and Jean-Jacques Marie, eds. *Les Bolcheviks Par Eux-Mêmes.* Paris, 1969.

Il'ina, L. I., et al., eds. *Geroi Oktiabria.* Leningrad, 1967.

Kitaeff, Michael. *Communist Party Officials: A Group of Portraits.* New York, 1954, Eastern European Fund, Mimeographed series, no. 67.

Koch, Hans, ed. *5,000 Sowjetköpfe.* Köln, [1959].

Krassnovsky, Dimitry M., ed. *Biographical Index of Slavic Men and Women of Letters, Science, Art, Politics, Army, Navy, etc.* 9 vols. Stanford and Los Angeles, 1943-1954.

Lazitch, Branko and Milorad M. Drachkovitch, eds. *Biographical Dictionary of the Comintern.* Stanford, 1973.

Lebed, A. I., ed. *Portraits of Prominent USSR Personalities.* Munich, 1966-.

Lensen, George Alexander. *Russian Diplomatic and Consular Officials in East Asia: A Handbook of Representatives of Tsarist Russia and the Provisional Government in China, Japan and Korea from 1858 to 1924 and of Soviet Representatives in Japan from 1925 to 1968.* Tallahassee, 1968.

Levytsky, Borys. *The Soviet Political Elite: Brief Biographies, Indices and Tables on 989 Members and Candidate Members of the CPSU Central Committee from 1912 to 1969, Together with an Overall Analysis.* Munich, 1969.

—— ed. *The Stalinist Terror in the Thirties: Documentation from the Soviet Press.* Stanford, 1974.

Lewytzkyj, Borys and Kurt Müller. *Sowjetische Kurzbiographien.* Hannover, 1964.

Lezhava, L. and G. Rusakov, eds. *Pamiatnik bortsam proletarskoi revoliutsii: pogibshim v 1917-1921gg.* 3rd edn. Moscow and Leningrad, 1925.

Malaia sovetskaia entsiklopediia. 3rd edn. Moscow, 1958-1960. 10 vols.

The Modern Encyclopedia of Russian and Soviet History. Gulf Breeze, 1976-.

Pamiatnik bortsam proletarskoi revoliutsii pogibshim v 1917-1921gg. Vypusk I. Moscow, 1922.

Politicheskii slovar'. 2nd edn. Moscow, 1940 and 3rd edn. Moscow, 1958.

Schulz, Heinrich E., Paul K. Urban and Andrew I. Lebed, eds. *Who Was Who in the USSR: A Biographical Directory Containing 5,015 Biographies of Prominent Soviet Historical Personalities.* Metuchen, 1972.

Schulz, Heinrich and Steven S. Taylor, eds. *Who's Who in the USSR, 1961-62.* New York, 1962.

Sovetskaia istoricheskaia entsiklopediia. Moscow, 1961-.

Vyshinskii, Andrei Ia. and S. A. Lozovskii, eds. *Diplomaticheskii slovar'.* 1st edn. Moscow, 1948-1950. 2 vols.

Collected Works, Memoirs and Commentary by Participants

Abrikossow [Abrikosov], Dmitrii I. *Revelations of A Russian Diplomat.* George Lensen, ed. Seattle, 1964.

Acheson, Dean. 'Of Men I Have Known: Part Two: The Russians', *Saturday Evening Post,* CCXXXIV, 12 (25 March 1961), pp. 31 and 69-71.

Agabekov, Grigorii S. *G.P.U.: zapiski chekista.* Berlin, 1930.

—— *O.G.P.U.: The Russian Secret Terror.* New York, 1931.

Aline. *Lénine à Paris.* Paris, 1929.

Aralov, Semen Ivanovich. *Vospominaniia sovetskogo diplomata, 1922-1923.* Moscow, 1960.

—— 'In the Turkey of Atatürk (Reminiscences of an Ambassador)', *International Affairs,* 1960, no. 8, pp. 80-87, no. 10, pp. 97-103 and no. 11, pp. 96-102.

—— 'On Lenin's Instructions', *International Affairs,* no. 4 (1960), pp. 10-15.

Bailey, F. M. *Mission to Tashkent.* London, 1946.

Balabanoff, Angelica. *My Life as a Rebel.* Bloomington, 1973 [1938].

Bajanov [Bazhanov], Boris. *Stalin: der Rote Diktator.* Berlin, n.d. [1931].

Barmine, Alexander. *One Who Survived.* New York, 1945.

—— 'A Russian View of the Moscow Trials', *International Conciliation: Documents for the Year 1938,* no. 337 (1938), pp. 43-52.

Beatty, Bessie. 'Chicherin', *New Republic,* vol. XXX (April 1922), pp. 335-38.

Berezhkov, V. *Gody diplomaticheskoi sluzhby.* Moscow, 1972.

—— *In diplomatischer Mission bei Hitler in Berlin 1940-1941.* Frankfurt a.M., 1967.

Bessedowsky [Besedovskii], Grigory. *Den Klauen der Tscheka entronnen: Erinnerungen.* Leipzig and Zürich, 1930.

—— *Na putiakh k termidoru: iz vospominanii sovetskogo diplomata.* Paris, 1931.

—— *Revelations of A Soviet Diplomat.* London, 1931.

Bickel, Karl A. 'How the Outside World Gets Its Information Concerning Events in Russia', in: *The Internal and External Problems of Russia: Proceedings of General Conference, August 1 and 2, 1930*. Williamstown, 1930.

Bilainkin, George. *Maisky: Ten Years Ambassador*. London, 1944.

Blum, Oscar. *Russische Köpfe*. Berlin, 1923.

Body, Marcel. 'Alexandra Kollontai', *Preuves*, no. 14 (April 1952), pp. 12-24.

—— 'Reminiscences of the Third International', *Studies on the Soviet Union*, IX, 1 (1969), pp. 26-30.

Bohlen, Charles E. *Witness to History, 1929-1969*. New York, 1973.

Bonch-Bruevich, V. *Na boevykh postakh fevral'skoi i oktiabr'skoi revoliutsii*. Moscow, 1930.

—— *Na slavnom postu: Pamiati V. V. Vorovskogo*. Moscow, 1923.

—— *Vospominaniia o lenine*. Moscow, 1968.

Bryant, Louise. *Mirrors of Moscow*. New York, 1923.

—— *Six Red Months in Russia*. New York, 1918.

Buchanan, George. *My Mission to Russia and Other Diplomatic Memoirs*. 2 vols. London, 1923.

Buchanan, Muriel. *The Dissolution of an Empire*. London, 1939.

Bukharin, Nikolai. *Imperialism and World Economy*. New York, 1973 [1929, 1918].

—— 'K teorii imperialisticheskogo gosudarstva', in: *Revoliutsiia prava: sbornik pervyi*. Moscow, 1925.

Bullitt, William C. *The Bullitt Mission to Russia: Testimony Before the Committee on Foreign Relations of the United States Senate of William C. Bullitt*. New York, 1919.

Chicherin, G. V. 'Chetyre kongressa', *Vestnik NKID*, no. 1 (1919).

—— *The Foreign Policy of Soviet Russia: Report Submitted by the People's Commissariat of Foreign Affairs to the Seventh All-Russian Congress of Soviets (Nov. 1918-Dec. 1919)*. London, 1919.

—— *Offener Brief Tschitscherins, des russischen Volkskommissars für auswärtige Angelegenheiten an den Präsidenten der Vereinigten Staaten von Nordamerika, Herrn Woodrow Wilson*. Berlin, n.d. [1919?].

—— 'Mezhdunarodnaia politika dvukh internatsionalov', *Kommunisticheskii internatsional*, no. 6 (1919), pp. 817-28.

—— 'Rossiia i aziatskie narody', *Vestnik NKID*, no. 2 (1919).

—— *Two Years of Foreign Policy: The Relations of The Russian Socialist Federal Soviet Republic with Foreign Nations from November 7, 1917 to November 7, 1919*. New York, 1920.

—— 'Lenin i vneshniaia politika', in: *Mirovaia politika v 1924g.: sbornik statei*. Moscow, 1925.

—— 'Za piat' let', *Mezhdunarodnaia zhizn'*, no. 15 (1922), pp. 4-6.

—— *Stat'i i rechi po voprosam mezhdunarodnoi politiki*. Moscow, 1961.

Cleveland, C. O. 'Memories of Chicherin', *Commonwealth*, XXIV (28 August 1936).

D'Abernon, Edgar V. *The Diary of an Ambassador*. Garden City, 1929-31.

Davies, Joseph E. *Mission to Moscow*. New York, 1941.

Dirksen, Herbert von. *Moscow, Tokyo, London: Twenty Years of German Foreign Policy*. Norman, 1952.

Dmitrievskii, S. _Dans les coulisses du Kremlin._ Paris, 1933.
Duranty, Walter. _Duranty Reports Russia._ New York, 1934.
—— _I Write As I Please._ New York, 1935.
Ehrenburg, Ilya. _Memoirs: 1921-1941._ Cleveland and New York, 1963 and 1964.
—— _The War: 1941-1945._ Cleveland and New York, 1964.
——_Post-War Years, 1945-1954._ London, 1966.
Ex-Insider, V. [pseud.], 'Raskolnikov', _Survey,_ no. 53 (October 1964), pp. 119-28.
Fedorov, L. _Diplomat i konsul._ Moscow, 1965.
Fischer, Louis. 'Litvinov's Diplomatic Years', _The Fortnightly Review._ (London). January 1934.
—— _Men and Politics: An Autobiography._ New York, 1941.
Fokke, D. G. 'Na stsene i za kulisami brestskoi tragikomedii', _Arkhiv russkoi revoliutsii._ V. Gessen, ed., vol. XX, pp. 5-208. The Hague and Paris, 1970.
Francis, David R. 'Ambassador Francis on Bolshevism: The League of Nations vs. Bolshevism', _Worlds Work,_ XXXVIII, 5 (September 1919), pp. 464-68.
—— _Russia From the American Embassy, April 1916-November 1918._ New York, 1921.
Fuse, Katsuji. _Rono Rokoku Yori Kaerite._ Tokyo, 1921.
Ganetskii, Iakov Stanislavovich, _V.V. Vorovskii: biograficheskii ocherk._ Moscow, 1925.
—— ed. _O Lenine: otryvki iz vospominanii._ Moscow, 1933.
Gnedin, E. 'Sud'ba evropeiskoy nasledstva', _Novyi mir,_ no. 1 (1964), pp. 202-22.
—— _Iz istorii otnoshenii mezhdu SSSR i fashistskoi germaniei: Dokumenty i sovremennye kommentarii._ New York, 1977.
Gregory, John Duncan. _On the Age of Diplomacy: Rambles and Reflections, 1902-1928._ London, 1929.
Grew, Joseph Clark. _Turbulent Era: A Diplomatic Record of Forty Years, 1904-1945._ Boston, 1952, Vol. I.
Herbette, Jean. _Un Diplomate Français Parle du Péril Bolchéviste._ Paris, 1943.
Hilger, Gustav. _Wir und der Kreml: Deutsch-sowjetische Beziehungen, 1918-1941: Erinnerungen eines deutschen Diplomaten._ Frankfurt a.M. and Bonn, 1964.
—— and Alfred G. Meyer. _The Incompatible Allies: A Memoir-History of German-Soviet Relations, 1918-1941._ New York, 1953.
Hodgson, Sir Robert M. 'Memoirs of an Official Agent', _History Today,_ IV, 8 (August 1954), pp. 522-28.
Ioffe, A. A. 'Germanskaia revoliutsiia i rossiiskoe posol'stvo', _Vestnik zhizni,_ no. 5 (1919), pp. 35-46.
—— 'Pervoe proletarskoe pravitel'stvo', _Kommunisticheskii internatsional,_ no. 6 (1919).
—— 'Pered genuei', _Vestnik NKID,_ no. 4-5 (1922), pp. 3-6.
Iranskii, S. 'Stranitsa iz istorii krasnoi diplomatii (pamiati t.I.I. Kolomiitseva)', _Novyi vostok,_ nos. 8-9 (1925), pp. 151-59.
Kantorovich, B. 'Organizatsionnoe razvitie NKID', _Mezhdunarodnaia zhizn',_ no. 15 (1922), pp. 51-5.
Kazanin, Mark. _Zapiski sekretaria missii i stranichka istorii pervykh let sovetskoi diplomatii._ Moscow, 1962.

Selected Bibliography 207

—— *China in the Twenties*. Moscow, 1973.

Kaznacheev, Aleksandr. *Inside A Soviet Embassy: Experiences of a Russian Diplomat in Burma*. Philadelphia and New York, 1962.

Kennan, George F. *Memoirs, 1925-1950*. Boston, 1967.

Khinchuk, L. M. *K istorii anglo-sovetskikh otnoshenii*. Moscow-Leningrad, 1928.

Khrushchev, N. S. *Khrushchev Remembers*. Boston, 1970.

Kiselev, K. *Zapiski sovetskogo diplomata*. Moscow, 1974.

Kennedy, Aubrey L. *Old Diplomacy and New*. London, 1922.

Kizel'shtein, G. 'Muchitel'no zhazhdu vysokoi tseli: iz arkhiva G.V. Chicherina', *Ogonek*, no. 48 (1963), p. 18.

Kollontai, A.M. 'Oppozitsiia i partiinaia massa', *Pravda* (30 October 1927).

Korostovetz, Vladimir Konstantinovich. *Seed and Harvest*. London, 1931.

Krasina, Liubov. *Leonid Krassin: His Life and Work*. London, n.d. [1929].

Kravchenko, Victor. *I Choose Freedom: The Personal and Political Life of A Soviet Official*. New York, 1946.

Krivitsky, Walter G. *In Stalin's Secret Service: An Exposé of Russia's Secret Policies by the Former Chief of the Soviet Intelligence in Western Europe*. New York, 1939.

Kroll, Hans. *Lebenserinnerungen eines Botschafters*. Berlin, 1967.

Krupskaia, N.K. *Vospominaniia o lenine*. Moscow, 1968.

Kulik, Ivan. *Zapiski konsula*. Moscow, 1964.

Larsons, M. J. *An Expert in the Service of the Soviet*. London, 1929.

Ladyzhenskii, A. 'Instruktsiia konsulam RSFSR', *Mezhdunarodnaia zhizn'*, no. 16, 134 (30 November 1922), pp. 22-27.

Lenin, V. I. *Leninskii sbornik*. Moscow, 1924-.

—— *Polnoe sobranie sochinenii*. 5th edn. Moscow, 1958-1965.

—— 'Ein neues Dokument W.I. Lenins', *Beiträge zur Geschichte der Arbeiterbewegung*, V, 4 (1963), pp. 79-86.

Liberman, Simon. *Building Lenin's Russia*. Chicago, 1945.

Litvinova, A. 'Vstrechi i razluki (Iz vospominanii o M. M. Litvinove)', *Novyi mir*, no. 7 (1966), pp. 235-50.

Litvinov, Maksim. *Vneshniaia politika SSSR: rechi i zaiavleniia, 1927-1937*. Moscow, 1937.

—— *Against Aggression: Speeches by Maxim Litvinov, Together with Texts of Treaties and of the Covenant of the League of Nations*. New York, 1939.

Liubimov, N. N. and A. N. Erlikh. *Genuezskaia konferentsiia: vospominaniia uchastnikov*. Moscow, 1963.

—— 'The 1922 Genoa Conference', *International Affairs*, no. 6 (1963), pp. 65-70; no. 8 (1963), pp. 97-103; no. 9 (1963), pp. 78-83; and no. 10 (1963), pp. 71-78.

Lockhart, Robert Bruce. *Memoirs of A British Agent*. London, 1932.

—— *Retreat from Glory*. New York, 1934.

—— *The Diaries of Sir Robert Bruce Lockhart*, vol I, *1915-1938*. London, 1973.

Luke, Harry C. J. *Cities and Men: An Autobiography*. 3 vols. London, 1953-1956.

Lunacharskii, Anatoly Vasilievich. *Stat'i i rechi po voprosam mezhdunarodnoi politiki*. Moscow, 1959.

—— *Revolutionary Silhouettes*. London, 1967.

Maiskii, I. M. 'Anglo-sovetskoe torgovoe soglashenie 1921 goda', *Voprosy istorii*, no. 5 (1957), pp. 60-77.
—— 'Diplomat leninskoi shkoly', *Izvestiia*, (27 October 1963).
—— B. *Shou i drugie: vospominaniia*. Moscow, 1967.
—— 'Diplomats of the Lenin School: Georgi Chicherin', *New Times*, no. 44 (1967), pp. 10-3.
—— 'Diplomats of the Lenin School: Ambassador Krasin', *New Times*, no. 3 (1968), pp. 23-7.
—— 'Diplomats of the Lenin School: Alexandra Kollontai', *New Times*, no. 4 (1968), pp. 20-2.
—— 'Iz londonskikh vospominanii', *Novyi mir*, no. 4 (1968), pp. 195-216; and no. 5 (1968), pp. 153-67.
—— *Vneshniaia politika RSFSR, 1917-1922*. Moscow, 1923.
—— *Journey into the Past*. London, 1962.
—— *Vospominaniia sovetskogo diplomata, 1925-1945gg*. Moscow, 1971.
—— *Memoirs of A Soviet Ambassador: The War, 1939-43*. London, 1967.
—— *Who Helped Hitler?* London, 1964.
Meyendorff, Alexander. 'My Cousin, Foreign Commissar Chicherin', *The Russian Review*, XXX, 2 (April 1971), pp. 173-78.
Monzie, Anatole de. *Destins hors serié*. Paris, 1927.
Murray, Nora. *I Spied for Stalin*. New York, 1951.
Nabokoff, C. [Konstantin Nabokov]. *The Ordeal of A Diplomat*. London, 1921.
Narischkine-Witte [Naryshkin-Vitte], V. *A Petrograd pendant la Revolution*. Paris, 1925.
Neymann, Alexei F. 'The Formulation and Administration of Soviet Foreign Policy', in: Samuel N. Harper, ed. *The Soviet Union and World Problems*. Chicago, 1935, pp. 224-33.
Noulens, Joseph. *Mon Ambassade en Russie Soviétique, 1917-1919*. Paris, 1933.
O'Malley, Owen St. Clair. *The Phantom Caravan*. London, 1954.
Orlov, Alexander. *The Secret History of Stalin's Crimes*. New York, 1953.
Oudendyk, W. J. *Ways and Byways in Diplomacy*. London, 1939.
Ozols, K. V. *Memuary poslannika*. Paris, 1938.
Pal'gunov, Nikolai Grigor'evich. *Tridtsat' let (vospominaniia zhurnalista i diplomata)*. Moscow, 1964.
Palencia, Isabel de. *Alexandra Kollontay: Ambassadress from Russia*. New York, London and Toronto, 1947.
Pestkovskii, S. 'Ob oktiabr'skikh dniakh v pitere', *Proletarskaia revoliutsiia*, no. 10 (1922).
Petrov, Vladimir and Evdokia. *Empire of Fear*. New York, 1956.
Popoff, George. *Ich sah die Revolutionäre: Moskauer Erinnerungen und Begegnungen während der Revolutionsjahre*. Bern, 1967.
Poretsky, Elisabeth K. *Our Own People: A Memoir of 'Ignace Reiss' and His Friends*. Ann Arbor, 1969.
Quaroni, Pietro. *Diplomatic Bags*. London, 1966.
Radek, Karl. *Die auswärtige Politik Sowjet-Russlands*. Hamburg, 1921.
—— *Die innere und äussere Lage Sowjetrusslands und die Aufgaben der KPR*. (Vortrag vor der Kommunistischen Fraktion des Generalstabes der Roten Armee am 27. Februar 1920). Leipzig, 1921.

—— Der Kampf der Kommunistischen Internationale gegen Versailles und gegen die Offensive des Kapitals. Hamburg, 1923.
—— Vneshniaia politika sovetskoi rossii. Moscow and Petrograd, 1923.
—— 'Noiabr' (stranichka iz vospominanii)', Krasnaia nov', no. 10 (1926), pp. 139-75.
—— 'Russia at Geneva', Living Age, CCCXL, 4378 (July 1931), pp. 438-43.
—— Portraits and Pamphlets. London, 1935.
—— La Situation internationale et la Politique extérieure du Pouvoir des Soviets. Geneva, n.d.
Rafaila, M., et. al. Lenin i vostok. 2nd edn. Moscow, 1925.
Rakovsky, C. G. [Rakovskii, Kh.G.] Roumania and Bessarabia. London, 1925.
—— 'The Foreign Policy of Soviet Russia', Foreign Affairs, IV, 4 (July 1926), pp. 574-84.
Reed, John. 'Foreign Affairs', The Liberator, I (June 1918).
Reswick, William. I Dreamt Revolution. Chicago, 1952.
Robien, Louis de. Journal d'un diplomate en Russie, 1917-1918. Paris, 1967.
Rotshtein, F. 'Desnitsa i shuitsa angliiskoi diplomatii (zametki nabliudatelia)', Vestnik NKID, no. 8 (1920), pp. 1-6.
—— ed. Mirovaia politika v 1924 g.: sbornik statei. Moscow, 1925.
Sabanin, A. V. Posol'skoe i konsul'skoe pravo: kratkoe prakticheskoe posobie. Moscow, 1934.
Sabanine, André. 'L'Organisation du service diplomatique et consulaire de la R.S.F.S.R.', Bulletin de L'Institut Intermediaire International, VIII (1923), pp. 197-216.
Sadoul, J. Notes sur la Révolution bolchévique. Paris, 1920.
—— Quarante lettres de Jacques Sadoul. Paris, 1922.
Saint-Aulaire, August F. C. de B., Comte de. Confession d'un Vieux Diplomate. Paris, 1953.
—— Je suis diplomate. Paris, 1954.
Scheffer, Paul. Augenzüge im Staate Lenins: Ein Korrespondent berichtet aus Moskau, 1921-1930. Munich, 1972.
—— 'Maxime Litvinov, Intimate Study', Current History (August 1931), pp. 670-7.
—— Seven Years in Soviet Russia. New York, 1932.
Schlesinger, Moritz. Erinnerungen eines Aussenseites im diplomatischen Dienst. Köln, 1977.
Schmidt-Pauli, Edgar von. Diplomaten in Berlin. Berlin, 1930.
Serge, Victor. 'Litvinov', Esprit, no. 81 (June 1939).
—— Memoirs of A Revolutionary, 1901-1941. London, 1963.
—— From Lenin to Stalin. New York, 1972.
Sheridan, Clare. Russian Portraits. London, 1921.
Shtein, Boris E. 'Russkii vopros' v 1920-1922gg. Moscow, 1958.
Shumiatskii, B. Z. Na postu sovetskoi diplomatii. Moscow, 1960.
Simonov, P. 'Tri s polovinoi goda sovetskogo diplomaticheskogo predstavitelstva', Mezhdunarodnaia zhizn', no. 15 (1922), pp. 61-66.
Socoline, Vladimir. Ciel et Terre soviétiques. Neuchâtel, 1949.
Sokol'nikov, G.Ia. Brestskii mir. Moscow, 1920.
Solomon, George. Sredi krasnykh vozhdei: lichno perezhitoe i vidennoe na sovetskoi sluzhbe. 2 vols. Paris, 1930.

—— *Among the Red Autocrats: My Experience in the Service of the Soviets.* New York, 1935.

Solov'ev, Iurii Iakovlevich. *Dvadtsat' piat' let moei diplomaticheskoi sluzhby,* [*1893-1918*]. Moscow and Leningrad, 1928.

—— *Vospominaniia diplomata, 1893-1922.* Moscow, 1959.

Stalin, J. V. *Sochineniia.* Moscow, 1946-1952. Vols. I-XIII. Stanford, 1967. Vols. XIV-XVI.

Sukhorukov, V. T. 'Nalet chankaishistov na general'noe konsul'stvo SSSR', *Na kitaiskoi zemle: vospominani* [sic] *sovetskikh dobrovol'tsev, 1925-1945.* Moscow, 1974.

Tanin, M. *Mezhdunarodnaia politika SSSR (1917-1924).* Moscow, 1925.

—— 'Anglo-sovetskii razryv i problema edinogo imperialisticheskogo fronta', *Bol'shevik,* no. 11-12 (1927), pp. 59-68.

—— *Desiat let vneshnei politiki SSSR, 1917-1927.* Moscow-Leningrad, 1927.

Tchimichkian, Satho. 'Extraits de la correspondance Mihail Kuzmin-Georgij Cicerin', *Cahiers du Monde Russe et Soviétique,* XV, 1-2 (Jan.-June 1974), pp. 147-81.

Trotskii, Lev D. 'Prospects of a Labor Dictatorship', in: Leon Trotsky. *Our Revolution: Essays on Working Class and International Revolution, 1904-1917.* Moissaye J. Olgin, tr. New York, 1918.

—— *Kak vooruzhalas' revoliutsiia.* Moscow, 1923-1925.

—— *Moia zhizn': opit avtobiografii.* Berlin, 1930. 2 vols.

—— *What is A Revolutionary Programme?* Colombo, 1956.

—— *Sochineniia.* Moscow [n.d.].

Turkan, G. A., ed. 'Doklad Ia.E. Rudzutaka o genuizkoi konferentsii', *Istoricheskii arkhiv,* no. 2 (1962), pp. 80-95.

Vansittart, Robert G. *The Mist Procession: The Autobiography of Lord Vansittart.* London, 1958.

Vorovskii, Vatslav V. *Stat'i i materialy po voprosam vneshnei politiki, 1903-1923.* Moscow, 1959.

Weizsäcker, Ernst von. *Erinnerungen.* Munich, 1950.

Williams, Albert Rhys. *Journey into the Revolution: Petrograd, 1917-1918.* Chicago, 1969.

Wilson, Hugh R. *Diplomat Between Wars.* New York and Toronto, 1941.

Ypsilon (pseud. of Karl Volk). *Pattern of World Revolution.* Chicago, 1947.

Zalkind, I. 'Iz pervykh mesiatsev narodnogo komissariata po inostrannym delam', *Mezhdunarodnaia zhizn',* no. 15 (1922), pp. 55-61.

—— 'NKID v semnadtsatom godu (Iz vospominanii ob Oktiabre)', *Mezhdunarodnaia zhizn',* no. 10 (1927), pp. 12-20.

Secondary Works

Adamec, Ludwig W. *Afghanistan's Foreign Affairs to the Mid-Twentieth Century: Relations With the USSR, Germany, and Britain.* Tucson, 1974.

Akhtamzian, A. *Ot bresta do kiliia: proval antisovetskoi politiki germanskogo imperializma v 1918 godu.* Moscow, 1963.

—— 'Lenin's Foreign Policy Activity (April-July 1918)', *International Affairs*, no. 2 (1969), pp. 100-3.

—— 'Lenin's Foreign Policy Activity (April-August 1920)', *International Affairs*, no. 8 (1969), pp. 82-86.

—— 'Lenin's Foreign Policy Activity (April-October 1921)', *International Affairs*, no. 11 (1969), pp. 50-53.

—— 'Profili rapall'skoi diplomatii', *Voprosy istorii*, no. 2 (1974), pp. 100-24.

—— *Rapall'skaia politika: Sovetsko-germanskie diplomaticheskie otnosheniia v 1922-1932 godakh*. Moscow, 1974.

Akzin, Benjamin. *Propaganda by Diplomats*. Washington, 1936.

Alexander, Robert J. 'Marx, Lenin and Developing Countries', *New Politics*, IX, 2 (1971), pp. 87-95.

Alexandrov, A. and L. Sergeyeva. '90th Anniversary of Valerian Dovgalevsky's Birth', *International Affairs*, no. 1 (1976), pp. 127-31.

Allard, Sven. *Stalin und Hitler: Die sowjetrussische Aussenpolitik, 1930-1941*. Bern and Munich, 1974.

Anderle, Alfred. *Die deutsche Rapallo-Politik: Deutschsowjetische Beziehungen, 1922-1929*. Berlin, 1962.

Andropov, I. 'Lenin's Ambassador in America (Ludwig Martens)', *New Times*, no. 17 (1970), pp. 28-32.

Angress, Werner T. *Stillborn Revolution: The Communist Bid for Power in Germany, 1921-1923*. Princeton, 1963.

Anti-Soviet Forgeries. London, 1927.

Armstrong, John A. 'Tsarist and Soviet Elite Administrators', *Slavic Review*, XXXI, 1 (March 1972), pp. 1-28.

Artem'ev, Viacheslav Pavlovich. *Selection and Training of Soviet Personnel for Trade Missions Abroad and the Soviet Trade Mission in Iran: Two Brief Studies*. New York, 1954.

Aspaturian, Vernon V. *The Union Republics in Soviet Diplomacy: A Study of Soviet Federalism in the Service of Soviet Foreign Policy*. Geneva, 1960.

—— *Process and Power in Soviet Foreign Policy*. Boston, 1971.

Asteriou, Socrates James. 'The Third International and the Balkans, 1919-1945'. Ph.D. thesis, University of California, Berkeley, 1959.

Avtorkhanov, Abdurakhman. *Stalin and the Soviet Communist Party: A Study in the Technology of Power*. New York, 1959.

—— *The Communist Party Apparatus*. Cleveland and New York, 1968.

Babel, Isaak. *Red Cavalry*. London, 1929.

Bailes, Kendall E. 'The Politics of Technology: Stalin and Technological Thinking among Soviet Engineers', *American Historical Review*, LXXIX, 2 (April 1974), pp. 445-69.

Bakhov, A. S. 'Organy vneshnikh snoshenii', in: *Istoriia sovetskogo gosudarstva i prava*. Vol. I. Moscow, 1963, pp. 234-42.

—— *Na zare sovetskoi diplomatii*. Moscow, 1966.

Balawyder, Aloysius. *Canadian-Soviet Relations between the World Wars*. Toronto, 1972.

Bassekhes, Nikolai. 'Izcheznuvshie sovetskie diplomaty', *Russkie zapiski* (July 1939), pp. 121-38.

Batsell, Walter Russell. *Soviet Rule in Russia*. New York, 1929.

Baumgart, Wilfried. *Deutsche Ostpolitik, 1918: Von Brest-Litowsk bis zum Ende des Ersten Weltkrieges.* Wien and München, 1966.

Bednarczyk, Chester Peter. 'Soviet-Comintern Relations with Poland, 1917-1939'. M.A. thesis, University of California, Berkeley, 1953.

Belkov, A. K. *Vatslav Vatslavovich Vorovskii.* Moscow, 1971.

Beloff, Max. *The Foreign Policy of Soviet Russia, 1929-1941.* 2 vols. London, 1947.

Bezumenskii, L. A. 'Vladimir Il'ich Lenin — rukovoditel' sovetskoi delegatsii na genuezskoi konferentsii', in: Alfred Anderle, ed. *Rapallskii dogovor i problema mirnogo sosushchestvovaniia.* Moscow, 1963, pp. 58-84.

Bishop, Donald G. 'Immunity of Diplomatic Establishment: Soviet Law and Practice', *Osteuropa-Recht,* V, 1 (1959), pp. 8-14.

Blackstock, Paul W. *Agents of Deceit: Frauds, Forgeries and Political Intrigue among Nations.* Chicago, 1966.

—— ' "Books for Idiots": False Soviet "Memoirs" ', *Russian Review,* XXV, 3 (July 1966), pp. 285-96.

—— *The Secret Road to World War II: Soviet versus Western Intelligence, 1921-1939.* Chicago, 1969.

Blinov, S. I. *Vneshniaia politika sovetskoi rossii: Pervyi god proletarskoi diktatury.* Moscow, 1973.

Blishchenko, I. P., and V. N. Durdenevskii. *Diplomaticheskoe i konsul'skoe pravo.* Moscow, 1962.

Bloom, Solomon F. *The World of Nations: A Study of the National Implications in the Work of Karl Marx.* New York, 1941.

Boersner, Demetrio. *The Bolsheviks and the National and Colonial Question, 1917-1928.* Geneva, 1957.

Booth, Ken. *The Military Instrument in Soviet Foreign Policy, 1917-1972.* London, 1973.

Borisov, Iu. V. *Sovetsko-frantsuzskie otnosheniia (1924-1945gg.).* Moscow, 1964.

Borkenau, Franz. *European Communism.* New York, 1953.

—— *World Communism.* Ann Arbor, 1962.

Bourcart, J. R. D. *L'Espionnage Soviétique.* Paris, 1962.

Brandt, Conrad. *Stalin's Failure in China: 1924-1927.* Cambridge, 1958.

Browder, Robert P. *The Origins of Soviet-American Diplomacy.* Princeton, 1953.

Buckholtz, Albrecht. 'Leonid Krasin und sein Verhältnis zu Deutschland', in: Uwe Liszkowski, ed. *Russland und Deutschland.* Stuttgart, vol. 22, 1974.

Bukhartsev, Dm. *7 let nashei vneshnei politiki.* Moscow, 1925.

Buriakov, V. A. 'Missiia V.V. Vorovskogo v Italii v 1921 godu', *Voprosy istorii,* no. 11 (1971), pp. 131-42.

—— 'Lenin's Diplomacy in Action', *International Affairs,* no. 5 (1972), pp. 92-7.

Burton, J. W. *Systems, States, Diplomacy and Rules.* London, 1968.

Busk, Douglas. *The Craft of Diplomacy: How to Run A Diplomatic Service.* New York, Washington, London, 1967.

Butterfield, H. 'The New Diplomacy and Historical Diplomacy', in: Herbert Butterfield and Martin Wight, eds. *Diplomatic Investigations: Essays in the Theory of International Politics.* Cambridge, 1968. pp. 181-92.

Buzinkai, Donald I. 'Soviet-League Relations, 1919-1939: A Survey and Analysis'. Ph.D. thesis, University of Chicago, 1961.

—— 'The Bolsheviks, the League of Nations and the Paris Peace Conference, 1919', *Soviet Studies*, XIX, 2 (October 1967), pp. 257-63.

Calhoun, Daniel F. *The United Front: The TUC and the Russians, 1923-1928.* London, 1976.

Carley, Michael Jabara. 'The Origins of the French Intervention in the Russian Civil War, January-May 1918: A Reappraisal', *Journal of Modern History*, XLVIII, 3 (September 1976), pp. 413-39.

Carr, Edward Hallett. *German-Soviet Relations Between the Two World Wars, 1919-1939.* Baltimore, 1951.

—— *The Bolshevik Revolution, 1917-1923.* 3 vols. Baltimore, 1966 [1950-1953].

—— *The Interregnum, 1923-1924.* Baltimore, 1969 [1954].

—— *Socialism in One Country, 1924-1926.* Baltimore, 1970 [1958-1964]. 3 vols.

Cattell, David T. 'Formulation of Foreign Policy in the USSR', in: Philip W. Buck and Martin Travis, Jr., eds. *Control of Foreign Relations in Modern Nations.* New York, 1957, pp. 657-82.

Cecil, Lamar. 'The Kindermann-Wolscht Incident: an Impasse in Russo-German Relations 1924-1926', *Journal of Central European Affairs*, XXI (July 1961), pp. 188-99.

—— *The German Diplomatic Service, 1871-1914.* Princeton, 1976.

Ceyrat, M. *La Politique russe et le Parti communiste français, 1920-1945.* Paris, 1946.

Chamberlin, William H. 'Meet the Real Litvinov', *American Mercury*, LIV (1942), pp. 273-83.

Chester, Lewis, Stephen Fay and Hugo Young. *The Zinoviev Letter: A Political Intrigue.* Philadelphia, 1967.

Chossudovsky [Chossudovskii], E. M. 'Genoa Revisited: Russia and Co-existence', *Foreign Affairs*, L, no. 3 (April 1972), pp. 554-77.

—— *Chicherin and the Evolution of Soviet Foreign Policy and Diplomacy.* Geneva, 1973.

—— 'Lenin and Chicherin: The Beginnings of Soviet Foreign Policy and Diplomacy', *Millennium*, III, 1 (Spring 1974), pp. 1-16.

Chubar'ian, A. O. *V. I. Lenin i formirovanie sovetskoi vneshnei politiki.* Moscow, 1972.

—— *Leninskie printsipy sovetskoi vneshnei politiki: istoriia i sovremennost'.* Moscow, 1974.

Clemens, Walter C., Jr. 'Origins of the Soviet Campaign for Disarmament: The Soviet Position on Peace, Security, and Revolution at the Genoa, Moscow, and Lausanne Conferences, 1922-1923'. Ph.D. thesis, Columbia University, 1961.

—— 'Lenin on Disarmament', *Slavic Review*, XXIII, 3 (September 1964), pp. 504-25.

Clements, Barbara Evans. 'The Revolution and the Revolutionary: Aleksandra Mikhailovna Kollontai, 1917-23'. Ph.D. thesis, Duke University, 1971.

Cohen, Stephen F. *Bukharin and the Bolshevik Revolution: A Political Biography, 1888-1938.* New York, 1973.

Conquest, Robert. *The Great Terror: Stalin's Purge of the Thirties.* New York, 1973.

Conte, F. 'Autour de la polémique Rakovskij-Staline sur la question nationale, 1921-1923', *Cahiers du Monde Russe et Soviétique*, XVI, 1 (January-March 1975), pp. 111-17.

Craig, Gordon A. *On the Diplomatic Revolution of Our Times*. Riverside, 1961.

—— and Felix Gilbert, eds. *The Diplomats, 1919-1939*. New York, 1965.

—— *War, Politics, and Diplomacy: Selected Essays*. New York and Washington, 1966.

Crowe, Sibyl. 'The Zinoviev Letter: A Reappraisal', *The Journal of Contemporary History*, X, 3 (July 1975), pp. 407-32.

Cristescu, Gheorghe. 'Amintiri despre dr. Cristian Racovski', *Anale de istorie*, XVIII, 1 (1972), pp. 145-54.

Dallin, David J. *Soviet Espionage*. New Haven, 1955.

—— *From Purge to Coexistence: Essays on Stalin's and Khrushchev's Russia*. Chicago, 1964.

Daniels, Robert V. *The Conscience of the Revolution*. New York, 1969.

Davies, Norman. *White Eagle, Red Star — the Polish-Soviet War, 1919-1920*. London, 1972.

—— 'The Genesis of the Polish-Soviet War', *European Studies Review*, V, 1 (1975), pp. 47-67.

—— 'The Missing Revolutionary War: The Polish Campaigns and the Retreat from Revolution in Soviet Russia, 1919-21', *Soviet Studies*, XXVII, 2 (April 1975), pp. 178-195.

Davis, Kathryn Wasserman. *The Soviets at Geneva: the USSR and the League of Nations, 1919-1933*. Chambéry, 1934.

Day, Richard B. *Leon Trotsky and the Politics of Economic Isolation*. London, 1973.

Debo, Richard K. 'George Chicherin: Soviet Russia's Second Foreign Commissar'. Ph.D. thesis, University of Nebraska, 1964.

—— 'The Making of A Bolshevik: Georgii Chicherin in England, 1914-1918', *Slavic Review*, XXV, 4 (December 1966), pp. 651-62.

—— 'Dutch-Soviet Relations, 1917-1924: The Role of Finance and Commerce in the Foreign Policy of Soviet Russia and the Netherlands', *Canadian Slavic Studies/Revue canadienne d'Études slaves*, IV, 2 (Summer 1970), pp. 199-217.

—— 'Lockhart Plot or Dzerzhinskii Plot', *Journal of Modern History*, XLIII, 3 (September 1971), pp. 415-39.

—— 'Litvinov and Kamenev — Ambassadors Extraordinary: The Problem of Soviet Representation Abroad', *Slavic Review*, XXXIV, 3 (September 1975), pp. 463-82.

Dennett, Raymond and Joseph E. Johnson, eds. *Negotiating With the Russians*. Boston, 1951.

Dennis, Alfred L. P. *Foreign Policies of Soviet Russia*. New York, 1924.

Deutscher, Isaac. *The Prophet Unarmed: Trotsky, 1921-1929*. New York, 1959.

—— *The Prophet Armed: Trotsky, 1879-1921*. New York, 1965.

—— *Stalin: A Political Biography*. New York, 1960.

Dipkur'ery: ocherki o pervykh sovetskikh diplomaticheskikh kur'erakh. Moscow, 1970 and 1973.

Draper, Theodore. 'The Strange Case of the Comintern', *Survey*, XVIII, 3 (84) (Summer 1972), pp. 91-137.

Duroselle, Jean-Baptiste. *Les Relations Germano-Soviétiques de 1933 à 1939.* Paris, 1954.

Dyck, Harvey L. *Weimar Germany and Soviet Russia, 1926-1933: A Study in Diplomatic Instability.* New York, 1966.

Eastman, Max. *Since Lenin Died.* London, 1925.

Epstein, Fritz T. 'Aussenpolitik in Revolution und Bürgerkrieg, 1917-1920', in: Dietrich Geyer, ed. *Osteuropa-Handbuch: Sowjetunion, Aussenpolitik 1917-1955.* Cologne and Vienna, 1972, pp. 86-149.

—— *Germany and the East: Selected Essays.* Robert F. Byrnes, ed. Bloomington, 1973.

Erickson, John. *The Soviet High Command, 1918-1941.* London, 1962.

Erickson, John Richard. 'International Law and the Revolutionary State: A Case Study of the Soviet Union and Customary International Law'. Ph.D. thesis, University of Virginia, 1971.

Ermolaeva, R. A. 'Iakov Stanislavovich Ganetskii (k 85-letiiu so dnia rozhdeniia)', *Voprosy istorii KPSS*, no. 3 (1964), pp. 96-100.

Evgen'ev, Georgii E. and B. Shapik. *Revoliutsioner, diplomat, uchenyi (o L.K. Martens).* Moscow, 1960.

Fainsod, Merle. *International Socialism and the World War.* Cambridge, 1935.

—— *How Russia is Ruled.* Cambridge, 1965.

Farnsworth, Beatrice Brodsky. 'Bolshevism, the Woman Question, and Aleksandra Kollontai', *The American Historical Review*, LXXXI, 2 (April 1976), pp. 292-316.

—— *William C. Bullitt and the Soviet Union.* Bloomington, 1967.

Fediukin, S. A. *Sovetskaia vlast' i burzhuaznye spetsialisty.* Moscow, 1965.

Fedorov, L. *Diplomat i konsul.* Moscow, 1965.

Fiddick, Thomas C. 'Soviet Policy and the Battle of Warsaw, 1920'. Ph.D. thesis, Indiana University, 1974.

Filene, Peter G. *Americans and the Soviet Experiment, 1917-1933.* Cambridge, 1967.

Fischer, Louis. *The Soviets in World Affairs: A History of the Relations Between the Soviet Union and the Rest of the World, 1917-1929.* 2 vols. Princeton, 1951.

—— *The Life and Death of Stalin.* New York, 1952.

Fisher, Ralph T. 'The Comintern in Russian Foreign Policy'. M.A. thesis, University of California, Berkeley, 1948.

Fitzpatrick, Sheila. *The Commissariat of Enlightenment.* London, 1970.

Freund, Gerald. *Unholy Alliance: Russian-German Relations from the Treaty of Brest-Litovsk to the Treaty of Berlin.* New York, 1957.

Fuller, Sterling Hale. 'The Foreign Policy of the Soviet Union in the League and United Nations'. Ph.D. thesis, University of Texas, 1952.

Furaev, V. K. 'Informatsionnoe biuro sovetskogo soiuza v vashingtone (1923-1933gg.)', *Problemy otechestvennoi i vseobshchei istorii*, no. 2 (1973), pp. 70-77.

Garamvölgyi, Judit. *Aus den Anfängen sowjetischer Aussenpolitik: Das britisch-sowjetrussische Handelsabkommen von 1921.* Köln, 1967.

Gasiorowski, Zygmunt J. 'The Russian Overture to Germany of December 1924', *Journal of Modern History*, XXX, 2 (June 1958), pp. 99-117.

Gatzke, Hans W. 'Dokumentation zu den deutsch-russischen Beziehungen im Jahre 1918', *Vierteljahrshefte für Zeitgeschichte*, III (1955), pp. 67-98.

Gaucher, Roland. *Opposition in the USSR, 1917-1967.* New York, 1969.

Gaworek, Norbert H. 'From Blockade to Trade: Allied Economic Warfare Against Soviet Russia, June 1919 to January 1920', *Jahrbücher für Geschichte Osteuropas,* XXIII, 1 (1975), pp. 36-69.

Gerson, Lennard. *The Secret Police in Lenin's Russia.* Philadelphia, 1976.

Gilbert, Felix. 'The "New Diplomacy" of the Eighteenth Century', *World Politics,* IV, 1 (October 1951), pp. 1-38.

Ginsburgs, George. 'The Theory and Practice of Neutrality in Soviet Diplomacy'. Ph.D. thesis, UCLA, 1959.

Girardet, Raoul. 'Litvinov et ses énigmes', in: *Les Relations Germano-Soviétiques de 1933 à 1939.* Paris, 1954.

Glassman, Jon D. 'Soviet Foreign Policy Decision Making', in Andrew W. Cordier, ed., *Columbia Essays in International Afairs,* vol. III, *The Deans Papers, 1967.* New York, 1968, pp. 373-402.

Glenny, M. V. 'The Anglo-Soviet Trade Agreement, March 1921', *The Journal of Contemporary History,* V, 2 (1970), pp. 63-82.

—— 'Leonid Krasin: The Years before 1917, An Outline', *Soviet Studies,* XXII, 2 (October 1970), pp. 192-221.

Goldbach, Marie-Luise. *Karl Radek und die deutsch-sowjetischen Beziehungen, 1918-1923.* Bonn-Bad Godesberg, 1973.

Gorodetskii, E. N. *Rozhdenie sovetskogo gosudarstvo, 1917-18gg.* Moscow, 1965.

Gorodetsky, Gabriel. *The Other "Zinoviev Letters" New Light on the Mismanagement of the Affair.* Tel-Aviv, 1976.

—— *The Precarious Truce: Anglo-Soviet Relations, 1924-27.* Cambridge, 1977.

—— 'The Soviet Union and Britain's General Strike of May 1926', *Cahiers du Monde Russe et Soviétique,* XVII, 2-3 (Avril-Septembre 1976), pp. 287-310.

Gorokhov, A. 'Leninist Diplomacy: Principles and Traditions', *International Affairs,* no. 4 (1968), pp. 38-44.

Gorokhov, I., L. Zamiatin and I. Zemskov.*G. V. Chicherin — diplomat leninskoi shkoly.* Moscow, 1966 and 1974.

Govorchin, Gerald Gilbert. 'The Voikov Affair', *International Review of History and Political Science,* IX, 1 (February 1972), pp. 76-94.

Grant, Natalie. 'The "Zinoviev Letter" Case', *Soviet Studies,* XIX, 2 (October 1967), pp. 264-77.

Graubard, Stephen R. *British Labour and the Russian Revolution, 1917-1924.* Cambridge, 1956.

Gregor, R. 'Lenin, Revolution, and Foreign Policy', *International Journal,* XXII (1967), pp. 563-75.

Griffiths, Franklyn. 'The Origins of Peaceful Coexistence: A Historical Note', *Survey,* no. 50 (January 1964), pp. 195-201.

—— 'Inner Tensions in the Soviet Approach to "Disarmament",' *International Journal,* XXII, 4 (Autumn 1967), pp. 593-617.

Gromyko, A. 'Diplomat leninskoi shkoly', *Izvestiia,* (5 December 1962).

—— and B. N. Ponomarev, eds. *Istoriia vneshnei politiki SSSR, 1917-1975, tom pervyi, 1917-1945gg.* 2nd edn. Moscow, 1976.

Grottian, Walter. *Lenins Anleitung zum Handeln: Theorie und Praxis sowjetischer Aussenpolitik.* Köln and Opladen, 1962.

Grzybowski, Kazimierz. *Soviet Public International Law: Doctrines and Diplomatic Practice.* Leyden, 1970.

Gvishiani, Liudmila. 'The Martens Mission (From the History of Soviet-American Relations, 1919-1920)', *International Affairs*, no. 10 (1964), pp. 62-65 and 98.

—— *Sovetskaia rossiia i SShA (1917-1920)*. Moscow, 1970.

Hague, Kaare. 'Alexandra Mikhailovna Kollontai: The Scandinavian Period, 1922-1943'. Ph.D. thesis, University of Minnesota, 1971.

Hard, William. *Raymond Robins' Own Story*. New York, 1920.

Harr, John Ensor. *The Professional Diplomat*. Princeton, 1969.

Haupt, Georges. *Socialism and the Great War*. London, 1972.

Heilbrunn, Otto. *The Soviet Secret Services*. New York, 1956.

Heitman, Sidney. 'Nikolai Bukharin's Theory of World Revolution'. Ph.D. thesis, Columbia University, 1963.

Helbig, Herbert. *Die Träger der Rapallo-Politik*. Göttingen, 1958.

Herman, Donald L. *The Comintern in Mexico*. Washington, 1974.

Heymann, Hans, Jr. 'Oil in Soviet-Western Relations in the Interwar Years', *American Slavic and East European Review*, VII, 4 (December 1948), pp. 303-16.

Himmer, Robert. 'Harmonicas for Lenin: The Development of German Economic Policy toward Soviet Russia, December 1918 to June 1919', *The Journal of Modern History*, XLIV, 2 (June 1977), pp. D1221-48.

—— 'Soviet Policy Toward Germany During the Russo-Polish War, 1920', *Slavic Review*, XXXV, 4 (December 1976), pp. 665-82.

Hopper, Bruce C. 'Narkomindel and Comintern: Instruments of World Revolution', *Foreign Affairs*, XIX, 4 (July 1941), pp. 737-50.

Horak, Stephan. 'Lenin on Coexistence: A Chapter in Soviet Foreign Policy', *Studies on the Soviet Union*, III, 3 (1964), pp. 20-30.

Hulse, James W. *The Forming of the Communist International*. Stanford, 1964.

Iakushevskii, A. S. *Propagandistskaia rabota bol'shevikov sredi voisk interventov v 1918-1920gg*. Moscow, 1974.

Ignat'ev, A. V. *Vneshniaia politika vremennogo pravitel'stva*. Moscow, 1974.

Ioffe, A. E. *Vneshnaia politika sovetskogo soiuza, 1928-1932gg*. Moscow, 1968.

—— *Internatsionalnye nauchnye i kul'turnye sviazi sovetskogo soiuza, 1928-1932*. Moscow, 1969.

—— 'Mezhdunarodnye nauchno-tekhnicheskie i kul'turnye sviazi sovetskoi strany (noiabr' 1917-1920g)', *Istoricheskie zapiski*, no. 91 (1973), pp. 27-80.

Iroshnikov, M. P. 'Iz istorii organizatsii narodnogo komissariata inostrannykh del', *Istoriia SSSR*, no. 1 (1964), pp. 105-16.

—— *Sozdanie sovetskogo narodnykh komissarov i narodnye komissariaty oktiabr' 1917g.-ianvar' 1918g*. Leningrad and Moscow, 1966 and Leningrad, 1967.

—— *Tainoe stanovitsia iavnym: ob izdanii sekretnykh dogovorov tsarskogo i Vremennogo pravitel'stva*. Moscow, 1970.

—— 'K voprosy o slome burzhuaznoi gosudarstvennoi mashiny v Rossii', in: Iu. S. Tokarev, ed. *Problemy gosudarstvennogo stroitel'stva v pervye gody sovetskoi vlasti: sbornik statei*. Leningrad, 1973, pp. 46-66.

—— 'O partiinom sostave sovetskogo gosudarstvennogo apparata v 1918g.', *Voprosy istorii KPSS*, no. 9 (1974), pp. 115-18.

Isaacs, Harold. *The Tragedy of the Chinese Revolution*. New York, 1966.

Itkina, A. M. *Revoliutsioner, tribun, diplomat: stranitsy zhizni Aleksandry Mikhailovny Kollontai*. Moscow, 1970 and 1964.

Iusupov, I. A. *Ustanovlenie i razvitie sovetsko-iranskikh otnoshenii (1917-1927gg.)*. Tashkent, 1969.

Jacobsen, Hans-Adolf. *Nationalsozialistische Aussenpolitik, 1933-1938*. Frankfurt, 1968.

Jacobson, Jon. *Locarno Diplomacy: Germany and the West, 1925-1929*. Princeton, 1972.

Jelavich, Barbara. *St. Petersburg and Moscow: Tsarist and Soviet Foreign Policy, 1814-1974*. Bloomington, 1974.

Joost, Wilhelm. *Botschafter bei den roten Zaren: die deutschen Missionschefs in Moskau 1918 bis 1941*. Vienna, 1967.

Kahan, Vilém. 'The Communist International, 1919-43: The Personnel of Its Highest Bodies,' *International Review of Social History*, XXI, 2 (1976), pp. 151-85.

Kapur, Harish. *Soviet Russia and Asia, 1917-1927: A Study of Soviet Policy towards Turkey, Iran and Afghanistan*. Geneva, 1966.

Kaplin, Anatolii Stepanovich. *V. I. Lenin — osnovopolozhnik diplomatii sotsialisticheskogo gosudarstva*. Moscow, 1970.

Karpova, Roza Fedorovna. *L. B. Krassin — sovetskii diplomat*. Moscow, 1962.

—— 'Zakliuchitel'nyi etap anglo-sovetskikh peregovorov', *Vestnik leningradskogo universiteta*, 'seriia istorii, iazyka i literatury', no. 14 (1962), pp. 34-46.

Kelly, David. *The Ruling Few: The Human Background to Diplomacy*. London, 1952.

Kennan, George. *Russia and the West Under Lenin and Stalin*. New York, 1961.

—— *American-Soviet Relations, 1917-1920*. Vol. I. *Russia Leaves the War*. Vol. II. *The Decision to Intervene*. New York, 1967 [1956 and 1958].

Kertesz, Stephen D. 'Reflections on Soviet and American Negotiating Behavior', *The Review of Politics*, XIX, 1 (January 1957), pp. 3-36.

Kharlamov, M. A., ed. *Leninskaia vneshniaia politika sovetskoi strany, 1917-1924*. Moscow, 1969.

Kheifets, A. N. *Sovetskaia rossiia i sopredel'nye strany vostoka v gody grazhdanskoi voiny (1918-1920)*. Moscow, 1964.

—— *Sovetskaia diplomatiia i narody vostoka, 1921-1927*. Moscow, 1968.

Klein, Fritz. *Die diplomatischen Beziehungen Deutschlands zur Sowjetunion, 1917-1923*. Berlin, 1953.

Kobliakov, I. K. *Ot bresta do rapallo: ocherki istorii sovetsko-germanskikh otnoshenii s 1918 po 1922g*. Moscow, 1954.

—— 'Bor'ba sovetskogo gosudarstva za normalizatsiiu otnoshenii s Germaniei v 1919-1929gg.', *Istoriia SSSR*, no. 2 (1971), pp. 17-31.

—— and M. Slavyanov. 'The Shaping of the All-Union Foreign Policy', *International Affairs*, no. 4 (1972), pp. 46-54.

Kochan, Lionel. *Russia and the Weimar Republic*. Cambridge, 1954.

—— *The Struggle for Germany*. New York, 1963.

Kol'tsov, A. V. *Lenin i stanovlenie akademii nauk kak tsentra sovetskoi nauki*. Leningrad, 1969.

Kondrat'ev, Nik. *Skvoz' revol'vernyi lai...* Moscow, 1962.

Korbel, Josef. *Poland Between East and West: Soviet and German Diplomacy toward Poland, 1919-1933*. Princeton, 1963.

Kordt, E., A. Kaznachejev and C. D. Kernig. 'Theorie und Praxis der kommunistischen Diplomatie', in: *Sowjetsystem und Demokratische Gesellschaft*. Vol. I. Freiburg, 1966, pp. 12-25.

Korn, Walter. *Der deutsch-russische Konsular-Vertrag*. Munich [1928?].

Kornev, N. *Litvinov*. Moscow, 1936.

Korovin, E. A., ed. *Mezhdunarodnoe pravo*. Moscow, 1951.

Kositsyn, A. P., et al., eds. *Istoriia sovetskogo gosudarstva i prava*. Vol. I. *Stanovlenie sovetskogo gosudarstva i prava (1917-1920gg.)*. Vol. II. *Sovetskoe gosudarstvo i pravo v period stroitel'stva sotsializma (1921-1935gg.)*. Moscow, 1968.

Kozhevnikov, I. F. *Sovetskoe gosudarstvo i mezhdunardnoe pravo*. Moscow, 1967.

Krasin, Liubov. *Leonid Krasin: His Life and Work*. London, 1929.

Kremnev, Boris Grigor'evich. *Krasin*. Moscow, 1968.

Kruglak, Theodore. *The Two Faces of TASS*. Minneapolis, 1962.

Krutitskaia, E. I. and L. S. Mitrofanova. *Polpred Aleksandr Troianovskii*. Moscow, 1975.

—— 'Posol sovetskogo soiuza A. A. Troianovskii', *Novaia i noveishaia istoriia*, no. 2 (1975), pp. 88-100 and no. 3 (1975), pp. 102-14.

Kulski, W. W. 'Soviet Diplomatic Techniques', *The Russian Review*, XIX, 3 (July 1960), pp. 217-26.

Kuz'min, M. S. *Deiatel'nost' partii i sovetskogo gosudarstva po razvitiiu mezhdunarodnykh nauchnykh i kul'turnykh sviazei SSSR, 1917-1932gg*. Leningrad, 1971.

Kuznetsova, S. I. *Ustanovlenie sovetsko-turetskikh otnoshenii (k 40-letiiu moskovskogo dogovora mezhdu RSFSR i turtsiei)*. Moscow, 1961.

Lahey, Dale Terence. 'Soviet Ideological Development of Coexistence: 1917-1927', *Canadian Slavonic Papers*, VI (1964), pp. 80-94.

Laqueur, Walter. *Russia and Germany: A Century of Conflict*. Boston, 1965.

Lasch, Christopher. *The American Liberals and the Russian Revolution*. New York, 1972.

Lauren, Paul Gordon. *Diplomats and Bureaucrats: The First Institutional Responses to Twentieth-Century Diplomacy in France and Germany*. Stanford, 1976.

Lazitch, Branko, and Milorad Drashkovitch. *Lenin and the Comintern*. Stanford, 1972.

Lebedinka, E. D. 'Mezhdunarodnye sviazi sovetskikh uchenykh v 1917-1924gg.', *Voprosy istorii*, no. 2 (1971), pp. 44-54.

Lederer, Ivo J., ed. *Russian Foreign Policy: Essays in Historical Perspective*. New Haven, 1962.

Lenczowski, George. *Russia and the West in Iran, 1918-1948*. Ithaca, 1949.

'Lenin's Foreign Policy Activity (October 1917-March 1918)', *International Affairs*, no. 1 (1969), pp. 110-14.

Lenin v bor'be za revoliutsionnyi internatsional. Moscow, 1970.

Leninskaia diplomatiia mira i sotrudnichestva (ustanovlenie diplomaticheskikh otnoshenii mezhdu SSSR i kapitalisticheskimi stranami v 1924-1925gg.). Moscow, 1965.

Lensen, George Alexander. *Japanese Recognition of the USSR: Soviet-Japanese Relations, 1921-1930.* Tallahassee, 1970.

—— *The Damned Inheritance: The Soviet Union and the Manchurian Crisis, 1924-1925.* Tallahassee, 1974.

Leong, Sow-Theng. *Sino-Soviet Diplomatic Relations, 1917-1926.* Honolulu, 1976.

Leonidov, A. 'Socialism's First Diplomats', *New Times*, no. 28 (1967), pp. 12-6.

Lerner, Warren. 'Karl Radek on World Revolution: A Study in Revolutionary Strategy and Tactics'. Ph.D. thesis, Columbia University, 1961.

—— 'Karl Radek and the Chinese Revolution, 1925-27', in: John Shelton Curtiss, ed. *Essays in Russian and Soviet History in Honor of Geroid Tanquary Robinson.* New York, 1962, pp. 270-82.

—— 'The Historical Origins of the Soviet Doctrine of Peaceful Coexistence', *Law and Contemporary Problems*, XXIX, 4 (Autumn 1964), pp. 865-70.

—— *Karl Radek: The Last Internationalist.* Stanford, 1970.

—— 'Poland in 1920: A Case Study of Foreign Policy Decision Making Under Lenin', *South Atlantic Quarterly*, LXXII, 3 (Summer 1973), pp. 406-14.

Lesnoi, V. M. *Sotsialisticheskaia revoliutsiia i gosudarstvennyi apparat.* Moscow, 1968.

Lewin, Moshe. *Political Undercurrents in Soviet Economic Debates: From Bukharin to the Modern Reformers.* London, 1975.

Liadov, Martyn Nikolaevich, ed. *Leonid Borisovich Krasin ('Nikitch'); gody podpol'ia: sbornik vospominanii, statei i dokumentov.* Moscow, 1928.

Lindemann, Albert S. *The 'Red Years', Bolshevism vs. European Socialism, 1919-1921.* Berkeley and Los Angeles, 1974.

Linder, I. 'Lenin's Foreign Policy Activity (October 1921-March 1922)', *International Affairs*, no. 12 (1969), pp. 46-51.

—— and M. Trush. 'Lenin's Foreign Policy Activity (August-December 1919),' *International Affairs*, no. 6 (1969), pp. 56-60.

Linke, Horst Günther. *Deutsch-sowjetische Beziehungen bis Rapallo.* Köln, 1970.

'Litvinov, Maxim' (pseudonym for Grigorii Besedovskii?). *Notes for A Journal.* New York, 1955.

Liubimov, N. N. 'O V.V. Vorovskom', *Voprosy istorii*, no. 10 (1971), pp. 138-43.

Loginov, M. 'Kul't lichnosti chuzhd nashemu stroiu!', *Molodoi kommunist*, no. 1 (1962), pp. 52-6.

London, Kurt. *The Making of Foreign Policy: East and West.* New York, 1965.

Macfarlane, L. J. 'Hands Off Russia: British Labour and the Russo-Polish War, 1920', *Past and Present*, no. 37 (December 1967), pp. 126-52.

Magerovsky, Eugene L. 'The People's Commissariat for Foreign Affairs, 1917-1923: Organization and Evolution'. M.A. thesis, Columbia University, 1957.

—— 'The People's Commissariat for Foreign Affairs, 1917-1946'. Ph.D. thesis, Columbia University, 1975.

Mahaney, W. L., Jr. *The Soviet Union, the League of Nations and Disarmament.* Philadelphia, 1940.

Maksimov, I. 'Lenin's Foreign Policy Activity (April-July 1919)', *International Affairs*, no. 5 (1969), pp. 54-58.

Marantz, Paul Joseph. 'The Soviet Union and the Western World: A Study in Doctrinal Change, 1917-1964'. Ph.D. thesis. Harvard University, 1971.

Margulies, Sylvia R. *The Pilgrimage to Russia: The Soviet Union and the Treatment of Foreigners, 1924-1937.* Madison, 1968.

Markert, Werner, ed. *Deutsch-russische Beziehungen von Bismarck bis zur Gegenwart.* Stuttgart, 1964.

Markus, Vasyl. *L'Ukraine soviétique dans les relations internationales et son statut en droit international, 1918-1923.* Paris, 1959.

Martin, Thomas S. 'The Urquhart Concession and Anglo-Soviet Relations, 1921-1922', *Jahrbücher für Geschichte Osteuropas,* XX, 4 (December 1972), pp. 552-70.

Mastny, Vojtech. 'The Cassandra in the Foreign Commissariat: Maxim Litvinov and the Cold War', *Foreign Affairs,* LIV, 2 (January 1976), pp. 366-76.

Mayer, Arno J. *Wilson vs. Lenin: The Political Origins of the New Diplomacy, 1917-1918.* Cleveland and New York, 1959.

—— *Politics and Diplomacy of Peacemaking: Containment and Counter-revolution at Versailles, 1918-1919.* New York, 1969.

McQuillen, David Karl. 'Soviet Attitudes towards China, 1919-1927'. Ph.D. thesis, Kent State University, 1973.

Medvedev, R. A. *Let History Judge: The Origins and Consequences of Stalinism.* New York, 1972.

—— *K sudu istorii.* New York, 1974.

Metzler, W. von. *Die auswärtige Gewalt der Sowjetunion.* Berlin, 1930.

Meyer, Alfred G. *Leninism.* New York, Washington and London, 1962.

Meyer, Klaus. 'Sowjetrussland und die Anfänge der Weimarer Republik', *Forschungen zur osteuropäischen Geschichte,* XX (1973), pp. 77-92.

Milioukov [Miliukov], Pavel. *La Politique Extérieure des Soviets.* Paris, 1936.

Miller, A. 'The Origin of Leninist Eastern Policy', *International Affairs,* no. 4 (1972), pp. 68-75.

Milton, Nan. *John Maclean.* N.p. [London], 1973.

Minasian, Nikolai Mikhailovich. *Pravovye osnovy leninskoi diplomatii.* Rostov n.D., 1970.

Mints, I. I., ed. *Sovetskaia rossiia i kapitalisticheskii mir v 1917-1923gg.* Moscow, 1957.

Mironov, N. V. *Pravovoe regulirovanie vneshnikh snoshenii SSSR, 1917-1970gg.* Moscow, 1971.

Mirovitskaia, R. 'An Example of Friendship and Cooperation (From the History of Soviet-Chinese Relations)', *International Affairs,* no. 12 (1974), pp. 95-98.

Mogilevskii, Boris L'vovich. *Nikitich (Leonid Borisovich Krasin).* Moscow, 1963.

—— *Prizvanie inzhenera Krasina.* Moscow, 1970.

Molchanov, Iu. L. *Komintern: u istokov politiki edinogo proletarskogo fronta.* Moscow, 1969.

Moore, Barrington, Jr. *Soviet Politics — The Dilemma of Power: The Role of Ideas in Social Change.* New York, 1950.

Morgan, R. P. 'The Political Significance of the German-Soviet Trade Negotiations, 1922-5', *The Historical Journal,* VI, 2 (1963), pp. 253-71.

Morris, Bernard S. *International Communism and American Policy.* New York, 1966.

Morse, William Perry, Jr. 'Leonid Borisovich Krasin: Soviet Diplomat, 1918-1926'. Ph.D. thesis, University of Wisconsin, 1971.

Mosely, Philip E. *The Kremlin and World Politics: Studies in Soviet Policy and Action*. New York, 1960.

—— ed. *The Soviet Union, 1922-1962*. New York, and London, 1963.

Mosse, W. E. 'Makers of the Soviet Union', *The Slavonic and East European Review*, XLVI, 106 (January 1968), pp. 141-54.

Nauchitel', Mikhail Veniaminovich. *Stranitsy zhizni i bor'by* [*o L.B. Krasine*]. Irkutsk, 1972.

Nekrich, Alexander. 'The Arrest and Trial of I. M. Maisky', *Survey*, XXII, 3-4 (Summer/Autumn 1976), pp. 313-20.

Nemzer, Louis. 'The Structure of Soviet Foreign Propaganda Organization'. Ph.D. thesis, University of Chicago, 1948.

—— 'The Kremlin's Professional Staff: The "Apparatus" of the Central Committee, Communist Party of the Soviet Union', *American Political Science Review*, XLIV, 1 (March 1950), pp. 64-85.

Nicolaevsky, Boris I. *Power and the Soviet Elite: "The Letter of an Old Bolshevik" and Other Essays*. Ann Arbor, 1975.

—— 'Stalin i ubiistvo kirova', *Sotsialisticheskii vestnik*, no. 10 (1956).

Nicolson, Harold. *Curzon: The Last Phase*. London, 1934.

—— *The Evolution of Diplomacy*. New York, 1962.

—— *Diplomacy*. New York, 1964.

Nikonova, S. V. *Antisovetskaia vneshniaia politika angliiskikh konservatorov, 1924-1927*. Moscow, 1963.

Nollau, Gunther. *International Communism and World Revolution: History and Methods*. New York, 1961.

North, Robert C. *Moscow and the Chinese Communists*. Stanford, 1963.

Ocherk istorii ministerstva inostrannykh del. St Petersburg, 1902.

Olenev, S. *Mezhdunarodnoe priznanie SSSR*. Moscow, 1962.

'On bral zimnii (dokumenty o V.A. Antonove-Ovseenko)', *Novyi mir*, XL, 11 (November 1964), pp. 200-12.

Organizatsiia nauki v pervye gody sovetskoi vlasti, 1917-1925. Leningrad, 1968.

Osakwe, Chris. *The Participation of the Soviet Union in Universal International Organizations: A Political and Legal Analysis of Soviet Strategies and Aspirations inside ILO, UNESCO and WHO*. Leiden, 1972.

Owen, Gail L. 'The Metro-Vickers Crisis: Anglo-Soviet Relations between Trade Agreements, 1932-1934', *Slavonic and East European Review*, XLIX, 114 (January 1971), pp. 92-112.

Pertzoff, Margaret Henderson. 'Lady in Red: A Study of the Early Career of Alexandra Mikhailovna Kollontai'. Ph.D. thesis. University of Virginia, 1968.

Petrov, G. D. 'Aleksandra Kollontai v SShA', *Novaia i noveishaia istoriia*, no. 3 (1972), pp. 128-42.

Petrov, V. 'The Sources of Leninist Diplomacy', *International Affaira*, no. 6 (1975), pp. 106-14.

—— V. Belov and A. Karenin. *Leninskaia vneshniaia politika SSSR: razvitie i perspektivy*. Moscow, 1974.

Pidhainy, Oleh S. 'Stalin's Negotiations on Behalf of the Soviet Government with the Ukraine, November 30, 1917, and Conversation with Bakinskiy: The Suppressed Text', *New Review of East-European History*, III, 6 (November 1963), pp. 4-12.

Pietsch, Walter. *Revolution und Staat: Institutionen als Träger der Macht in Sowjetrussland, 1917-1922,* Köln, 1969.

Pistrak, Lazar M. 'Lenin and "Peaceful Coexistence",' *Problems of Communism,* VIII, 6 (November-December 1959), pp. 53-56.

Polenov, V. A. 'Obezrenie prezhnego i nyneshnego sostoianiia ministerstva inostrannykh del'. *Sbornik imperatorskogo russkogo istoricheskogo obshchestva.* St Petersburg, 1867-1917. Bol. XXXI, pp. 163-96.

Ponomaryov [Ponomarev], B., et al., eds. *History of Soviet Foreign Policy, 1917-1945.* Moscow, 1969.

Poole, DeWitt C. *The Conduct of Foreign Relations Under Modern Democratic Conditions.* New Haven, 1924.

Pope, Arthur Upham. *Maxim Litvinoff.* New York, 1943.

Popov, A. 'Diplomatiia vremennogo pravitelstva v bor'be s revoliutsiei', *Krasnyi arkhiv,* XX, 1 (1927), pp. 3-38.

Popov, M. V. *Missiia E. A. Babushkina v irane.* Moscow, 1974.

Popov, V. I. *Anglo-sovetskie otnosheniia (1927-29).* Moscow, 1958.

—— *Diplomaticheskie otnosheniia mezhdu SSSR i Angliei, 1929-1939gg.* Moscow, 1965.

—— ed. *Leninskaia diplomatiia mira i sotrudnichestva (ustanovlenie diplomaticheskikh otnoshenii mezhdu SSSR i kapitalisticheskimi stranami v 1924-1925gg.).* Moscow, 1965.

—— ed. *Dipkur'ery: ocherki o pervykh sovetskikh diplomaticheskikh kur'erakh.* Moscow, 1970.

Potemkin, Vladimir P., ed. *Istoriia diplomatii.* 1st edn. Moscow, 1941-1945. 3 vols.

Pragmaticus. 'The Lessons of Brest Litovski', *Slavonic and East European Review,* XV, 44 (1937), pp. 328-43.

Problemy gosudarstvennogo stroitel'stva v pervye gody sovetskoi vlasti: sbornik statei. Leningrad, 1973.

Quigley, John. *The Soviet Foreign Trade Monopoly: Institutions and Laws.* Columbus, 1974.

Rakitin, A. 'Soviet Diplomacy — One of the Pioneers', *New Times,* no. 32 (9 August 1967), pp. 18-20.

Ravasani, Schapour. *Sowjetrepublik Gilan: Die sozialistische Bewegung im Iran seit Ende des 19. Jhdt. bis 1922.* Berlin, n.d.

Rigby, T. H. *Communist Party Membership in the USSR, 1917-1967.* Princeton, 1968.

—— 'The Birth of the Council of People's Commissars', *Australian Journal of Politics and History,* XX, 1 (April 1974), pp. 70-75.

Riha, Thomas. *A Russian European: Paul Kiliukov in Russian Politics.* Notre Dame, 1969.

Roberts, Henry L. 'Marxim Litvinov', in: Gordon A. Craig and Felix Gilbert, eds. *The Diplomats, 1919-1939.* New York, 1963, pp. 344-77.

Roberts, James W. 'Lenin's Theory of Imperialism in Soviet Usage', *Soviet Studies,* XXIX, 3 (July 1977), pp. 353-72.

Rosenbaum, Kurt. 'The German Involvement in the Shakhty Trial', *The Russian Review,* XXI, 3 (July 1962), pp. 238-60.

—— *Community of Fate: German-Soviet Diplomatic Relations, 1922-1928.* Syracuse, 1965.

Rosenfeld, Günter, *Sowietrussland und Deutschland, 1917-1922.* Berlin, 1960.

Rosenko, I. S. *Sovetsko-germanskie otnosheniia (1921-1922gg.).* Leningrad, 1965.

Rosenstone, Robert A. *Romantic Revolutionary: A Biography of John Reed.* New York, 1975.

Rossow, Robert. 'The Professionalization of the New Diplomacy', *World Politics,* XIV, 4 (July 1962), pp. 561-75.

Rubinshtein, N. L. *Sovetskaia diplomatiia v bor'be protiv izoliatsii SSSR i ustanovlenie diplomaticheskikh otnoshenii s kapitalisticheskimi stranami.* Moscow, 1947.

—— *Sovetskaia rossiia i kapitalisticheskie gosudarstva v gody perekhoda ot voiny k miru (1921-1922gg.).* Moscow, 1948.

—— *Ukreplenie mezhdunarodnykh pozitsii sovetskogo soiuza v period perekhoda na mirnuiu rabotu po vosstanovleniiu khoziaistva (1921-1925gg.).* Moscow, 1951.

Ruge, Wolfgang. *Die Stellungnahme der Sowjetunion gegen die Besetzung des Ruhrgebietes: Zur Geschichte der deutsch-sowjetischen Beziehungen von Januar bis September 1923.* Berlin, 1962.

Ruland, Bernd. *Deutsche Botschaft Moskau: 50 Jahre Schicksal zwischen Ost und West.* Bayreuth, 1964.

Sabanin, A. V. *Posol'skoe i konsul'skoe pravo: kratkoe prakticheskoe posobie.* Moscow, 1934.

Schapiro, Leonard. *The Communist Party of the Soviet Union.* New York, 1960 and 1971.

—— *The Origin of the Communist Autocracy.* New York and Washington, 1965.

Schlesinger, Rudolf. 'Litvinov's Ghost', *Soviet Studies,* VII, 4 (April 1956), pp. 373-83.

Schmid, Alex P. *Churchills privater Krieg: Intervention und Konterrevolution im russischen Bürgerkrieg, November 1918-März 1920.* Zurich, 1974.

Schram, Stuart. 'Christian Rakovskij et le premier rapprochement franco-soviétique', *Cahiers du Monde Russe et Soviétique,* I, 2 (January-March 1960), pp. 205-37 and I, 4 (July-December 1960), pp. 584-629.

Schüddekopf, Otto-Ernst. 'Karl Radek in Berlin: Ein Kapitel deutsch-russischer Beziehungen im Jahre 1919', *Archiv für Sozialgeschichte,* II (1962), pp. 87-166.

—— 'Deutschland zwischen Ost und West: Karl Moor und die deutsch-russischen Beziehungen in der ersten Hälfte des Jahres 1919', *Archiv für Sozialgeschichte,* no. 3 (1963), pp. 223-63.

Schulzinger, Robert D. *The Making of the Diplomatic Mind: The Training, Outlook, and Style of United States Foreign Service Officers, 1908-1931.* Middletown, 1975.

Schütz, Walter J., ed. *Aus der Schule der Diplomatie.* Dusseldorf and Vienna, 1965.

Scott, George. *Rise and Fall of the League of Nations.* London, 1973.

Scott, William Evans. *Alliance Against Hitler: The Origins of the Franco-Soviet Pact.* Durham, 1962.

Seabury, Paul. *The Wilhelmstrasse: A Study of German Diplomats under the Nazi Regime.* Berkeley and Los Angeles, 1954.

Senn, Alfred Erich. 'The Rakovsky Affair: A Crisis in Franco-Soviet Relations, 1927', *Slavic and East-European Studies,* III-IV (1965-66), pp. 102-17.

—— *Diplomacy and Revolution: The Soviet Mission to Switzerland, 1918.* Notre Dame, 1974.

Shabanov, Iu. V. *Leninskie printsipy raboty gosudarstvennogo apparata.* Minsk, 1971.

Shakhova, N. 'Partiinye organizatsii v narkomatakh', *Partiinoe stroitel'stvo*, no. 7 (1941), pp. 13-18.

Sharp, Alan J. 'The Foreign Office in Eclipse, 1919-1922', *History*, LXI, 202 (June 1976), pp. 198-218.

Sheviakov, A. A. 'Ustanovlenie diplomaticheskikh otnoshenii SSSR so stranami tsentral'noi i iugo-vostochnoi evropy', *Voprosy istorii*, no. 1 (1975), pp. 23-31.

Shishkin, V. A. *Sovetskoe gosudarstvo i strany zapada v 1917-1923gg.: ocherki istorii stanovleniia ekonomicheskikh otnoshenii.* Leningrad, 1969.

Shub, D. 'Iz davnikh let', *Novyi zhurnal*, no. 105 (1971), pp. 232-39.

Silverman, Saul Norman. 'A World to Win: A Study in the Roots of Pre-Revolutionary Development of the Bolshevik Approach to World Affairs'. Ph.D. thesis, Yale University, 1963.

Sizonenko, A. I. *V strane atstekskogo orla.* Moscow, 1969.

—— *Ocherki istorii sovetsko-latinoamerikanskikh otnoshenii 1924-1970gg.* Moscow, 1971.

—— 'Sovetskaia rossiia i latinskaia amerika v 1917-1924gg.', *Voprosy istorii*, no. 6 (1973), pp. 81-92.

—— *Sovetskii soiuz i meksika — 50 let.* Moscow, 1974.

Skaba, A. D. *Parizhskaia mirnaia konferentsiia i inostrannaia interventsiia v strane sovetov (ianvar'-iiun' 1919 goda).* Kiev, 1971.

Slessinger, Seymour. 'The Idea of Nationalism in Soviet Foreign Policy'. Ph.D. thesis, Boston University, 1960.

Slusser, Robert M. 'The Role of the Foreign Ministry', in: Ivo Lederer, ed., *Russian Foreign Policy.* New Haven, 1962, pp. 197-239.

Sokolov, V. 'Break Through the Diplomatic Blockade (Fiftieth Anniversary of the Period of the Recognition of the USSR)', *International Affairs*, no. 6 (1974), pp. 81-90; no. 8 (1974), pp. 89-95; and no. 12 (1974), pp. 94-102.

Solov'ev, O. F. 'Iz istorii bor'by sovetskogo pravitel'stva za mirnoe sosushchestvovanie s Angliei', *Voprosy istorii*, no. 2 (1965), pp. 54-64.

Sonkin, Moisey Evelevich. *Kliuchi ot bronirovannykh.* Moscow, 1966.

Sontag, John P. 'The Soviet War Scare of 1926-27', *The Russian Review*, XXXIV, 1 (January 1975), pp. 66-77.

Sostav rukovodiashchik rabotnikov i spetsialistov soiuza SSR. Moscow, 1936.

Spector, Ivor. *The Soviet Union and the Moslim World, 1917-1958.* Seattle, 1959.

Spoerry, Philip S. 'The Central Rabkrin Apparatus: 1917-1925'. Ph.D. thesis, Harvard University, 1968.

SSSR i latinskaia amerika, 1917-1967. Moscow, 1967.

Startsev, A. *Russkie bloknoty Dzhona Rida.* Moscow, 1968.

Steiner, Zara S. *The Foreign Office and Foreign Policy, 1898-1914.* London, 1969.

—— and M. L. Dockrill. 'The Foreign Office Reforms, 1919-1921', *The Journal of History*, XVII, 1 (March 1974), pp. 131-56.

Stepanov, A. 'The Historical Experience of Co-operation Between the USSR and Germany: The 1926 Berlin Treaty', *International Affairs*, no. 8 (1963), pp. 91-96.

—— 'Diplomatic practice: Forms and Methods', *International Affairs*, no. 12 (1972), pp. 43-49.

—— 'Leninskie printsipy partiinogo rukovodstva vneshnei politikoi i torcheskoe razvitie', *Voprosy istorii KPSS*, no. 12 (1976), pp. 57-69.

Stepanov, G. 'Pervoe torgovoe otnoshenie (s Angliei)', *Vneshniaia torgovlia*, no. 2 (1967), pp. 12-14.

Stern-Rubarth, Edgar. *Graf Brockdorff-Rantzau: Wanderer zwischen zwei Welten.* Herford and Bonn, 1968.

Struger, Marlene. 'Nikolai Nikolaievich Krestinskii and Soviet German Relations, 1921-1930'. Ph.D. thesis, University of Wisconsin, 1973.

Tang, Peter S. H. *Russian and Soviet Policy in Manchuria and Outer Mongolia, 1911-1931.* Durham, 1959.

Taracouzio, T. A. *The Soviet Union and International Law.* New York, 1935.

—— *War and Peace in Soviet Diplomacy.* New York, 1940.

Teplinskii, L. B. *Sovetsko-afganskie otnosheniia, 1919-1960: kratkii ocherk.* Moscow, 1961.

—— *50 let sovetsko-afganskikh otnoshenii, 1919-1969.* Moscow, 1971.

Thayer, Charles W. *Diplomat.* New York, 1959.

Thompson, John M. *Russia, Bolshevism and the Versailles Peace.* Princeton, 1966.

Thornton, Richard C. *The Comintern and the Chinese Communists, 1928-1931.* Seattle, 1969.

Tokarev, Iu. S., et al., eds. *Problemy gosudarstvennogo stroitel'stva v pervye gody sovetskoi vlasti: sbornik statei.* Leningrad, 1973.

Towster, Julian. *Political Power in the USSR, 1917-1947.* New York, 1948.

Trani, Eugene P. 'Woodrow Wilson and the Decision to Intervene in Russia: A Reconsideration', *The Journal of Modern History*, XLVIII, 3 (September 1976), pp. 440-61.

Triska, Jan F. and David D. Finley. *Soviet Foreign Policy.* New York, 1968.

Triska, Jan F. and Robert M. Slusser. *The Theory, Law and Policy of Soviet Treaties.* Stanford, 1962.

Trofimova, L. I. 'Vstupitel'naia stat'ia', in: G. V. Chicherin, *G. V. Chicherin: stat'i i rechi po voprosam mezhdunarodnoi politiki.* Moscow, 1961.

—— 'Pervye shagi sovetskoi diplomatii', *Novaia i noveishaia istoriia*, no. 6 (1971), pp. 37-52 and no. 1 (1972), pp. 63-79.

—— 'Stranitsa diplomaticheskoi deiatel'nosti G. V. Chicherina', *Voprosy istorii*, no. 2 (1973), pp. 114-23.

—— 'Moskva i parizh obemenivaiutsia poslami (50 let ustanovleniia diplomaticheskikh otnoshenii mezhdu SSSR i frantsiei)', *Novaia i noveishaia istoriia*, no. 6 (1974), pp. 86-95.

—— 'Genuezskaia konferentsiia', *Novaia i noveishaia istoriia*, no. 5 (1977), pp. 109-34.

Trukhanovskii, V. G. *Istoriia mezhdunarodnikh otnoshenii i vneshnei politiki SSSR, 1917-1967gg.* Moscow, 1967.

—— 'Lenin's Foreign Policy Activity (January-March 1919)', *International Affairs*, no. 4 (1969), pp. 111-14.

—— 'Lenin's Foreign Policy Activity (January-March 1921)', *International Affairs*, no. 10 (1969), pp. 36-9.

—— et al., eds. *Diplomaticheskaia deiatel'nost' V.I. Lenina.* Moscow, 1970.

Trush, M. *Vneshnepoliticheskaia deiatel'nost' V.I. Lenina, 1917-1923.* 2 vols. Moscow, 1963.

—— 'Lenin's Foreign Policy Activities (September-December 1920)', *International Affairs*, no. 9 (1969), pp. 46-49.

—— 'Lenin's Foreign Policy Activity (January-March 1920)', *International Affairs*, no. 7 (1969), pp. 67-70.

—— 'Lenin's Foreign Policy Activity (April-July 1922)', *International Affairs*, no. 1 (1970), pp. 63-66.

—— 'Lenin's Foreign Policy Activity (August 1922-March 1923)', *International Affairs*, nos. 2-3 (1970), pp. 34-37.

—— 'A Diplomat of the Leninist School: For the 100th Anniversary of the Birth of G. V. Chicherin', *International Affairs*, no. 12 (1972), pp. 66-72.

—— *Soviet Foreign Policy: Early Years*. Moscow, n.d.

Trutko-Gul, F. I. 'O sovetskom konsule i konsul'skom kodekse', *Sovetskoe pravo*, no. 1 (1925), pp. 79-84.

Tucker, Robert C. 'Stalin, Bukharin and History as Conspiracy', in: Tucker and Stephen F. Cohen, eds. *The Great Purge Trial*. New York, 1956, pp. ix-xlviii.

—— *The Soviet Political Mind: Studies in Stalinism and Post-Stalin Change*. New York, Washington, London, 1963.

—— *Stalin as Revolutionary, 1879-1929*. New York, 1973.

Tykh, F. and Kh. Shumaker. *Iulian Markhlevskii*. Moscow, 1968.

Ulam, Adam. *The Bolsheviks*. New York, 1968.

—— *Stalin: The Man and His Era*. New York, 1973.

—— *Expansion and Coexistence: A History of Soviet Foreign Policy, 1917-1973*. New York, 1974 [1968].

Ullman, Richard H. *Anglo-Soviet Relations, 1917-1921*. Vol I. *Intervention and the War*. Vol. II. *Britain and the Russian Civil War*. Vol. III. *The Anglo-Soviet Accord*. Princeton, 1961, 1968 and 1973.

Unger, A. L. 'Stalin's Renewal of the Leading Stratum: A Note on the Great Purge', *Soviet Studies*, XX, 3 (January 1969), pp. 321-30.

Uralov, Alexander (pseudonym for Abdurakhman Avtorkhanov). *The Reign of Stalin*. London, 1953.

Valentinov, Nikolai. 'Non-Party Specialists and the Coming of the NEP', *The Russian Review*, XXX, 2 (April 1971), pp. 154-63.

Vidnye sovetskie kommunisty — uchastniki kitaiskoi revoliutsii. Moscow, 1970.

Vigor, P. H. *The Soviet View of War, Peace and Neutrality*. London and Boston, 1975.

Völgyes, Iván. 'Hungarian Prisoners of War in Russia, 1916-1919', *Cahiers du Monde Russe et Soviétiques*, XIV, 1-2 (January-June 1973), pp. 54-85.

Volkov, F. D. *Anglo-sovetskie otnosheniia, 1924-1928gg*. Moscow, 1958.

Von Laue, Theodore H. 'Soviet Diplomacy: G. V. Chicherin, Peoples Commissar for Foreign Affairs, 1918-1930', in: Gordon A. Craig and Felix Gilbert, eds., *The Diplomats, 1919-1939*. New York, 1965, pp. 234-86.

Vygodskii, S. Iu. *V.I. Lenin — rukovoditel' vneshnei politiki sovetskogo gosudarstva, (1917-1923gg.)*. Leningrad, 1960.

—— *U istokov sovetskoi diplomatii*. Moscow, 1965.

Wade, Rex A. 'War, Peace and Foreign Policy During the Russian Provisional Government of 1917'. Ph.D. thesis. University of Nebraska, 1963.

—— *The Russian Search for Peace: February-October 1917*. Stanford, 1969.

Walters, F. P. *A History of the League of Nations*. London, 1952.

Wandycz, Piotr S. *France and Her Eastern Allies, 1919-1925: French-Czechoslovak-Polish Relations from the Paris Peace Conference to Locarno.* Minneapolis, 1962.
—— *Soviet-Polish Relations, 1917-1921.* Cambridge, 1969.
Warth, Robert D. 'The Mystery of the Zinoviev Letter', *South Atlantic Quarterly*, XLIX, 4 (October 1950), pp. 441-53.
—— *The Allies and the Russian Revolution: From the Fall of the Monarchy to the Treaty of Brest-Litovsk.* Durham, 1954.
—— 'The Arcos Raid and the Anglo-Soviet "Cold War" of the 1920's', *World Affairs Quarterly*, XXIX, 2 (July 1958), pp. 115-51.
Waterfield, Gordon. *Professional Diplomat: Sir Percy Loraine of Kirkharle Bt., 1880-1961.* London, 1973.
Watt, D. C. 'The Initiation of the Negotiations Leading to the Nazi-Soviet Pact: A Historical Problem', in: Chimen Abramsky, ed. *Essays in Honour of E. H. Carr.* Hamden, 1974, pp. 152-70.
Weissman, Benjamin M. *Herbert Hoover and Famine Relief to Soviet Russia: 1921-1923.* Stanford, 1974.
Weinberg, Gerhard. *Germany and the Soviet Union, 1939-1941.* Leiden, 1954.
—— *The Foreign Policy of Hitler's Germany: Diplomatic Revolution in Europe, 1933-36.* Chicago, 1970.
Wheeler-Bennett, John W. *Brest-Litovsk: The Forgotten Peace, March 1918.* London, 1966 [1929].
White, Stephen. 'Communism and the East: the Baku Conference, 1920', *Slavic Review*, XXXIII, 3 (September 1974), pp. 492-514.
—— 'Colonial Revolution and the Communist International, 1919-1924', *Science and Society*, XL, 2 (Summer 1976), pp. 173-93.
—— ' "Anti-Bolshevik Control Officers" and British Foreign Policy, 1918-20', *Co-existence*, XIII, 2 (October 1976), pp. 144-56.
Whiting, Allen S. *Soviet Politics in China, 1917-1924.* Stanford, 1953.
Wilbur, C. Martin. *Sun Yat-sen: Frustrated Patriot.* New York, 1976.
Williams, William Appleman. 'American Intervention in Russia, 1917-1920', in: David Horowitz, ed., *Containment and Revolution.* Boston, 1967, pp. 26-75.
—— *American-Russian Relations, 1781-1947.* New York, 1952.
Wilson, Edward T. *Russia and Black Africa before World War II.* New York, 1974.
Wilson, Joan Hoff. *Ideology and Economics: U. S. Relations with the Soviet Union, 1918-1933.* Columbia, 1974.
Wolfe, Bertram D., 'The Case of the Litvinov Diary', *Encounter*, VI, 1 (January 1956), pp. 39-47.
—— 'Nationalism and Internationalism in Marx and Engels', *American Slavic and East European Review*, XVII, 4 (December 1958), pp. 403-17.
—— *Strange Communists I Have Known.* New York, 1965.
Wolin, Simon, and Robert M. Slusser, eds. *The Soviet Secret Police.* New York, [1957].
Wollenberg, Erich. *The Red Army: A Study of the Growth of Soviet Imperialism.* London, 1949.
—— *Der Apparat: Stalins Fünfte Kolonne.* Bonn, [1951].

Yakhontov, Victor A. *Russia and the Soviet Union in the Far East.* Westport, 1973 [1931].

Zaitsev, V. S. 'Geroi oktiabria i grazhdanskoi voiny', *Voprosy istorii KPSS*, no. 12 (1963), pp. 90-94.

Zakharov, S. A. *Komissar — diplomat (Petr Lazarevich Voikov).* Sverdlovsk, 1962.

Zarnitskii, S. V. and L. I. Trofimova. *Sovetskoi strany diplomat.* Moscow, 1968.

Zarnitsky, S. and A. Sergeyev. 'The Birth of Soviet Diplomacy', *International Affairs*, no. 6 (1967), pp. 58-66 and 95.

—— *Chicherin.* Moscow, 1966 and 1975.

Zhukov, E. M., et al., eds. *Voprosy istorii vneshneipolitiki SSSR i mezhdunarodnykh otnoshenii: sbornik statei pamiati akademika Vladimira Mikhailovicha Khvostova.* Moscow, 1976.

Zhukovskii, N. *Na diplomaticheskom postu.* Moscow, 1973.

Zimmerman, William. *Soviet Perspectives on International Relations, 1956-1967.* Princeton, 1969.

Zorin, Valerian A., et al., eds. *Istoriia diplomatii.* 2nd edn. Moscow, 1959-.

—— *Osnovy diplomaticheskoi sluzhby.* Moscow, 1964.

Zvezdin, Z. K. 'Iz istorii deiatel'nost Gosplana v 1921-1924gg.', *Voprosy istorii KPSS*, no. 3 (1967), pp. 45-56.

INDEX

Shtein, Boris, 36, 176-7
Shtern, D. G., 171, 175
Shumiatskii, Boris Z., 157
Siberia, 49-50, 132
Siemens-Schuckert factory, workers, 21
Simonov, P., 23-4
Skevensyrev (Soviet diplomat), 23
Skvirskii, Boris E., 74, 171, 184n.8
Smolnyi Institute, 17-8, 26, 32
Sobolev, Arkadii, 177, 186n.32
Socialism in one country, 130
Socialist Party of Germany (SPD), 35, 52, 62
Socialist Revolutionary Party, 29, 32, 48-9, 52; and NKID, 98 table 1, 190; in Soviet government, 99; uprising of, 32, 49, 51
Sokol'nikov, Grigorii I., 38, 122, 128-9, 132, 135, 157, 171, 184n.8
Solf, H., 52
Solomon, Georgii, 39, 85, 88
Solov'ev, Iurii, 22, 106
Soviet-Afghan Treaty of Friendship, 22
Soviet Information Bureau, in Washington, 74
Soviet-Persian Treaty, 72
Soviet Union, blockade of, 58; censorship in, 80; foreign policy formulation, 78, 117-27; formed 77-8; structure of, 70, 100, 117-8, 144, 176; isolated, 47, 59, 70-2, 173; protection of, 40, 155, 189, 193; recognition of, 74, 77, 80, 125, 132, 154, 159, 164n.9, 170, 193; and foreign trade, 57. *See also* Commissariat of Foreign Affairs; Central Executive Committee
Sovnarkom. *See* Council of People's Commissars
Spain, 151, 170-2
Spartakus Bund, 58, 60, 62, 159
Stakelberg, Count, 29
Stalin, I. V., 84, 108, 119-20, 128-30, 132, 136n.8 & 12, 138n.43, 140n.50, 141n.69, 142n.72, 150, 170, 178; and Chicherin, 128, 130,

140n.59; on diplomacy, 122, 149; and foreign policy, 133, 137n.21, 151, 175, 182-3; and Litvinov, 64, 140-1n.64, 176; and NKID, 128, 133-4, 138n.25, 177, 180-1, 183; and opposition, 129, 131, 181; and purges, 171, 176, 179, 181-4, 185-6n.31, 187n.44, 188n.51
State and Revolution (Lenin), 97
State Bank, 131
Stern, David. *See* Shtern, D. G.
Stomoniakov, Boris, 154, 169
Stuchka, Petr I., 34, 157
Supreme Council of National Economy (VSNKh), 56, 99, 131-2
Supreme Court, 90
Surits, Iakov Z., 38, 53, 65n.24, 72, 176-7
Sverdlov, Ia. M., 17
Sweden, 23-4, 47, 58, 72, 74, 81, 107-8, 176; Soviet missions in, 38, 56, 85, 112 table 6, 175
Switzerland, 24, 38, 46, 81, 102, 138n.44, 169

Tairov, V. K., 171
Talleyrand, C. M. de, 123
Tannu-Tuva Republic, 81, 169
Tartu, Treaty of (Dorpat), 70-1
Tatishchev (Chancellery chief), 19
Teheran Conference, 185-6n.31
Tereshchenko, M. I., 11
Tibet, 81
Tikhmenev, N. S., 171
Tomskii, Mikhail P., 119
Trades Union Council, 146, 162
Trotskii, Lev D., 15, 17-9, 22, 29-30, 88, 119, 129-30, 137n22, 157, 172; and Chicherin, 29, 88, 159; and Lenin, 15-7, 29, 132, 137n.19; and NKID, 17-8, 20, 27, 41n.8, 108, 130, 189-90; and Soviet diplomacy, 26, 31, 38, 61, 67n.52, 122, 152, 165n.33; on world revolution, 12, 60, 130, 140n.61, 144
Troianovskii, Aleksandr A., 22, 86, 109, 135, 176-7

Teddy James Uldricks is presently an Associate Professor of History at the University of California, Riverside, USA. Professor Uldricks was educated at Valparaiso University and the University of California, Berkeley, from which he received an A.B. in history. He also has an M.A. and a Ph.D. in Russian history from Indiana University. Teddy Uldricks has published a number of articles in scholarly journals dealing with Soviet diplomacy and with the Russian revolution.